REPUTATION

A Leader's Path to Career Success

Rodney Warrenfeltz, PhD
Trish Kellett, MBA

Hogan Press

© 2017 Hogan Assessment Systems, Inc.
11 S Greenwood Ave
Tulsa, OK 74120

Rodney Warrenfeltz, PhD
Trish Kellett, MBA

No part of this work may be copied or transferred to any other form or expression without the expressed written consent from Hogan Assessment Systems, Inc.

Hogan Personality Inventory ™
Hogan Development Survey ™
Motives, Values, Preferences Inventory ™

are the exclusive registered trademarks of
Hogan Assessment Systems, Inc.

www.hoganassessments.com

First printing May 2017

ISBN 978-0-692-86222-3

Contents

Cases	vii
Foreword	ix
Preface	xi
Acknowledgments	xv

PART I — REPUTATION FUNDAMENTALS 1

    Chapter 1: Reputation and Development 3
    Chapter 2: Pillars of Reputation Change 13
    Chapter 3: Assessing the Dark Side 25
    Chapter 4: Development Case Studies 53

PART II: DEVELOPMENT TECHNIQUES FOR REPUTATION CHANGE 75

    Chapter 5: Excitable 77
        High Excitable: Controlling Your Emotions 77
        Low Excitable: Generating Passion 84

Chapter 6: Skeptical — 91
- High Skeptical: Staying Positive — 91
- Low Skeptical: Trust, but Verify — 99

Chapter 7: Cautious — 107
- High Cautious: Leveraging Risk — 107
- Low Cautious: Becoming Prudent — 115

Chapter 8: Reserved — 123
- High Reserved: Ensuring Your Approachability — 123
- Low Reserved: Taking Tough Stands — 131

Chapter 9: Leisurely — 139
- High Leisurely: Maintaining Your Commitments — 139
- Low Leisurely: Establishing a Personal Agenda — 149

Chapter 10: Bold — 157
- High Bold: Managing Your Overconfidence — 157
- Low Bold: Strengthening Your Resolve — 166

Chapter 11: Mischievous — 175
- High Mischievous: Building Trust — 175
- Low Mischievous: Becoming Adventuresome — 184

Chapter 12: Colorful — 193
- High Colorful: Lowering Your Profile — 193
- Low Colorful: Getting Noticed — 202

Chapter 13: Imaginative — 209
- High Imaginative: Controlling Ideation — 209
- Low Imaginative: Appearing Innovative — 217

Chapter 14: Diligent — 225
- High Diligent: Empowering Others — 225
- Low Diligent: Managing the Details — 234

Chapter 15: Dutiful — 243
- High Dutiful: Charting Your Path — 243
- Low Dutiful: Keeping Others Informed — 251

PART III: CHARTING A PATH FOR CAREER SUCCESS   261

Chapter 16: Building an Aspiration Plan   263
Chapter 17: Development Tips for All Leaders   283
Chapter 18: Closing Thoughts   291

Bibliography   *297*
Index   *299*
About Hogan Assessment Systems   *309*

Cases

Case 1	Rex, Vice President of Sales (Low Cautious)	56
Case 2	Phil, Logistics Technician (High Skeptical)	58
Case 3	Robert, Design Engineer (High Reserved)	60
Case 4	Tanya, Insurance Professional (High Mischievous)	62
Case 5	Janis, Customer Service Manager (Low Bold)	64
Case 6	Mark, District Account Manager (High Colorful)	66
Case 7	James, Marketing Manager (High Dutiful)	68
Case 8	Courtney, Assistant Operations Manager (Low Diligent)	70
Case 9	Kelly, Chief Financial Officer (High Diligent)	72

Foreword

At its core, leadership and organization development is about using data to enhance self-awareness and drive a commitment to individual growth and behavior change. It is that simple. Or is it? For decades, organizational psychologists, executive coaches, and organization development (OD) professionals have focused on using data-based tools to provide feedback to individuals so that they can learn about their strengths and their opportunities (weaknesses). Psychological assessments, process observations, stakeholder interviews, and 360-degree feedback, for example, have become the staples by which organizations operate and facilitate this agenda in their talent development efforts.

Why? The basic premise has always been that leaders will find ways to build on their strengths and address their opportunities through experiential learning, developmental coaching and mentoring, or formal training. This approach assumes, however, that the individual knows and is focused on enhancing a specific set of knowledge, skills, and abilities required for success. These might be based on a leadership competency model, a profile of a high-potential executive, a functional specialty area, or a set of core values that are important to an organization. In other situations, individuals might receive feedback on their foundational traits such as cognitive skills or personality characteristics as well, with an emphasis on developing "work-around" skills. In other words, they identify ways to avoid or overcome their shortcomings.

All these approaches rely on the individual to move his or her own agenda forward by changing behavior (or even changing him- or herself). But the question often is, to what end? Moreover, the motivation to change on the part of the individual is often quite limited. Sure, the idea of improving one's leadership skills to be more effective or ready for more senior roles is appealing. But the outcome measured is often a higher rating on a 360-survey report or informal feedback obtained from others.

While these outcomes are clearly important, as Rodney and Trish demonstrate in *Reputation: A Leader's Path to Career Success,* we have been missing a critical component in our leadership development efforts all these years. That is, the role of one's reputation in the organizational milieu. It is not that understanding one's personality and leadership behaviors and building specific capabilities are not critical; they are. But if we want to move the needle on individuals achieving their full potential in the workplace, it is time now to focus on something that matters to them—that is, their careers. Anyone wanting to advance his or her career trajectory will find the reputational approach to behavior change particularly compelling and a real motivator to acting on his or her opportunities once and for all.

As the authors point out so eloquently, one's reputation goes far beyond the individual behaviors demonstrated in the workplace. Their approach to utilizing the 11 personality derailers in the context of preventing reputational damage shows there can be a profound influence on the perceptions of colleagues, team members, customers, managers, and even senior leadership of an individual. Exhibiting these characteristics is more than just "behaving badly" in a meeting—it reflects who the individual is as a leader. Moreover, reputation is both viral and cumulative at the same time. As the authors demonstrate in case after case, one set of bad behaviors (which we normally might coach against in isolation) can cascade into a negative view or aura of a leader that will put a dead stop to his or her career.

Yes, this book is all about the impact of personality derailers. Those familiar with the Hogan Development Survey will find a wealth of new information, tips, and tactics that can be applied across a wide range of development challenges. The entire emphasis of the discussion, though, is about derailing at a higher level of magnitude. As Rodney and Trish point out, reputation and reputation change vis-à-vis targeted behavior change should be the focus for leaders interested in improving their career success—not development for development's sake.

The role of reputation management is the missing link in the leadership development equation. This book represents a huge step forward in the development and coaching of individuals as leaders and as human beings. As an organizational psychologist and OD professional working with personality and behavioral feedback for over 25 years, I believe that Rodney and Trish have set us on a new path and a new way of thinking about helping our clients and ourselves grow as leaders. They also have included a wealth of knowledge in this book to help us all get there. Well done and enjoy the journey.

Allan H. Church, PhD
Senior Vice President
Global Talent Assessment and Development
PepsiCo

Preface

Metamorphosis in Our Thinking

We have learned a lot since publishing *Coaching the Dark Side of Personality* in 2016. As authors, we learned that there is much more to publishing a book than just writing it. Writing is the fun part. Everything that comes after it takes knowledge, skills, and, most of all, patience. Beyond what we have learned as authors, we have learned a tremendous amount about leadership development and coaching. We titled the opening section of the preface in *Coaching the Dark Side of Personality*, "Evolution in Our Thinking." That title was quite accurate because our thinking really did evolve during the course of the four years it took to get the book written and published. Today, "evolution" is simply not a strong enough word to capture what we have undergone as professionals who have dedicated our careers to helping leaders become more effective. We have truly undergone a metamorphosis in our thinking. There is no better way to illustrate this than with a recent coaching case involving a chief marketing officer (CMO) we will call Mark.

> *Mark is like many of our coaching cases these days. He was quite successful, but he had reached a plateau in his career. He was considered an outstanding marketing person and was well respected for his knowledge, ideas, and the passion that he brought to the CMO position. Unfortunately for Mark, his reputation was such that his superiors did not see him as ready for a position at the next level and were content to pay him well for his work as a CMO. Two comments would regularly come up in any discussion regarding the possibility of*

promoting Mark to a division president position. First, Mark's reputation as a passionate marketing guy had evolved into one of an emotional guy who lacked executive maturity. Second, people all around Mark described him as marching to his own drummer and very poor at keeping others informed.

At this point, we would like to describe the masterful coaching that Mark received that transformed him into a calm, even-tempered executive who became a good soldier supporting the company agenda, keeping others well informed, and generally becoming a model executive who was promoted to division president. That may yet be the story that is told about Mark, but it is certainly not the point of relating this case as an exemplar of why we, as authors and professional coaches, have undergone a metamorphosis in our thinking. The fact is that Mark fell off the rails shortly after this coaching engagement got underway. Mark had undermined his manager to the point that Mark was in danger of being fired, and the coaching engagement was essentially put on hold for a period of time until his manager figured out if he even wanted Mark in the company anymore. Eventually, the coaching engagement was restarted, and the initial restart conversation is why we think this case stands out as an example of our metamorphosis. In that initial restart conversation, Mark opened the conversation with his coach by relating the following critical incident:

> "... I read the two chapters you sent me related to excitable behaviors and leisurely behaviors. You could have used me as the case study because those behaviors are my biggest problems. I have a reputation for getting overly emotional, and I tend to work on my own agenda and don't bother keeping others informed. It was so apparent to me in a recent situation where I failed to keep a customer informed about an invoice I sent her. She called my manager to complain, and my manager and I got into a huge, emotional fight over the situation. As I looked back, the whole situation was my fault. I should have done a better job of keeping the customer informed. I was just attending to my own agenda with little concern for my customer. I also should not have let my emotions get out of hand as I do when I get excitable. The really bad thing about this entire incident is it finally dawned on me that I have a really bad reputation. My manager told me that the reason my customer did not come to me directly was because I never keep her informed, and any time she is critical of my performance, I get emotional. Furthermore, my manager told me that my whole department has a reputation for not following up, and many of my team members think it is okay to scream and yell at people the way I do."

So why is this conversation so profound? It is an excellent illustration of the importance of reputation to success in the workplace. Mark's reputation caused the customer to go around him directly to his manager. Mark's reputation had contaminated his entire department. Mark's reputation had even contaminated his team members. The actual behaviors had become secondary for Mark because his reputation had taken over as the driving force behind the way others treated him, his department, and even his team members. Behavior change alone was not going to turn the situation around; only reputation change could make a meaningful difference.

To borrow a line from James Carville (strategist for Bill Clinton's 1992 successful presidential campaign), "It's the economy, stupid!" In our case, the quote should read, "It's the leader's reputation, stupid." Reputation should be the real focus of change for any leader interested in improving his or her career success.

It is the simple notion that behavior change is only a means to an end, not the end itself, that started the metamorphosis in our thinking. The more we talked about it, the more we realized just how important reputation is in the success equation. We began to see the theme of reputation change permeate all aspects of our thinking with respect to leadership development. Even more interesting was the impact we began to see among the leaders we coached when we used reputation as the central focus of change. They have no trouble seeing the direct link between their reputation and their career success. They just get it!

The purpose in writing this book became more and more clear with each step we took down the path of reputation focused leadership development. We wanted to create a book that leaders could use as a guide in building a winning reputation. We did not want to create a one-time read that was cast away to collect dust on a bookshelf. We wanted to create a book that leaders would go back to time and time again with each new reputational challenge they face as they chart their path to career success. For us, the reputational vision for this book is one of an indispensable guide, lying dog-eared on a desk, ready to be put to use when a leader has an "It's reputation, stupid!" moment requiring developmental attention.

STRUCTURE OF THE BOOK

The structure of the book follows directly from our vision. We wanted to achieve three very practical objectives:

- Provide a basic understanding of reputation as the focus of development.
- Outline development content that can be easily applied to make reputational changes.
- Offer leaders detailed guidance on how to put the development content to work.

The book is divided into three parts, with each part addressing one of the three objectives.

Part I—Reputation Fundamentals

In Part I, we take a deep dive into the concept of reputation as the focal point of a leader's development. Our development model is outlined, we provide the pillars of reputation change, we set the stage for measuring the characteristics that cause reputational damage, and we present the nine case studies used to organize the development content in Part II.

Part II—Development Techniques for Reputation Change

Part II is a thorough review of the development content that a leader can call upon to make a reputational change. The content is organized according to 11 personality characteristics that are consistently associated with reputational damage. The development techniques offered throughout Part II have been fully vetted by professional executive coaches and have been proven in terms of their effectiveness in helping leaders achieve the improvements necessary for career success.

Part III—Charting a Path for Career Success

Part III is essentially a how-to guide for taking the development content in Part II and putting it to work to achieve a reputational vision. Part III also includes a summary of the "go-to" development techniques that are commonly employed when leaders engage in a change effort, and we conclude with our closing thoughts on the takeaways from the book.

Audience

The audience for this book is simple. The book was written for leaders and those they lead. Leaders will be able to apply the content to chart their own path to career success. They also will be able to use the content in their efforts to build talented leaders around them. Great leaders develop great leaders. They do that by building their own reputation and then coaching those they lead on the same fundamentals that led to their success. We hope leaders will find this book to be an essential companion on their career success journey.

ACKNOWLEDGMENTS

The foundation for this book was *Coaching the Dark Side of Personality*. Following the publication of that book in 2016, we decided we needed a book that was written specifically for leaders to use for their own development and the development of those they lead. Many of the development tips and techniques covered in this book were drawn from *Coaching the Dark Side of Personality*. For that content, we again want to acknowledge the contribution of the members of the Hogan Coaching Network (HCN) who continue to contribute to the growth of Hogan Assessment Systems as the industry leader in personality-based leadership development. These coaches include David Brookmire, Margaret Butteriss, Cheryl Cerminara, Ben Dattner, Andrea Facchini, Jorge Fernandez, Ron Festa, Karin Fulton, Jill Geehr, Fraser Clark, Dale Hayden, Bill Hector, Terry Hollon, Andreas Janz, Jennifer Johnson, Elaine Kamm, Warren Kennaugh, Ed Marks, Sid Nachman, Mary Nelson, Pradnya Parasher, Tom Patterson, Mirna Perez Piris, Diarmuid Ryan, Mitch Shack, Julie Shuman, Alan Siegel, Audrey Wallace, Valerie White, Kristie Wright, and Nicole Zucker.

We want to give special thanks to the coaches who authored some of the chapters dedicated to the Hogan Development Survey (HDS) scales: Lisa Aronson, Ray Harrison, Doug Klippel, Patrick Lagutaris, Joy McGovern, Dan Paulk, Betsy Reeder, and Susan Toback.

A book of this scope also requires a great deal of work behind the scenes with respect to layout, formatting, and editing. We would like to thank the team at Adept Content Solutions, who were great partners in the production of this book. In particular, we want to acknowledge the contribution of Lori Martinsek, president of

Adept Content Solutions, who took the time to understand our business needs and was instrumental in helping us finish this book well ahead of schedule. In addition, we want to thank Kelly Thomas and Julie Warrenfeltz for their diligence in helping us through the final editing process. Finally, we would like to thank our colleagues for their willingness to review the book and provide us with their thoughts and ideas. Their contributions helped us make significant improvements to the final version of the book and ensure that the content fully aligned with the philosophy that is central to the success of Hogan Assessment Systems. Many thanks to all those who helped!

Rodney Warrenfeltz

Trish Kellett

April 2017

PART I

REPUTATION FUNDAMENTALS

Chapter 1	Reputation and Development	3
Chapter 2	Pillars of Reputation Change	13
Chapter 3	Assessing the Dark Side	25
Chapter 4	Development Case Studies	53

CHAPTER 1

REPUTATION AND DEVELOPMENT

INTRODUCTION

The truth is reputation drives career success! Leaders who believe otherwise are likely to find themselves drawing the short straw when the next promotion comes along or when they are head-to-head in any competition with their peers for an advancement opportunity. The importance of reputation is a hard lesson for many leaders to accept. It is counter to pretty much everything most of us were taught growing up, especially in relation to the workplace where hard work and solid performance were drilled into us as the cornerstones of career success. In today's workplace, such thinking is, at best, naïve. It is not that working hard, building on strengths, and ameliorating weaknesses have lost their merit when it comes to getting ahead. They are, for the most part, necessary ingredients but fall far short of being sufficient ingredients for leaders interested in working their way up the career ladder.

The reputation of a leader is the litmus test for career outcomes. The working world is littered with thousands of people who did not reach their full potential because they failed to attend to this critical outcome variable. It is such a simple idea that it is hard to believe it has received so little attention by the leadership development industry. The focus of this industry is almost exclusively on performance in the form of measurable behavior. Meanwhile, careers are made or broken based on reputation. We are not ignoring the fact that behavior and reputation are inextricably linked to one another. After all, the behavior a leader exhibits on the job represents an important contributing factor to his or her reputation. However, behavior is by no means the only contributing factor. It may not even be the primary contributing factor.

Consider for a moment the number of people for whom you have a reputational image embedded in your mind. It is actually an impossible task because we have a reputational image for every person, place, or thing we come in direct (or indirect) contact with in our lives. Reputation is the way we organize our understanding of the world around us. We confer a reputational image on virtually everything, be it person, place, or thing. Furthermore, all subsequent contacts with that person, place, or thing are approached with an eye toward reputation confirmation (i.e., we seek to confirm our initial reputational image in all subsequent contacts). Interestingly, once a reputational image becomes stable in our minds (and it does not take much for that to happen), the only thing that really registers in our minds concerning that reputational image in the future is a significant piece of disconfirming information. What constitutes disconfirming information depends upon the stability of the image in our minds. The more stable the image, the more powerful the disconfirming information must be in order for the reputational image to change.

Let us return to the notion that reputation is the litmus test for career outcomes using our view of reputation as the lens through which we interpret the success (or lack of success) a leader experiences. Reputation in the workplace works in a manner very similar to a highly contagious virus. It starts to spread upon the very first contact a leader has with an organization. The contact may even occur before the individual joins the organization. Résumés, references, interviews, and even word of mouth can initiate the spread of the reputational virus. Its spread is perpetuated with each subsequent contact among individuals within the workplace. Contact does not have to be direct; hearsay information spreads the reputational virus just as direct observation can perpetuate the spread. It is important to keep in mind that we have not mentioned a word about "accuracy." Reputation is based on the perception of others, and while perception is reality, perception is often distorted. That is the insidious aspect of reputation. It can form in a moment. It can last a lifetime. And it can be totally off base!

For the moment, let us assume that perception is reality as the reputational virus is introduced into the workplace for a leader and begins to spread. A simple example can serve to illustrate how an innocent reputational characteristic can morph into a career-derailing reputational scar. We will use a newly hired sales manager whom we will call Brian for this example. Brian was initially hired into the organization to manage a 20-person sales team. One of the most talked-about characteristics that Brian displayed during the interview process was the passion and excitement he had for the product line his team would be selling. From his first day on the job, his passion and excitement were evident to all those he interacted with, and it was not long before this aspect of reputation had spread beyond his department to other parts of the organization. Brian was becoming known for being a passionate, even excitable guy.

Early in his tenure as sales manager, the business was underperforming, and Brian was put under increasing pressure to get things turned around. He would act a bit despondent when the weekly sales numbers were not as good as expected, and he would display a degree of elation when the numbers were in the right direction. People began to notice that his emotions could rise and fall based on relatively minor changes in business performance. His team members also began to wonder which "Brian" would show up when they had to deliver good or bad news to him. Over time, people got used to Brian's tendency to ride an emotional roller coaster, especially his team members who observed the behavior regularly. On occasion, they would even experience an emotional outburst from Brian when certain issues did not go his way. Brian's manager had coached Brian on numerous occasions to do a better job of controlling his emotions, but her coaching only had minimal impact. In addition, the business began to perform well, and Brian's emotional demeanor appeared to take a back seat.

When Brian's manager, VP of sales for the company, decided to take a job with another organization, it opened an important promotion opportunity for Brian. Unfortunately, with the departure of his manager, the decision on who should fill the position fell to other members of the executive team who were only tangentially familiar with Brian's performance. They were, however, quite familiar with Brian's reputation for being volatile, as they had heard rumors to that effect, observed his passionate behavior in presentations, and were even asked for suggestions from his former manager on how she should coach Brian regarding his emotional demeanor. In essence, Brian's reputation with the executive team had become one of a good sales manager who lacked the executive maturity necessary to be an effective member of the executive team. A decision was made to go outside the organization to fill the VP of sales job, and Brian, now labeled as lacking emotional maturity, had his career derailed based on his reputation.

You might be thinking that, "Well, he displayed the behaviors that led to the reputational scar for lacking emotional maturity," and that would be true. We would like you to think beyond that for a moment and ask the question, "What needs to change for Brian to have a better career outcome?" Does Brian need to become more emotionally mature? Alternatively, does Brian need to change his reputation for emotional maturity? These are fundamentally different questions. Becoming more emotionally mature is an *introspective* issue that very well could take years of counseling to achieve meaningful progress. Developing a reputation for emotional maturity is an *extrospective* issue that requires the manipulation of the perceptions of others, which is an entirely different and far more achievable developmental objective for a leader such as Brian.

Reputation in the Workplace

The traditional definition of *reputation* is the accumulation of past behaviors observed by others that are used to form their opinion of an individual. We believe this definition in the context of the workplace is far too narrow. It is too narrow because of its focus on "observed" behavior. When you use a viral model to understand reputation in the workplace, observed behavior becomes a much less significant aspect of the definition. The reality is that reputation in the workplace often begins to form long before people directly observe behavior. Furthermore, even when a leader's behavior is directly observed, people see it through their own lens, which may or may not lead to an accurate interpretation. Let us consider the formation of a leader's reputation in the workplace from both a direct and indirect perspective as seen through the eyes of others. When we use the term "others," we are referring to anyone in the workplace who has formed a reputational image of the leader, including, but not limited to, the leader's manager, direct reports, peers, superiors, and colleagues.

Direct observation as seen through the eyes of others is relatively straightforward. It means that there are no variables besides what others witness. The leader displays a behavior, and others see it in real time. The only question with respect to direct observation is, "How was the behavior perceived?" Two people can directly observe a leader's behavior, but that observed behavior gets translated into what each individual perceived it to mean. Since perception is reality when considering reputation through the eyes of others, how a person perceives the observed behavior of a leader will be what accumulates in the formation of his or her reputation. Accurate or not, it is the perception of observed behavior that forms a reputational image.

Two additional points are important with respect to the perception of observed behavior. First, the old adage, "You never get a second chance to make a first impression," has its roots in the perception of observed behavior. When others observe the behavior of a leader, they cannot unsee it. In fact, most of their perceptional energy with respect to that leader goes into confirming what they initially perceived. All of us have a natural bias to believe that what we initially perceive about someone is accurate. Therefore, we strive to incorporate future information into our initial perception. The accuracy of our perception becomes secondary to our need to confirm an initial perception.

Second, the perception of every individual is different because of the influence of our personal bias. Personal bias is the result of everything from our upbringing to personality characteristics; hence, every individual is different in this regard. It is at the heart of why eyewitness testimony is notoriously unreliable. Two people witness exactly the same thing, and yet they may have completely different descriptions because their personal bias colors their perception.

While direct observation of a leader's behavior will most certainly affect his or her reputation, indirect reputational information may potentially have an even greater impact in the workplace. Indirect reputational information spreads through the workplace via second-hand contact. Others may spread this type information about a leader by actively engaging coworkers in a discussion of the leader's behavior. It also spreads in subtler ways like seeing the results of a leader's performance or being on the receiving end of a leader's decision.

Indirect reputational information suffers from the same personal bias that affects the perception of direct observation of behavior by others. In addition, when more than one individual is involved in spreading reputational information, the motivation of those spreading the information can have serious consequences for a leader. For example, a peer may spread negative reputational information about a leader as a means of garnering a competitive advantage in the pursuit of future opportunities. Even idle gossip may be passed along, and as it spreads through the workplace, it can be twisted in ways that have all sorts of reputational consequences for a leader. In short, the workplace is a hotbed for indirect reputational information, and this type of information can be quite insidious when multiple individuals are involved in spreading it.

The foregoing discussion suggests the need for refining the definition of reputation as it applies to the workplace. We prefer to define the *reputation* of a leader or any individual in the workplace as:

The perception held by others regarding the characteristics of an individual based on the accumulation of ANY behavioral information.

This definition has far-reaching consequences when considering potential career outcomes. Leaders must come to realize that reputation is reality, and their reputation is the foundation upon which others will make decisions regarding their career. Therefore, any development effort aimed at improving a career outcome must have the reputation of the leader as its target for change. Anything short of that will simply represent change for change's sake. This point bears repeating. Development efforts that target behavior change without consideration of reputation change are like throwing darts with a blindfold on. You might hit the target, but you are just as likely to put a hole in your wall.

IMPLICATIONS FOR DEVELOPMENT

Our focus on reputation change significantly alters the way leaders should approach their own development. In the past, leadership development efforts were person centered with an emphasis on skill development. Emphasizing reputation change means that leaders need to look beyond skill development and focus on those behaviors that are likely to have the greatest positive impact on their reputation and, consequently, will enhance their career outcome opportunities. To leverage our focus on reputation change, we created the Leader Development Cycle (See Figure 1).

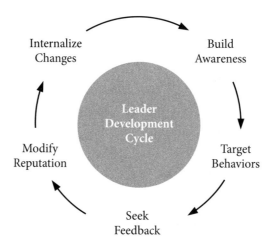

Figure 1 Leader Development Cycle

The Leader Development Cycle (LDC) is unique in several ways. First, it emerged from more than 25 years of experience working with leaders using a personality-based approach to assessment that has resulted in considerable insight regarding the development of leaders. The study of personality as it relates to leader performance started to take off in the early 1990s when it became apparent that personality characteristics were largely responsible for the reputation an individual acquired in the workplace. This brought personality out of the clinical shadows to a place where people could measure the consequences of specific personality characteristics via reputation. For example, an individual who scores high on the personality characteristic known as conscientiousness typically develops a reputation in the workplace for being detail oriented. As we gained greater understanding of the link between personality characteristics and reputation, it became apparent to us that reputation should be the primary target for leadership development because it was easily measured and critical in terms of career outcomes.

A second unique aspect of the LDC regards our perspective on learning—that it is couched in terms of a development cycle. Educators often talk of lifelong learning. The concept of a development cycle is that it involves continuous learning. It goes on throughout our daily lives whether we are aware of it or not. The key is raising awareness to actively incorporate worthwhile lessons into our behavioral repertoire and, ultimately, into the development of our reputation. Keep in mind that not all learning contributes to a positive reputation. It can be a difficult challenge to determine the impact behavior will have on a person's reputation. For this reason, you will see considerable emphasis placed on awareness in our development cycle and the important connection we make between behavior and reputation.

Finally, we emphasize the importance of internalizing change. One of the most common questions that we receive regarding personality in general and leadership in particular is, "How stable is personality or leadership style over time?" It is our contention that both are stable and require changes to be internalized to the point that they impact reputation; one's reputation is then modified to the point that not only do others think about the individual differently, but the individual also thinks about him- or herself differently. One of the reasons leaders' results on a personality assessment are so stable is that they truly must think differently about themselves before those changes will be reflected in the results. This transformation can take a considerable amount of time and is not something that happens in months, but in years.

The LDC contains five steps that operate continuously throughout a leader's career. Change behaviors are happening at all different stages of the model and at many different levels of awareness. The steps we describe below are from an active learning perspective in which it is assumed that the leader is actively pursuing learning or behavior change as would be the case in a coaching engagement, learning event, or the leader pursuing an active course of behavior change.

Building Awareness requires a person to fully understand "the what and the how" associated with a development need. Targeting Behaviors involves the identification of behaviors to be changed and the development techniques that will be brought to bear in making the change. Seeking Feedback is necessary in order to calibrate progress. Reputation Modification will occur as others observe or become aware of the changes and begin to respond or act differently around the person. These changes are often subtle, but they do accumulate over time. Finally, a person will begin to Internalize Changes to reputation, allowing them to become a part of the person's identity. Internalizing the changes is not something a person does actively. It comes as a consequence of the reputation modifications the person has achieved. Internalizing the changes comes as others treat the person in ways that are consistent with the reputation modifications.

For example, consider a common coaching engagement in which a leader (we will call her Christine) has a problem with being argumentative and not taking time to understand the position of those who interact with her. Perhaps she has had some general feedback that has caused her to understand her reputation and, as a result, wants to make a change. A coach, in working with her, might provide some specific examples of the problem behavior gathered through interviews. The coach might also conduct a personality assessment that suggests that Christine is very outgoing, but lacks interpersonal sensitivity. Christine has now built considerable awareness around the problem behavior, including what the offending behavior is, how it is manifested, and even the behavioral tendencies that underlie the behavior. The coach then helps Christine target specific behaviors that she needs to change (e.g., overusing "tells" during interactions) and provides alternative behaviors (e.g., using more soft "seeks" and clarifying behaviors to understand the position of others).

Initially, the new behaviors may look forced and somewhat unnatural. Seeking and listening to feedback will allow Christine to begin to calibrate the effectiveness of using the new behaviors.

Those around Christine will see and likely talk about the effort and the changes and begin to consider the possibility that her behavior is changing. As Christine's new behavior becomes more consistent, those around her start to form a different opinion of her that slowly accumulates in the form of a reputation change. Others begin to think of and talk about Christine as someone who is truly interested in their views, seeks their opinions, and works to understand their positions. They may even come to expect these behaviors from her. Such changes will inevitably result in Christine thinking differently about herself to the extent that even her own identity becomes one of a person who looks to seek and understand before considering a "tell."

This description is quite linear and rarely happens that way in the real world. As stated at the outset of this section, the Leader Development Cycle is a continuous process that happens at many levels across many types of behavior. However, the cycle serves as a way to consider learning as a discrete set of steps that can be actively planned and executed by a leader to make positive changes. Furthermore, the validity of the cycle can be easily demonstrated from an empirical standpoint using before-and-after multi-rater assessments that can do a great job of measuring reputational information. Even something as fuzzy as internalizing changes can be seen in a leader's self-ratings. As the leader begins to think differently about him- or herself, the differences will be reflected in self-ratings of performance. A similar process will occur with respect to personality assessment results, although it may take a leader a bit longer to internalize change to a point where his or her personality profile changes in a substantive way.

REPUTATION AND THE LEADER DEVELOPMENT CYCLE

Our focus on reputation has specific implications for how the Leader Development Cycle would unfold for a leader interested in enhancing his or her career opportunities. When we started following the LDC as a pure-behavior change model, we consistently achieved positive behavior change. That should not come as much of a surprise, as the model was built upon proven adult learning principles. However, behavior change should not be thought of as the primary focus of leader development. Behavior change is simply a means to an end, and the real end should be enhancing the career opportunities for a leader that are inevitably tied to the leader's reputation.

There are implications for each step of the LDC that must be considered when reputation is the target for change. The first step in the process is to build awareness. Building Awareness with a focus on reputation change means having a clear understanding of the leader's reputation and how it is viewed in the context of future opportunities. It is not good enough to know, for example, that a leader needs to improve his or her executive maturity. The leader needs to know what his or her reputation is among specific stakeholders, how they developed that reputational image, and what it would take to change that reputational image. That is a far more complex task than just focusing on the leader's need to improve his or her executive maturity.

The second step in the model involves Targeting Behaviors for change. When reputation is added to the development equation, the behavior Change Targets are more specific. They are the behaviors responsible for driving the reputational image held by key stakeholders. Thus, the behavior change tactics should be far more surgical and may even differ between stakeholders. For example, one stakeholder may view the leader as too emotional, while another stakeholder might appreciate the passion but disagree with the way it is displayed in the workplace. A situation such as this would require different behavioral tactics depending on the stakeholder involved.

The third step in the model involves Seeking Feedback. This is always challenging because people are reluctant to give honest feedback. Plus, the situation gets worse as a leader climbs the corporate ladder. The higher the position is in the organization, the more difficult it becomes to obtain feedback. Reputational feedback is even more problematic than feedback involving a behavior. It is one thing to tell a leader that a particular behavior is unproductive and making a change would strengthen the leader's performance. It is a completely different matter to tell a leader that, for example, he or she has a reputation for being a bully. It may even be the case that the reputation is the result of a single behavioral incident, and many of those who hold that reputational image for the leader have based it on second-hand information. The important point here is not the accuracy of the reputational image possessed by others. Perception is reality, and it is incumbent upon the leader to be persistent in his or her effort to uncover existing reputational information.

Reputation Modification is the fourth step in the model and presents many of the same challenges as third step, Seeking Feedback. At this stage, the leader needs to open a reputation change pipeline. It typically involves the identification of an individual(s) who can act as a surrogate(s) and gather information regarding the leader's reputation change efforts. This is a fairly strategic activity because the right person can not only gather information, he or she can plant thoughts about the leader's effort to make a change, which can start a reputational virus to spread. Interestingly, this can be done with a surrogate who is "in the know" regarding the change effort or by using a surrogate who is an unwitting link in the reputation chain that the leader uses to pass along information. For example, the surrogate could simply be a person who is well networked in the organization and has a propensity for passing along information. The leader could impact the surrogate's reputational image by demonstrating (or not demonstrating) the behaviors at the heart of the reputational image in the presence of the surrogate to initiate the spread of new reputational information. It is like seeding a cloud in the hope that it will start a rainstorm.

The final step in the model is Internalizing Change. Once a leader has initiated a reputation change, it is important to start internalizing the behaviors responsible for the change. The leader needs to start incorporating the new behaviors into his or her ongoing repertoire and display them in a natural, authentic manner. This process will be helped along as the leader experiences reactions and comments from those developing a new reputational image for him or her. It is almost a cycle within the cycle. The leader practices new behaviors, others witness and comment on what they are seeing, and the information filters back to the leader, thereby reinforcing the change effort.

Much of what we covered regarding the five steps in the Leader Development Cycle and the role of reputation in each step was presented in a linear fashion. It can be that linear, especially if the leader is trying to make a specific change to his or her reputational image. However, it is equally important to realize that the development cycle is very dynamic. Changes are occurring constantly, and the reputational information is flowing into and out of each step whether the leader is aware of it or not. Most of the information is accumulating in a reputational image held by others regarding the leader. The more stable the reputational image, the more likely new information is simply reinforcing the image that is held. It is up to the leader to stay in touch with the reputation information and manage its flow and impact to achieve positive career outcomes.

Summary

For many of those reading this chapter, our view of reputation as a central focus of leader development is likely a radical departure from the traditional view that begins and ends with behavior change. We are in a world today where the flow of information is more like drinking from a fire hose than sipping from a cup. People need ways to organize information now more than ever. That means they are inclined to develop a reputational image more quickly and hold on to that image with greater zeal. It is increasingly becoming an important control mechanism for information overload. For a leader, it suggests the need for careful attention to reputational information and close monitoring of how it is affecting his or her career outcomes. One Tweet©. One Facebook© post. Or, heaven forbid, one negative YouTube© clip could mean the difference between a rapid rise to the top of the corporate ladder or a seat at an empty table in the back of the lunchroom. In the coming chapters, we will explore some of the key issues leaders need to be aware of as they shape their reputations. More important, we will provide the guidance necessary to shape (or reshape) a reputational image to achieve positive career outcomes.

CHAPTER 2

PILLARS OF REPUTATION CHANGE

INTRODUCTION

There are five pillars upon which leadership development rests when reputation is the central focus of change. These pillars include Strategic Self-awareness, Situational Context, Change Targets, Self-Monitoring, and Calibration. We call these "pillars" because failing to attend to any one of them can jeopardize the ability of a leader to achieve positive career outcomes. While these pillars are implied within the components of the Leadership Development Cycle, they are so critical to the success equation that they warrant the attention we devote to them in this chapter.

STRATEGIC SELF-AWARENESS

Self-awareness is arguably one of the oldest terms ever associated with the field of psychology. It is typically thought of as becoming in touch with one's feelings and emotions that are trapped in the unconscious waiting to be brought to the surface. This view has its roots in the intrapsychic approaches to personality dating back to the early 1900s. For example, it is the cornerstone of traditional psychotherapy, which continues to flourish in clinical training programs throughout the world.

More recently, *self-awareness* has been defined by social psychologists as "a psychological state in which people are aware of their characteristics, feelings, and behavior" (Crisp & Turner, 2010). Unfortunately, even this view of self-awareness does not go far enough in bringing the concept out of the recesses of the mind to a place where it is a useful component in the process of leadership development.

Hogan and Benson (2009) argued that despite its dominance in the mainstream of psychology, the popular view of self-awareness is incorrect. In fact, they go further, stating, "It takes the process of guided individual development in the wrong direction." Their view of self-awareness takes a decidedly different direction that is much more behavioral and, for that matter, measurable.

Self-awareness, or as Hogan and Benson (2009) refer to it, "Strategic Self-awareness," involves knowing your strengths and weaknesses in comparison to those of your competitors in various activities. There are three important distinctions between Strategic Self-awareness and the view of self-awareness held by those who adhere to intrapsychic approaches to personality. First, strengths and weaknesses must be understood in behavioral terms and, as such, can be observed and measured. This is quite different from feelings or emotions that are the purview of intrapsychic approaches to self-awareness where understanding comes through various forms of introspection.

Second, for self-awareness to be truly strategic, strengths and weaknesses can only be fully understood when compared with those of others, particularly those who form a defined reference group. For example, a soccer player playing at the high school level may be viewed as having superior ball-handling skills. At the college level, those same ball-handling skills might be viewed as average. At the European Premier League level, those same ball-handling skills might not even get the player a tryout. For our soccer player to gain true Strategic Self-awareness, ball-handling skills would have to be evaluated in terms of the level to which the individual aspires, or at least to the level of a defined reference group.

Interestingly, the roots of this view of Strategic Self-awareness actually date back to the writings of Socrates. Hogan and Benson (2009) describe this early take on Strategic Self-awareness among Greek philosophers as follows:

> *Socrates' maxim was "know thyself"; he also famously maintained that the unexamined life is not worth living. However, Socrates and the ancient Greeks meant something very specific by self-knowledge. They were a practical people and they defined self-knowledge in terms of understanding the limits of one's performance capabilities—i.e., knowing one's strengths and shortcomings vis-à-vis one's competitors in various activities. (p. 120)*

This view of Strategic Self-awareness has considerable utility as the starting point in any leadership development effort. It forms the baseline from which to evaluate current performance and establish a target for future performance. It is important to understand that Strategic Self-awareness cannot be acquired through introspection as mainstream psychology would have you believe. It can only be acquired through systematic, performance-based, behavioral feedback.

Third, when reputation is the focus of leadership development, Strategic Self-awareness must be considered from the point of view of the observer. In other words, it is not enough to understand behavioral strengths and weaknesses even if they are considered in light of one's competition. Reputation is derived from the perspective of others and the way they may see behavioral strengths and weaknesses. It is incumbent upon a leader who takes a reputational approach to development to go beyond understanding strengths and weaknesses in comparison to the competition. Success depends upon even deeper self-awareness that includes an understanding of how others perceive a leader's strengths and weaknesses.

SITUATIONAL CONTEXT

Reputation does not occur in a vacuum. It is important to consider some of the key situational factors that impact job performance and the lens through which people form a reputational image of a leader. Three factors are especially relevant to this discussion, including the culture of the organization in which the job is being performed (Culture Context), the personality characteristics of the person managing a leader (Manager Context), and the role in which a leader is performing (Role Context). The following is a brief description of these contextual factors and how they impact a leader in terms of both performance and reputation.

> **Culture Context—***This contextual factor includes the norms, values, taboos, and success factors associated with the culture of an organization. No two organizations are alike, regardless of whether they happen to produce competing products or they are part of the same industry. What sets organizations apart from one another is culture. While it can be defined in a variety of ways, Ravasi and Schultz (2006) view organizational culture as a set of shared mental assumptions that guide interpretation and action in organizations by defining appropriate behavior for various situations. One of those situations involves evaluating the job performance of those working for the organization. The combined aspects of the culture will influence the way job performance is evaluated. For example, in some organizations the only thing that matters is results. In other organizations, how those results are achieved may be equally important. Even the way rating scales used to evaluate performance are utilized in an organization can be influenced by the culture. Some organizations are lenient in their ratings, while others can be very tough.*
>
> *The Culture Context can have a dramatic impact on the success of an employee. Consider a hard-working new supervisor who performs his or her job in a very competent fashion. However, the new supervisor happens to be very colorful and garners a lot of attention as the result of his or her colorful behavior. Some of the behaviors the new supervisor demonstrates on the job include being very dramatic, seeking the attention of others, overcommitting on assignments, and generally looking for ways to stand out as a leader. All of these*

behaviors contribute to the new supervisor's reputation for being colorful and an attention-seeker.

Let us say that the organization this new supervisor works for happens to have a very strong sales and marketing type of culture. Furthermore, attention-seeking behaviors are quite common among many employees, and employees who fail to call attention to themselves often go unnoticed. In other words, the Culture Context not only supports the colorful behaviors demonstrated by the new supervisor, they are almost a prerequisite for getting noticed and advancing in the organization. The new supervisor with a reputation for demonstrating colorful behaviors would not only survive but may thrive.

In contrast, let us say that our new supervisor joined a different organization. This organization supports a more engineering-oriented culture versus one that is sales and marketing oriented. In this culture, colorful attention-seeking behaviors are shunned. Perhaps they are even shunned at what might otherwise be considered an acceptable level in many organizations. The behaviors supported in this organization would look much more introverted, reserved, and even quiet. Despite being hard working and performing competently, there is every chance that our new supervisor would garner considerable negative attention for demonstrating colorful behaviors. At the very least, he or she would likely get feedback to dial back the colorful behaviors. It might even be the case that without making the appropriate behavior changes, the new supervisor could be let go on the basis of a poor cultural fit.

These two examples illustrate how the Culture Context can play such a central role in determining an employee's success. In one organization, the colorful behavioral tendencies worked to the advantage of the employee. In the second situation, those same behavioral tendencies could result in quite a different outcome. In other words, the evaluation of the job performance and the reputation of the new supervisor could be dramatically impacted by the Culture Context.

Manager Context—*This contextual factor includes the style of the manager evaluating performance, his or her core values, and priorities. All managers vary in the way they approach the task of evaluating performance. Training and sound performance evaluation strategies can improve consistency across managers, but differences in evaluating performance will always be present. It is interesting that this contextual factor can even come into play within an organization. Employees are often confronted with leadership changes, and at times, their performance may be evaluated by more than one manager. Situations like this will bring the Manager Context into play, and it may have an impact on employee success that rivals that of the Culture Context.*

The impact of Manager Context can clearly be illustrated using the previous example of the new supervisor who exhibited colorful behaviors. Consider a situation in which the new supervisor reports to a manager who demonstrated similar behaviors. Some of these behaviors might include attention-seeking or being overly dramatic. If the new supervisor demonstrates similar colorful behaviors, it is likely to go unnoticed by the manager. Interestingly, there may be some additional dynamics at work. For example, the manager may become annoyed with the new supervisor because each is competing for attention. Alternatively, the manager may encourage the new supervisor to demonstrate attention-seeking behaviors as he or she may view them as an essential ingredient for success. Dynamics such as these underscore the "awareness" challenge employees face on a regular basis. They may not realize it in the concrete terms described above, but it is quite prevalent throughout the career of an employee.

Now consider what would happen if there was a leadership change for the new supervisor with the incoming manager possessing a more introverted, low-profile style. It is entirely possible that the incoming manager would have disdain for colorful behaviors. It may even be the case that such behaviors would elicit negative feedback from the manager in the form of a poor performance evaluation. In any case, the new supervisor's colorful behaviors and reputation for attention seeking in relation to the incoming manager's introverted, low-profile style could have serious ramifications for the new supervisor's career success.

Role Context—This contextual factor is related to the role a person occupies or a role to which the individual aspires. Roles are often not as clear-cut as Culture or Manager contextual factors. In fact, they can vary by situation and place a significant burden on an individual to maintain a high degree of vigilance regarding behaviors that are appropriate, or more importantly, inappropriate. Again, the example of colorful behaviors will help illustrate the impact of this factor. A new supervisor will play a variety of roles as part of his or her job. Two of the most common will be leader to those reporting to him or her and team member working with peers who report to a common manager at the next level. It may be the case that the new supervisor's colorful behaviors will be tolerated differently in these two roles. Subordinates may be quite tolerant of some colorful behaviors from their supervisor. Peers, on the other hand, may view the colorful behaviors through a more competitive lens and have little tolerance for them. In either case, it is crucial for the new supervisor to maintain a degree of situational awareness that includes an understanding of the roles that are part of the job and the behavioral expectations that accompany them.

The notion of Situational Context and its relation to employee success can be quite overwhelming when one considers myriad possibilities that are ever-present in the workplace. The fact of the matter is that employees confront situational factors daily and find ways to cope with them. The purpose of highlighting Culture, Manager, and Role contextual factors is that they play such an important part in the success or failure of an employee at every career stage and are ever-present in the evaluation of job performance. Employees who maintain a high degree of awareness regarding their reputation within the context of their situation hold a decided edge over those who simply focus on performance and leave their reputation to chance.

SELF-MONITORING

Self-Monitoring with respect to one's reputation refers to the practice of remaining vigilant regarding the circumstances under which certain negative behaviors could contribute to a reputational scar. A simple example would be to increase a person's workload over an extended period of time without a sufficient break or recovery time. Conditions such as this increase the probability that a problem behavior might surface in the workplace. A person who is highly excitable is more likely to have an emotional outburst; a person who is overly self-confident is more likely to blame others if something goes wrong, and so on. The fact is any condition that causes individuals to reduce their Self-Monitoring opens the door for negative, derailing behaviors to emerge. An excessive workload is just one of many conditions that could allow derailing behaviors to enter a person's repertoire. Furthermore, when people are heavily engaged in Self-Monitoring, they can often prevent or control a negative, derailing behavior from being exhibited and creating reputational damage.

Perhaps one of the best examples can be found in an interview situation. Generally speaking, during a job interview, people attempt to put their best foot forward. They are in a heightened state of Self-Monitoring and will do their best to make sure the interviewer only sees the "bright side" of their personality. That is not to say that the derailing behaviors are not lurking in the background. It just means that for a period of time, the person's heightened state of Self-Monitoring is standing guard, attempting to make sure that certain behaviors do not emerge. A job interview is a microcosm of what goes on in everyday life. The only difference is the degree to which people monitor their behavior. When Self-Monitoring goes up, the risk of a negative, derailing behavior emerging declines. When Self-Monitoring goes down, the risk increases.

This is actually very good news from a leadership development standpoint. Leaders who possess self-awareness regarding their reputation (including potential reputational scars) and can effectively self-monitor these behaviors have an excellent chance of maintaining control over them. In fact, when you talk to effective leaders about their reputation, you will often hear stories about how their negative, derailing behaviors might have impacted them early in their career and how they learned to control them.

CHANGE TARGETS

Up to this point, we have mainly focused on leaders displaying negative, derailing behaviors and their potential for creating a reputational scar. There has been a lot of interest recently regarding the absence of certain behaviors and the impact it can have on career success. Much of the interest has been generated because of a Hogan workshop titled, "The Leadership Formula" (contact training@hoganassessments.com for more information on this workshop). The workshop is designed for leaders and combines the power of Hogan assessment insights with coaching tips to achieve positive behavior change.

Early in the development of the Leadership Formula workshop, there were extensive discussions about a number of executive coaching cases that had been conducted over the past couple of decades and the role negative, derailing behaviors played in these cases. These cases typically involved helping executives learn to control these behaviors as a means of becoming more successful in the workplace. One case stood out as particularly intriguing. It involved a C-suite executive who exhibited virtually no negative, derailing behaviors, but this executive was described as having an ongoing struggle with a tendency to be overly trusting. That led to a discussion about his failure to be even moderately skeptical with respect to those around him. It was apparent that certain behaviors associated with being moderately skeptical such as "paying attention to the motives of others" were missing, or at least underused, in his day-to-day performance. In other words, he was at no risk of derailing because he was overly distrustful. His performance was suffering because he was unable to benefit from effective skeptical behaviors that lead to insight about the motives of others.

This brings us to an important point about negative, derailing behaviors that can undermine the reputation of a leader. They are not really discrete behaviors. In fact, they are behaviors mixed in with an overall pattern of behavior. The pattern has many positive behaviors as well as negative behaviors, and even the negative behaviors have positive elements that can work to one's advantage if they do not go over the top. For example, everyone has encountered people when they are experiencing an excitable moment. They may talk fast, use words that convey passion, use hand gestures, and so on. When they go over the top, they may yell, bang desks, throw things, and so on. These are all behaviors associated with being excitable, but at some point, an acceptable level of excitable behavior becomes a derailing level of behavior. This leads inevitably to the conclusion that, for many potentially negative, derailing behaviors, there is an acceptable level of behavior that may, in fact, be important in a leader's performance.

For example, there is a certain pattern of excitable behavior that would likely be acceptable under many circumstances and, potentially, a strength when it appears as something as acceptable as passion. However, what might happen if a person demonstrates few (if any) excitable behaviors even when the situation calls for it? For all practical purposes, it is the absence of certain excitable behaviors that becomes the problem.

The "throwaway line" that captures the essence of this perspective is, "Excessive or overuse of certain derailing behaviors can get you fired, and the absence or underuse of those same behaviors can get you passed over." Although this is a simplistic view, it is not too far from the truth. If you ask a group of coaches to give behavioral examples of executives who have been fired, you will quickly fill up a flipchart. If you ask the same group of coaches to tell you about an executive fired for failing to demonstrate the same behaviors for which they have observed executives get fired, they likely will have very little to report. However, they can easily cite examples where the lack or absence of certain behaviors resulted in an executive being passed over. The point here is that Change Targets often involve the ability of a leader to control or eliminate negative, derailing behaviors that contribute to a poor reputational image. It can also be the case that a change target can involve the addition of behaviors to build a more positive reputational image. In either case, whether eliminating a negative, derailing behavior or adding a behavior that contributes to success, it is incumbent upon a leader to focus on Change Targets that impact his or her reputational image and successful career outcomes.

CALIBRATION

This brings us to the last, and perhaps most important, of the five pillars of reputation change—Calibration. The reputation of a leader is not a static concept. It is not static because the Situational Context is ever-changing. If the situation a leader found him- or herself in was a constant, the leader could simply focus on creating a good first impression among relevant others and allow that impression to be reinforced over time. Unfortunately, quite the opposite is true. New players come and go. Job requirements evolve. Even the stability of a strong culture can be upset by a merger, acquisition, or changes in business environment. It is incumbent upon a leader who is interested in career success to be cognizant of his or her reputation and to calibrate the management of his or her reputation using performance feedback.

Performance feedback comes to us in all different forms. Perhaps the biggest challenge for someone trying to manage his or her reputation is determining the useful feedback versus feedback that is just noise, or worse, inaccurate. Hogan and Benson (2009) suggest that the only useful feedback is negative feedback, which comes via frustration, failure, and defeat. They go so far as to say that there is "no news in good news." This seems to be a somewhat limited perspective and is even a bit inconsistent with the notion that Strategic Self-awareness involves knowing one's weaknesses *and* strengths (i.e., is one supposed to assume one's strengths are those things for which we have not received negative feedback?). It would also run counter to most leadership development efforts that include accentuating the positive as a method of achieving positive career outcomes.

An alternative view that has a better fit with the notion of Strategic Self-awareness is that feedback has a motivational component that can be positive or negative and an informational component that can be quantitative and/or qualitative.

According to Connellan and Zemke (1993), "Quantitative feedback tells us how much and how many. Qualitative feedback tells us how good, bad, or indifferent." This approach can be illustrated using the soccer example. Consider the following 2 x 2 matrix (Table 1) upon which a coach might draw to give a player feedback regarding ball-striking ability with the left leg.

If the player is interested in improving ball-striking ability with the left leg, any of the four cells would provide useful feedback. The "Informational" component clarifies the focus of the feedback. Combining qualitative with quantitative information typically enhances the feedback simply by virtue of the specificity and behavioral nature of the feedback. Equally important is the fact that the "Motivational" component of feedback could be quite important to the player's Strategic Self-awareness in that the player can gauge the fact that the work being done to improve ball striking with the left leg is producing results. When the "Motivational" component is positive, it encourages the player to build upon what has been accomplished. When the component is negative, it sets up a performance gap that needs to be closed.

		Informational Component	
		Qualitative	Quantitative
Motivational Component	Positive	**Feedback**—I am pleased with the improvement in your ball-striking ability with your left leg. **Impact**—Qualitative guidance is provided that left leg work was needed and that results are being achieved, and motivation is provided to build on the performance improvement.	**Feedback**—I am pleased with the 20% improvement in your ball-striking force with your left leg. **Impact**—Quantitative guidance is provided that left leg work was needed, a 20% performance improvement has been achieved, and motivation is provided to build on the performance improvement.
	Negative	**Feedback**—Your ball-striking ability with your left leg still needs more improvement. **Impact**—Qualitative guidance is provided that left leg work was needed and that results are being achieved, and motivation is provided to close the performance shortfall.	**Feedback**—The ball-striking force with your left leg still needs to improve by 20%. **Impact**—Quantitative guidance is provided that left leg work was needed and that results are being achieved, and motivation is provided to close the 20% performance shortfall.

Table 1   Components of Feedback

The question is which is more important from the standpoint of Strategic Self-awareness and helping leaders calibrate how they are doing with respect to building a solid reputation in the workplace. First, specific behavioral feedback from an "Informational" standpoint is better in nearly every feedback situation. Beyond that, individual differences start to play a significant role. Some people respond better to positive "Motivational" approaches and may even shut down when negative approaches are overused. Other people are perfectly fine with negative approaches and tire of the overuse of positive approaches, viewing them as just a form of "blowing smoke." One thing for certain is that Strategic Self-awareness and Calibration are critical to the process of guided individual development, and feedback is the only way an individual acquires it.

Consider the following example that illustrates just how important it is for a leader to detect feedback and remain vigilant because it does not take much to ruin a reputation.

> *Tim was a marketing vice president who was asked to take over as general manager of a restaurant chain. Tim possessed plenty of marketing experience but very little experience as a general manager. The situation was clearly a turnaround as the restaurant chain was seriously underperforming. Tim took over and made some minor changes to the rest of the leadership team, but basically kept the old team intact. Tim was quite outgoing and had a reputation for being long-winded at times. His team meetings were becoming lengthy, and he began to notice he was doing a lot of talking, and other team members were disengaging, and using laptops and cell phones. As the business challenges mounted, the CEO decided that Tim could use a coach. The coach did several interviews and began to hear a theme that Tim was arrogant and seemed more interested in hearing himself talk as opposed to hearing what others had to say. Tim was shocked when he got that feedback from the coach. He reported that he was never thought of as arrogant and worked to avoid such a label. The coach went back to his previous team members to check for the behavior, and sure enough, the last thing they considered Tim to be was arrogant. They did report, however, that he could be long-winded at times. After discussing this with Tim, two things became apparent. First, he recognized that he had a reputation for being long-winded. Second, he admitted that he was probably trying to prove himself too much in the new role and was going too far in explaining and justifying his thoughts and actions to the members of his team.*
>
> *Tim's failure to recognize and calibrate the impact his behavior was having on his team members resulted in his garnering a reputation for being arrogant. He did not pick up on the fact that his efforts to try to prove himself in conjunction with his tendency to be long-winded had almost the opposite impact. Not only did he fail to detect the feedback from his team members in the form of their disengaging, he compounded the situation by stepping up his tendency to talk too much. Furthermore, Tim's team members misinterpreted the behavior as his being arrogant and self-absorbed.*

With a bit more vigilance and greater outreach to calibrate the potential impact of talking too much, Tim could have avoided the negative impact to his reputation. A simple change of behavior involving the use of more "seeks" in place of his "tells" helped Tim to turn the situation around. This is certainly not an elaborate behavior change, but it could not take place without Tim being vigilant regarding his tendency to talk too much, calibrating its impact on team members, and Self-Monitoring his "seek" versus "tell" behavior.

Summary

The five pillars upon which leadership development rests, including Strategic Self-awareness, Situational Context, Self-Monitoring, Change Targets, and Calibration, are essential for a leader to understand when reputation is the central focus of a change effort. Each pillar underscores the dynamic nature of the workplace and the challenge a leader faces in maintaining a reputation that will result in positive career outcomes. In the past, this challenge was compounded by the fact that personality characteristics were given short shrift when it came to understanding the reasons for managerial or leadership failure. Today, quite the opposite is true. Reputation is based on the "you that we know" that stems from the expression of our personality characteristics in the form of behavior interpreted by others. By effectively attending to the five pillars within the context of the Leadership Development Cycle, leaders can effectively manage their reputation. In Chapter 3, we will provide an Overview of the Hogan Development Survey (HDS), which offers a taxonomy of the personality characteristics most often associated with managerial failure. Armed with this taxonomy, our approach to leadership development, and the development content outlined in Part II, leaders can effectively manage their reputation to achieve positive career outcomes.

Chapter 3

Assessing the Dark Side

Introduction

As with any journey, it is essential that an individual have a clearly defined starting point that ensures the path chosen will lead to a successful outcome. Never is that more true than when a leader pursues a development path that has reputation as its focal point. The assessment of behavior-based competencies has traditionally been the gold standard for identifying the strengths and weaknesses of a leader. The assessment technique most often cited as the best at measuring performance against behavior-based competencies is an assessment center. An assessment center can best be thought of as a combination of situational simulations in which a leader is asked to demonstrate behaviors that are evaluated by trained assessors. The approach can be quite effective but suffers from two basic problems when reputation is in the development equation. First, an assessment center is an expensive, time-consuming approach that is counter to the fast-paced, ever-changing world that is today's workplace. Second, behavior-based competencies tend to be organization specific. Therefore, a competency-based approach to development is fine from an organization standpoint; however, it does not serve the development interests of a leader who is likely to change organizations multiple times throughout his or her career. It also is not nearly as flexible as a reputation-based taxonomy that transcends the idiosyncrasies of any one organization.

An alternative to the assessment of behavior-based competencies that was developed specifically to measure reputational characteristics is the Hogan Development Survey (HDS; Hogan & Hogan, 1997, 2009). The HDS measures eleven characteristics that, if under- or over-demonstrated by a leader through his or her behavior, could have a negative impact on the leader's reputation. The more negative the impact, the more likely the behavior will result in a "reputational scar" that could impede career success. These characteristics are associated with what is called the Dark Side of personality. The HDS was the first assessment designed to measure these characteristics and, to this day, remains the only assessment structured around a reputation-based taxonomy that accurately measures potential career derailers.

HDS Development

While early versions of the HDS were not commonly in use until the mid-1990s, the roots of the inventory date back much further. In the early 1980s, Robert Hogan wrote about the concepts of socio-analytic theory and the need for people to "get along" and "get ahead" (Hogan, 1983). The HDS is essentially an assessment of the barriers to getting along and getting ahead. Also during the 1980s, Hogan was doing extensive development work on the Hogan Personality Inventory (HPI; Hogan & Hogan, 2007). Between 1979 and 1984, Hogan assessed more than 1,700 working adults with the HPI. This research legitimized the use of personality inventories in the workplace, and showed how to go beyond the Five-Factor Model (FFM) to gain insights into the personality characteristics associated with reputational scars that often result in managerial failure (e.g., Hogan, Hogan, & Busch, 1984).

The original model for the HDS was the PROFILE, developed by Warren Jones (1988) shortly after the appearance of the DSM-III, Axis 2 personality disorders (American Psychiatric Association, 1987). Jones intended to use the PROFILE as a psychometrically defensible alternative to the inventories of personality disorders available at the time. Hogan used the PROFILE for about five years, conducting validity studies with business clients. This research revealed associations between high-risk PROFILE scores, managerial misbehavior, and the resulting reputational scars that limited career potential.

The data from the PROFILE led Robert and Joyce Hogan to conclude that there was a role for the assessment of performance risks in the workplace. However, they had concerns about the PROFILE's emphasis on anxiety and depression. They decided to develop a nonclinical inventory to assess interpersonal behaviors that adversely affect the performance or reputation of people at work. They envisioned a tool to be used primarily for professional development and coaching, although even that vision has since expanded to include managerial selection—particularly considering the high-profile executive derailments that made headlines in the early 2000s.

The Hogans began working on the HDS in the fall of 1992. They developed items one scale at a time. They created an initial set of items, tested samples of people, computed internal consistency reliabilities and correlations with other well-established measures, reviewed the data, and revised the items to (a) enhance internal consistency reliability and (b) sharpen validity. They also received valuable input from colleagues in the United States and Europe concerning the content of the scales. The HDS is the product of six cycles of item writing, revision, testing, and further revision. The final set of items was defined during the summer of 1995. From 1995 to 1996, the Hogans assessed more than 2,000 people, including employed adults, job applicants, prisoners, and graduate students. The ages in these samples ranged from 21 years to 64 years with a mean of 38.5 years. There were 1,532 men and 322 women, 620 Caucasians, and 150 African Americans.

The inventory that emerged from this research was an assessment of 11 dysfunctional personality characteristics that form the foundation of a reputation-based performance taxonomy. From the beginning, the HDS was never intended to be used only with leaders. Rather, it was determined that these dysfunctional personality characteristics can be found in employees at any level and can negatively impact performance and reputation. The characteristics are not discrete behaviors; they are patterns of behavior that disrupt performance and tend to arise when a person (employee) fails to self-monitor and exert active behavioral control. All employees experience such moments to some degree. When leaders have these moments and one or more of the characteristics emerge as part of their reputation, they can destroy morale, derail a team, or even degrade an entire organization.

The potential impact of personality on leader performance and reputation led Rodney Warrenfeltz, PhD, founder of Development Dimensions International's (DDI) Executive Development Practice, to conclude that personality assessment was essential in providing leaders with development feedback. Between 1992 and 1996, Warrenfeltz incorporated the HPI; the Motives, Values, Preferences Inventory (MVPI; Hogan & Hogan, 2010); and the PROFILE (all measures of leader reputation in the workplace) into a comprehensive executive assessment program. In 1996, Warrenfeltz substituted the new HDS for the PROFILE. This was important for two reasons. First, DDI, a world leader in behaviorally based assessments, had adopted the HDS as a standard component of its Executive Development Practice. Second, it was the beginning of widespread acceptance of the HDS as an essential tool for understanding the reputation of leaders and their potential development needs.

Growing Acceptance

For 15 years following the development of the HDS, Hogan research demonstrated that performance risks are common among all working adults, and those risks often emerge as reputational scars. Furthermore, using coaching data collected after most HDS administrations, it has been well documented that (1) leaders gain considerable insight regarding their performance risks, and (2) focused development efforts can alter behavior and the associated reputational issues, resulting in enhanced career outcomes.

To date, nearly two million employed adults have taken the HDS. They represent every sector of the global economy, including manufacturing, communications, health care, retail, banking and finance, construction, transportation, security, law enforcement, and many others. The research involves more than 200 validation studies covering a wide range of job categories. Most of these studies link HDS scores with reputational ratings of managerial/professional incompetence.

The accumulated research regarding the HDS has been thoroughly documented in the technical manual (Hogan & Hogan, 1997, 2009). Perhaps more impressive is the way the HDS has been embraced by the business community. The HDS is now used in more than 70 percent of Fortune 100 companies, and more than 50 percent of Fortune 500 companies have used the HDS. It has become the standard assessment tool for leaders interested in establishing a clear understanding of their performance risks and the way they may be perceived by others in the workplace.

INTERPRETATION, PERFORMANCE, AND CAREER IMPACT

Leaders interested in building a foundation upon which they can craft a winning reputation in the workplace should start with a clear understanding of the characteristics measured by the HDS. The HDS essentially provides a research-based taxonomy of the characteristics commonly associated with management failure. These characteristics can emerge in the workplace in the form of dysfunctional behaviors when leaders are not adequately monitoring their performance. When these dysfunctional behaviors are exhibited, they get attached to a leader's reputation. As these behavioral incidents accumulate, a reputational scar begins to form. As we pointed out in Chapter 1, others will define a leader based on their direct or indirect perception of his or her reputation. If that reputation happens to include a reputational scar, the scar will undoubtedly be a focal point of the leader's reputation and could have significant career consequences.

The HDS epitomizes the notion of "forewarned is forearmed." Leaders who have completed an assessment involving the HDS have consistently reported a new, higher level of understanding regarding the way the potential dysfunctional characteristics measured by the HDS can impact their reputation. Leaders who have not taken the HDS but are interested in doing so can go to the Hogan website (hoganassessments.com) for the information necessary to gain access to the assessment.

The purpose of this chapter is to expand the understanding leaders have for the eleven scales of the HDS and the dysfunctional behaviors the inventory measures. For those unfamiliar with the HDS, the following provides a scale-by-scale description of the HDS that will introduce the fundamentals necessary for interpreting assessment results. It will also provide leaders with a behavioral taxonomy and lexicon for recognizing dysfunctional behaviors in the workplace, including the impact they can have on one's reputation.

For those familiar with the HDS, including those who have their own HDS assessment results, the information that follows will expand their understanding of the dysfunctional behaviors. We learn more about these behaviors, their impact in the workplace, and the reputational damage they can inflict each time we review them and see them being exhibited by leaders. We believe those leaders familiar with the HDS will significantly deepen their understanding of these dysfunctional behaviors and become even better equipped to prevent them from emerging to inflict reputational damage.

We begin each of the scale descriptions of the 11 dysfunctional characteristics measured by the HDS with a general definition including the range of behaviors possible at both ends of the main scale and the associated subscales. One of the most important recent advances in the understanding of the dysfunctional behaviors is the recognition that those scoring at the low end of a scale can encounter reputational problems just as those scoring at the high end of a scale. The best way to think about this concept is that high-end behaviors are typically overused or exaggerated in the way they are exhibited in the workplace. Those scoring at the low end of a scale tend to have an absence of scale behaviors that are necessary for career success. For example, a leader scoring high on the Excitable scale may demonstrate an excess of emotion in the workplace, earning him or her a reputation for lacking executive maturity. In contrast, those scoring low on the Excitable scale may demonstrate a lack of emotion to the point others label them as unable to be inspiring or motivational. The throwaway line that we referred to in Chapter 2 was that high score behaviors will get you fired, while low score behaviors will get you passed over.

In addition to the descriptive information, we provide the leadership and reputational implications for each scale with some major watch-outs that leaders should consider. Finally, the watch-outs are summarized in a chart, indicating how behaviors may impact a leader from a career and performance standpoint. This chart is not an exhaustive summary of scale-by-scale interpretation information. Rather, it is designed to set the stage for a leader to consider the development alternatives presented in Part II of this book.

EXCITABLE

Description: The Excitable scale not only concerns working with passion and enthusiasm but also being easily frustrated, moody, irritable, and inclined to give up on projects and people.

Low scorers seem calm to the point of appearing to lack passion or urgency ⟵ Behavior Range ⟶ High scorers display dramatic emotional peaks and valleys regarding people and projects

Subscale	Low Score	High Score
Volatile	Self-controlled; demonstrates strong emotional regulation but may seem overly restrained	Tempermental, easily angered or upset, tendency to lose control of emotions and react in interpersonally harsh ways
Easily Disappointed	Tolerant, steady, and resilient, but may seem to lack passion or "fire in the belly"	Demonstrates initial passion for people and projects, but becoming easily disappointed, frustrated, and losing interest
No Direction	Seems steady, self-assured, and clear about beliefs; unlikely to dwell on past mistakes	Cooperative and helpful, but may lack focus or have few well-defined beliefs or interests; tends to regret past behavior

Leadership and Reputation Implications

Leaders are expected to motivate and inspire others. Highly effective leaders are able to call on their emotions as part of delivering a message in either group or one-on-one situations as a way of adding excitement and urgency. They also can dial it back or avoid overusing their emotions as a motivating force. Without this versatility, leaders are at a deficit when it comes to motivating and inspiring others.

The Excitable scale suggests how even-keeled or steady a leader is across a variety of task and people situations. All leaders vacillate to one degree or another with respect to emotional highs or lows. When the amplitude of a leader's emotional sine wave is too great or too narrow regarding task or people situations, it can negatively impact his or her reputation. Too great, and people will regard the leader as unpredictable. Too narrow, and people will regard the leader as repressed or lacking passion. In colloquial terms, the latter is often referred to as "no fire in the belly."

Emotionality and steadiness are usually quite visible to those who work closely with a leader; however, that may not be the case with respect to beliefs as measured by the No Direction subscale. At the high end, a leader may just feel adrift with little clear sense of direction. At the low end, a leader may lack reflection, especially regarding mistakes, because of an entitled sense of direction. In both cases, reputational impact may be slow in coming but potentially just as problematic as more visible Excitable behaviors.

Risk Summary

	Low Scores	High Scores
Career	May be challenged to inspire people as a leader	Emotional outbursts may intimidate or alienate others
Career	Lack of emotion or flat affect may be misread as disinterest or a lack of concern	Emotional "roller coaster" may cause people to disregard opinions or concerns
Performance	Superiors may wonder if there is any "fire in the belly"	Superiors may see moodiness as "high maintenance" or a lack of executive maturity
Performance	Peers may look to others for passionate support on important issues	Peers may be concerned about consistency and predictability
Performance	Direct reports may have trouble reading the urgency of situations	Direct reports may avoid delivering bad news or avoid situations that create stress
Performance	Opponents may fuel a misperception of no passion or urgency	Opponents may "press one's buttons" to provoke inappropriate emotional responses

SKEPTICAL

Description: The Skeptical scale concerns being alert for signs of deceptive behavior in others and taking action when it is detected.

Low scorers seem trusting to the point of naiveté ⟷ Behavior Range ⟷ High scorers are negative or cynical and expect to be betrayed

Subscale	Low Score	High Score
Cynical	Seems positive and steady, but may not examine others' true intentions carefully enough; prone to naiveté	Perceptive about others' intentions but tends to assume they have bad ulterior motives; prone to negativity; quarrelsome
Mistrusting	Generally trusting; seems practical, cooperative, and follows through, but may get taken advantage of by others	Generalized mistrust of people and institutions; worrisome and alert for signs of perceived mistreatment
Grudges	Forgiving of others and understanding; others may take advantage of this accepting nature	Prone to holding grudges and unwilling to forgive real or perceived wrongs; unsympathetic and fault-finding

Leadership and Reputation Implications

One of a leader's most valuable assets is the ability to accurately size up people, an expertise that applies to everything from identifying talent to reviewing job performance. Leaders who approach the tasks associated with evaluating people from a "trust, but verify" standpoint typically outperform those who are ever on the watch for the Dark Side or, perhaps worse, tend to start from an unrealistic and stubbornly persistent Bright Side view.

The Bright Side versus Dark Side perspective that is measured by the Skeptical scale actually cascades across most situations for leaders. Leaders who start from the Bright Side tend to uplift people as long as they are viewed as sincere and not gullible. Leaders who start from the Dark Side usually do not fall victim to deception, but their questioning inclination can drain the energy out of people because of their often negative perspective. Behaviors associated with either extreme on this scale can be quite damaging to a leader's performance; however, it is probably fair to say that a healthy dose of skepticism should serve a leader well.

Interestingly, the subscales give some useful insights regarding leader challenges at the low end of the scale. It is easy to see how people who are not cynical, who trust others, and who do not hold grudges would generally be held in high regard. Unfortunately, there are times when leaders must be negative, and certainly there are times when they should not trust people. There are even times when leaders need a long memory of past transgressions to make sure history does not repeat itself.

Risk Summary

	Low Scores	High Scores
Career	May be taken advantage of by those who lack integrity or have an agenda	May be viewed as a negative force who drags people down
	May go too far in looking for the best in people who do not deserve it	May spend too much time looking for the Dark Side rather than for opportunities
Performance	Superiors may perceive a degree of naiveté	Superiors may tire of the negative or cynical views
	Peers may look for opportunities to advance their own agenda	Peers may use the negativism to advance their agendas
	Direct reports may prey on trust by taking performance liberties	Direct reports may have their morale depressed or lowered
	Opponents may feel comfortable using deception to achieve their interests	Opponents may prey on distrust to divide and conquer

CAUTIOUS

Description: The Cautious scale concerns risk aversion, fear of failure, and avoiding criticism.

| Low scorers are willing to take risks without adequate risk assessment | ⬅ Behavior Range ➡ | High scorers are reluctant to take risks regardless of risk assessment |

Subscale	Low Score	High Score
Avoidant	Open, warm, enthusiastic, and eager to meet new people but may overpower others or seem uninhibited	Avoids new people and situations to avoid potential embarrassment; may seem aloof, inhibited, uninterested in others
Fearful	Willing to try new things; seems original, inventive, and confident; may be overly forceful when expressing opinions or ideas	Afraid of being criticized for making mistakes and reluctant to act or make decisions independently; prefers to cooperate rather than assert oneself; may seem unoriginal
Unassertive	Decisive, assertive, and willing to express opinions; may come across as abrasive, inconsiderate, or unsympathetic	Unwilling to act assertively; tendency to be indecisive and slow to act; may seem cooperative but overly compliant

Leadership and Reputation Implications

Decision-making is an essential part of being a leader. It is a process that includes the consideration of alternatives, selecting from among those alternatives, and taking action (or not taking action) based on the alternative selected. Behaviors associated with the Cautious scale can impact a leader's decision-making process at any or all steps along the way. Overly cautious behavior can limit alternatives, slow the selection from among alternatives, and even thwart a leader's willingness to take action. In contrast, risky or low Cautious behavior can result in impulsive actions that stem from a lack of rigor in the decision-making process.

Perhaps more than any other HDS scale, the leadership implications of the Cautious scale can potentially impact the entire organization. Furthermore, behaviors associated with the scale are significantly impacted by the Situational Context in which they occur. This makes it difficult to pin down general leadership implications for low or high scores without the gratuitous "it depends." Nonetheless, behaviors at either extreme are not helpful to leaders under most circumstances. It is also true that others learn to take advantage of a leader's behavioral patterns at either extreme—at the low end to obtain agreement for action without due diligence and at the high end as a means to gain endorsement for no action.

The Avoidant subscale suggests a social cautiousness or fear of interacting with people, while the Fearful subscale tends to be more task focused or associated with decision-making fear. Both subscales will cause leaders to either approach or avoid situations based on the potential for failure. The Unassertive subscale tends to be driven more by a leader's self-confidence, and can be moderated to an extent by interpersonal skills in terms of how the assertiveness (or lack of assertiveness) is expressed.

Risk Summary

	Low Scores	High Scores
Career	Decision-making may seem impulsive or overly risky	May miss career opportunities because of the potential risk
Career	A history of bad decisions could be associated with poor judgment	May be seen as a blocker and not a mover in getting things done
Performance	Superiors may be concerned about due diligence in decision-making	May not be consulted by superiors regarding important decisions
Performance	Peers may be reluctant to support decisions that are seen as impulsive	Peers who want to get things done will find work-arounds
Performance	Direct reports may delay implementing decisions as a safety net	Direct reports may use slow decision-making to avoid work
Performance	Opponents may use risky decision-making as cover for their own risk taking	Opponents may use slow decision-making to stop initiatives they do not like

RESERVED

Description: The Reserved scale concerns seeming tough, aloof, remote, and unconcerned with the feelings of others.

Low scorers are too concerned about the feelings of others ←— Behavior Range —→ High scorers are indifferent to the feelings of others

Subscale	Low Score	High Score
Introverted	Socially engaging, enthusiastic, and enjoys being around others; may be seen as socially boisterous	Values private time and prefers to work alone; may seem withdrawn, unapproachable, or lacking in energy
Unsocial	Relationship oriented, accessible, warm, and highly cooperative; may seem conflict-avoidant	Keeps others at a distance; limits close relationships, and seems generally detached, aloof, and potentially harsh/argumentative
Tough	Sympathetic, sensitive to others' feelings, but may seem overly diplomatic or too soft on people issues	Seems indifferent to others' feelings and problems; focused on tasks rather than people; may seem cold or unfeeling

Leadership and Reputation Implications

Leaders must make tough calls on a daily basis. Often these decisions involve placing the good of the organization above the desires of individuals. Behaviors associated with the Reserved scale concern how leaders deal with these calls. At times, leaders need thick skin. Low-score behaviors may cause leaders to delay people calls or avoid delivering bad news. Higher score behaviors generally enable making tough calls as leaders will see people concerns as only one of several considerations.

High-score behaviors primarily impact a leader's communication style. Leaders displaying high-score behaviors often avoid interacting with others, and when they do interact, they may seem terse, curt, and uninterested. Because effective leadership depends on relationship building, this communication style can limit a leader's ability to approach and be approached by others.

The first two subscales speak to the social aspects of Reserved. They tend to negatively correlate with the Sociability and Interpersonal Sensitivity scales of the HPI. The Tough subscale is a bit different and really speaks to the notion of heart, or more specifically, heartlessness when it comes to leader behavior. Too high or too low scores have obvious drawbacks from a leadership standpoint. Too high and the leader may develop a reputation for being heartless, which can diminish followership. Too low and the leader may develop an "old softy" reputation as a person who is easily hornswoggled.

Risk Summary

	Low Scores	High Scores
Career	May avoid making tough but important decisions	May miss opportunities to network and build relationships
Career	May avoid interpersonal conflicts or confrontations that are necessary for advancement	May misread situations that have a large people component
Performance	Superiors may see excessive people concerns as soft on performance issues	Superiors may resist engaging a loner in important initiatives
Performance	Peers may employ aggressive or confrontational tactics as a means of influence	Peers may not reach out to network because of aloofness
Performance	Direct reports may misread messages that are too diplomatic and not sufficiently direct	Direct reports may not disclose concerns because of a perceived lack of empathy
Performance	Opponents may use conflict avoidance to gain tacit agreement	Opponents may insert themselves in stakeholder relationships as gatekeepers

LEISURELY

Description: The Leisurely scale concerns appearing to be friendly and cooperative, but actually following one's own agenda and quietly but stubbornly resisting those of others.

Low scorers appear to lack an agenda or direction ← Behavior Range → High scorers are passive aggressive and agenda driven

Subscale	Low Score	High Score
Passive Aggressive	Seems steady, cooperative, and forgiving; comfortable expressing feelings and opinions	Overtly pleasant and compliant but privately resentful and subversive regarding requests for improved performance; seems moody and easily upset
Unappreciated	Cooperative, efficient, reliable, and willing to help others; likely to believe hard work will speak for itself	Believes that one's talents and contributions are ignored or underappreciated; perceives inequities in assigned workloads
Irritated	Open to feedback, willing to assist others; easily distracted or too readily agrees to help others and loses focus on own agenda	Privately but easily irritated by interruptions, requests, or work-related suggestions; not easily coached

Leadership and Reputation Implications

Effective leaders have explicit agendas. The real question concerns whether their agendas serve the needs of the organization or their own needs. Behaviors at the low end tend to overserve the needs of the organization, or worse, the needs of a given individual, such as a manager. In essence, this scale is a marker for some of the negative aspects of followership, namely, following others simply because one has no agenda that offers any resistant or alternative direction. A further downside to low Leisurely behaviors is the lack of resistance to agenda change, which can create a reputation as a leader who just goes with the flow.

It is interesting to consider how high Leisurely behaviors play out for a leader. They seem to be tolerated more if the leader's agenda is in line with the needs of the organization, rather than needs characterized as personal self-interest. In some respects, unwavering adherence to an agenda aligned with the direction of the organization will even garner admiration from followers. Unfortunately, if high Leisurely behaviors are out of sync with the direction of the organization, derailment may be likely regardless of the degree to which the agenda is correct.

The emotional component of the Leisurely scale is often forgotten from an interpretation standpoint. The subscales clearly reinforce this aspect of the scale with respect to leader behavior. All three contain an emotional component, with the Irritated subscale leading the way in terms of visibility from the observer's perspective.

Risk Summary

	Low Scores	High Scores
Career	May be rudderless in seeking career advancement	May resist key opportunities because of adherence to an agenda
Career	Career decisions may be excessively influenced by others	Paying lip service to offers may diminish future opportunities
Performance	Superiors may tire of wishy-washy or unclear stands on issues	Superiors may become frustrated with passive resistance
Performance	Peers may assume followership regarding their positions on issues	Peers may perceive lip service as political angling
Performance	Direct reports may flounder in the face of an unclear or ambiguous agenda	Direct reports may view stated positions as not credible, conflicts not resolved, or lacking true alignment
Performance	Opponents may seize the lack of an agenda to enlist support for their personal agenda	Opponents may use passive-aggressive behavior as way to park issues they don't want to address

BOLD

Description: The Bold scale concerns seeming fearless, confident, and self-assured, always expecting to succeed, and unable to admit mistakes or learn from experience.

Low scorers appear to lack self-confidence and resolve ← Behavior Range → High scorers seem assertive, self-promoting, and overly self-confident

Subscale	Low Score	High Score
Entitled	Unassuming, unpretentious, and helpful; lacking in outward confidence; may not actively seek out more challenging work assignments	Feels that one has special gifts and accomplishments and therefore deserves special treatment; seems combative, self-important, and unrealistically expectant of deference from others
Overconfidence	Seems modest and realistic about abilities but may have low standards for work quality or seem to lack focus and drive	Unusually confident in one's abilities; believes that one will succeed in anything; highly organized and systematic, but overestimates one's level of competence and worth
Fantasized Talent	Practical, content, and realistic about abilities; may seem to prefer more routine work or come across as uninventive	Believes that one has unusual talents or gifts and has been born for greatness; seems original and inventive, but arrogant, hypercompetitive, and unrealistic

Leadership and Reputation Implications

The behaviors associated with the Bold scale concern the most visible aspects of a leader's style. Followers look to leaders to instill confidence, especially when it is backed up with a track record of success. Moreover, it is in the toughest of times that these behaviors create memories in followers that become a virtually intractable component of a leader's reputation, which is why the Bold scale offers so much insight into a leader's effectiveness.

Behaviors associated with low Bold scores, particularly when they suggest a lack of self-confidence that is directly measured by the Overconfidence subscale, will cause a leader to rely heavily on position power as a way to motivate others—that is, "do it because I am the boss." High Bold behaviors cause people to believe, and when they believe, they can accomplish more than they imagine. Unfortunately, there is a fine line between confidence and arrogance. Leaders who cross that line can demotivate their followers to the point of tempting them to subvert the leaders' effectiveness. Blaming or credit-grabbing behaviors are among the worst associated with the high end of the Bold scale, and they are virtually assured to diminish a leader's effectiveness.

Risk Summary

	Low Scores	High Scores
Career	Lack of apparent self-confidence will create a follower reputation	Self-promotion may work in the short run, but can do career damage in the long run
	May miss opportunities because of an unwillingness to be assertive	Arrogance can breed resentment and revenge when opportunities arise
Performance	Superiors may overlook views presented without confidence	Superiors may lose confidence when they see an inability to learn from mistakes
	Peers may see insecurity as a sign of weakness or a person easily influenced	Peers may tire of excessive self-confidence or arrogance
	Direct reports may mirror a lack of confidence in ideas or positions	Direct reports may leave when victimized by blaming or credit grabbing
	Opponents may easily sway potential supporters when they see a leader who lacks confidence	Opponents may easily enlist others in efforts to undermine a leader who seems arrogant

Mischievous

Description: The Mischievous scale concerns seeming bright, attractive, adventurous, risk-seeking, and limit-testing.

Low scorers are conservative, compliant, and potentially boring ← Behavior Range → High scorers are impulsive, limit-testing, and at times, devious

Subscale	Low Score	High Score
Risky	Compliant, conservative, and cooperative; avoids unneccesary risk and makes few mistakes; may seem unadventurous or overly conforming	Prone to taking risks and testing limits; deliberately bends or breaks inconvenient rules; may seem unconcerned with risk
Impulsive	Dependable, reliable, and focused; may seem overly reserved, conventional, or predictable	Tends to act without considering the long-term consequences of one's actions; seems disorganized, impetuous, and unpredictable
Manipulative	Seems genuine, straightforward, and trustworthy; may seem overly inhibited; may struggle to gain influence or persuade others	Uses charm to manipulate others and demonstrates no remorse for doing so; may be persuasive and interesting but may potentially seem insincere or deceptive

Leadership and Reputation Implications

Trust is the foundation on which leadership effectiveness depends. Without trust, there is little chance a leader will succeed. If leaders are trusted, many leadership mistakes will be forgiven. On the surface, behaviors associated with the Mischievous scale do not seem to concern trust issues. In fact, it is the cumulative effect of behaviors associated with high-end scores that will erode trust, especially if all three subscales are elevated. Followers do not necessarily trust or distrust a leader at the outset of a relationship. The trust equation is relatively neutral unless a leader has a reputation as trustworthy or devious. In either case, followers have their antennae up to detect whether or not a leader can be trusted.

High-end behaviors accumulate very fast in their ability to diminish trust. These behaviors may appear as interesting, provocative, and even charismatic, but as they are overdone, followers are keeping score. Low-end behaviors will not create an interesting, charismatic reputation for a leader. They might even lead to a reputation for being boring. However, they will not detract from a leader's reputation for being trustworthy. The balance point for behaviors associated with the Mischievous scale is for a leader to be charismatic (or at least interesting) without engaging in the limit-testing, impetuous, or devious behaviors that can contribute to a reputation of untrustworthiness.

Risk Summary

	Low Scores	High Scores
Career	May miss opportunities that exist outside official channels	May erode the trust needed with increasingly responsible positions
Career	May lack the spirit of adventure necessary to seize opportunities	May create a reputation as a rebel, reducing career opportunities
Performance	Superiors may tire of a rule-compliant, conservative approach	Superiors may see limit-testing as unreliable
Performance	Peers may not network with a dull and boring person	Peers may see devious activities as untrustworthy
Performance	Direct reports may develop a "corporate attitude"	Direct reports may see limit testing as a license for them to break rules
Performance	Opponents may use the conservative mind-set to slow or derail progress	Opponents may seek support and cover when their actions appear too risky

Colorful

Description: The Colorful scale concerns enjoying being in the spotlight and seeming gregarious, fun, and entertaining.

Low scorers are modest, unassuming, quiet, and self-restrained ←— Behavior Range —→ High scorers are attention-seeking, dramatic, and socially prominent

Subscale	Low Score	High Score
Public Confidence	Self-restrained, quiet, and controlled; may seem socially reserved, inhibited, and lacking in outward confidence	Outgoing, confident, engaging; presents ideas with energy and enthusiasm, but is attention-seeking, dominates conversation, and talks over others
Distractible	Focused, task oriented, and methodical; may seem unable to shift gears quickly or multitask effectively	Energetic, curious, and idea oriented; easily bored, distractible, lacks focus; needs constant stimulation; confuses activity with productivity
Self-Display	Restrained, adherent to social norms and expectations; may not make a strong impression on others	Expressive, entertaining, and dynamic; enjoys the spotlight; uses dramatics to attract attention to oneself; may seem self-absorbed

Leadership and Reputation Implications

Leaders are often the center of attention. Behaviors associated with the Colorful scale predict the degree to which a leader embraces those situations. Leaders who exhibit behaviors at the low end seem to believe that their performance should speak for itself. This is unrealistic because their competitors are more than willing to call attention to themselves and their accomplishments. Being socially reticent can turn a leader into a gray spot on a gray wall—someone who goes unnoticed.

More often, however, leaders need to avoid excessive use of high-end behaviors. It is one thing to discreetly draw attention to oneself and one's accomplishments. It is another thing to suck the oxygen out of a room. From management's perspective, high Colorful behaviors create noise that can diminish a leader's credibility. From the direct reports' perspective, it can be demotivating when a leader constantly upstages them with excessive attention seeking that can be seen as credit grabbing. It is also important not to forget behaviors associated with an elevation on the Distractible subscale. These behaviors cause leaders to lose focus, or worse, jump from task to task or meeting to meeting, failing to get anything tangible accomplished.

Risk Summary

	Low Scores	High Scores
Career	May be underestimated	May be too self-focused and not a team player
	May seem to lack impact and not appear leader-like	Drama and exaggerations may create mistrust
	Vunerable to others' taking credit for contributions	Self-promotion can cloud real accomplishments
Performance	Superiors may overlook views and opinions	Over-promising may lead to a credibility gap with superiors
	Peers may take the unassuming approach as tacitly supporting them	Peers may tire of being upstaged
	Direct reports may see the unassuming approach as a lack of advocacy	Direct reports may see attention seeking as credit grabbing
	Opponents may steal the limelight even when it is undeserved	Opponents may use attention seeking as cover for their own actions

IMAGINATIVE

Description: The Imaginative scale concerns seeming innovative, creative, possibly eccentric, and sometimes self-absorbed.

Low scorers are practical, rely on routine, and often lack new ideas ⟷ Behavior Range ⟷ High scorers may seem impractical and unpredictable, and offer unusual ideas

Subscale	Low Score	High Score
Eccentric	Conventional, practical, and organized; may seem unoriginal or lacking in creativity	Curious and imaginative, but disorganized, distractible, and lacking in follow-through; expresses unusual views that can be either creative or merely strange
Special Sensitivity	Seems open to others' ideas and perspectives, but others may not perceive a strong sense of vision	Belief that one has special abilities to see things others don't and understand complex issues that others cannot
Creative Thinking	Pragmatic and grounded; may seem uninspired or lacking in curiosity and creativity	Highly creative, inventive, and idea oriented; easily bored, and potentially overconfident in one's problem-solving ability

Leadership and Reputation Implications

Generating ideas, exhibiting creative problem solving, and seeing around corners are all components of a leader's reputation for being strategic. One of the most common development needs cited for a leader is the need to be more strategic. It is also one of the most misunderstood characteristics of an effective leader. Nonetheless, leaders who offer new ideas (especially when they cause others to think) increase the probability that they will be viewed as strategic. It is also clear that having a reputation for being strategic significantly increases the probability that a leader will be viewed as a high-potential or a candidate for advancement.

Leaders with high Imaginative scores who blather about their ideas and offer impractical solutions will not develop a reputation for being strategic; rather, they may be seen as eccentric or even strange. At the low end of the Imaginative scale, a leader's reputation will likely be one of being excessively practical or stuck in past routines, a particularly salient issue when the Creative Thinking subscale is depressed, indicating a very strong propensity for problem solving to be grounded in routine, well-known alternatives. Regardless, in a world that sometimes seems to value innovation more than leadership fundamentals, leaders need to overcome low-end Imaginative behaviors without crossing the line into the eccentric in order to avoid the career-limiting label "not strategic."

Risk Summary

	Low Scores	High Scores
Career	May garner a reputation for lacking creativity or strategic thinking	May diminish credibility with eccentric ideas
Career	May miss chances to inject new thinking	Lack of predictability may cause a reputation as an erratic leader
Career	May stifle creativity by pursuing routine alternatives	Excessive ideation may confuse those implementing ideas
Performance	Superiors may overlook views when discussing strategy	Superiors may miss the good ideas that are disguised in excessive ideation
Performance	Peers may not seek or may even ignore problem-solving ideas	Peers may dismiss input as often too impractical
Performance	Direct reports may become complacent regarding innovation	Direct reports may be confused by frequent changes of direction
Performance	Opponents may use reliance upon routine to thwart change they fear or don't want	Opponents will cite unusual or eccentric ideas to discredit good ideas

DILIGENT

Description: The Diligent scale concerns being hardworking and detail oriented, and having high standards of performance for self and others.

Low scorers have poor attention to detail and tend to over-delegate ← Behavior Range → High scorers are picky and overly conscientious, and tend to micromanage

Subscale	Low Score	High Score
Standards	Seems relaxed and forgiving with respect to performance standards; may seem careless and disorganized	Exceptionally high standards of performance for oneself and others; practical, systematic, and exacting
Perfectionistic	Action-oriented; works quickly; may neglect important details or seem expedient	Perfectionistic about the quality of work products and obsessed with the details of their completion; precise and competitive
Organized	Flexible; able to work comfortably in ambiguous situations; seems inattentive to rules/policies, may not demonstrate strong planning skills or adequate follow-through	Meticulous and inflexible about schedules, timing, rules, and procedures; organized, thorough, and efficient, but management style marked by excessive control

Leadership and Reputation Implications

People are often promoted into leadership roles because they exhibit high Diligent behaviors. It is far less common for people to get promoted because they were not or delegated too freely, behaviors common at the low end of the Diligent scale. The behaviors associated with this scale speak to the need for a leader to evolve over time. Early in the career of a leader, high-end Diligent behaviors are quite valued and in many instances essential, given that direct reports may be young or involved in a variety of lower-level tasks. As a leader's career progresses, it is essential to let go of high-end behaviors in favor of greater empowerment of direct reports.

Effective leaders rarely engage in excessive empowerment or what has been called abandonment. They understand how to stay close without taking over. This ability has several important side benefits: (1) it creates a growth environment for subordinates, allowing them to take on more responsibility, and (2) it also frees up the leader to take on more responsibility without sacrificing work-life balance.

An underlying theme related to this scale is the sheer volume of work a leader is able to handle. All three subscales contribute to this theme. At the high end, leaders often cannot keep up with all the challenges that come their way. At the low end, a leader may let go of tasks too soon or fail to adequately follow up on task completion.

Risk Summary

	Low Scores	High Scores
Career	May delegate tasks requiring more oversight	May become overwhelmed with trying to manage everything
Career	May not give feedback or follow up adequately	True priorities may suffer as all priorities are emphasized equally
Career	May miss steps or actions essential for successful implementation	Micromanagement may cause work-life balance to suffer
Performance	Superiors may be uneasy with a lack of detail approach	Superiors may see an implementer, not a leader
Performance	Peers may look for more details or substance in projects affecting them	Peers may see the excess focus on details as a bottleneck
Performance	Direct reports may feel cast adrift with little oversight or feedback	Direct reports may be demotivated by micromanagement
Performance	Opponents may use poor follow-up as a way to advance their own agenda	Opponents may rely on conscientiousness to avoid work they should be doing

DUTIFUL

Description: The Dutiful scale concerns seeming to be a loyal and dependable subordinate and organizational citizen.

Low scorers are overly independent and seem to resent authority ← Behavior Range → High scorers are excessively eager to please superiors

Subscale	Low Score	High Score
Indecisive	Independent and self-sufficient, and may fail to solicit advice or gain buy-in from others when making decisions; may be too quick to dismiss others' input	Overly reliant on others for advice, and reluctant to act independently; careful to seek approval and/or consensus before making decisions
Ingratiating	Self-reliant and tough-minded; may seem insubordinate, may contradict others, or seem unwilling to play politics	Excessively eager to please one's superiors, telling them what they want to hear and never contradicting them; seems overly deferential and hesitant to express strong opinions
Conforming	Challenging; willing to express opinions, but may come across as rebellious, defiant, or disloyal at times; may be inappropriately challenging or contentious	Takes pride in supporting one's superiors and following their orders, regardless of one's personal opinion; seems overly cooperative, obedient, and excessively concerned with compliance

Leadership and Reputation Implications

Leaders need to avoid overly dependent followership behaviors that are associated with the high end of the Dutiful scale. A reputation for high Dutiful behaviors will put a ceiling on a leader's career because of his or her perceived inability to take independent action, or worse, being seen as the "yes person" for the manager. An interesting corollary to the challenges of high Dutiful behaviors is the way a manager might take advantage of the individual by limiting opportunities just to keep the individual in the fold doing the manager's bidding.

Low-end Dutiful behaviors do not seem to be nearly as problematic for a leader. The most significant risk is the potential for friction to develop with authority figures. Leaders exhibiting low Dutiful behaviors may resent management controls and seem rebellious or insubordinate. Managers who have a need for control may be intolerant of these behaviors or even see them as a form of disloyalty. It may seem counterintuitive to consider disloyalty in a conversation about the Dutiful scale, but leaders have a strong need for a degree of followership from direct reports. Decisive, tough, and even rebellious behaviors are inconsistent with behaviors associated with loyalty.

Risk Summary

	Low Scores	High Scores
Career	May miss lessons learned or coaching from those with situational knowledge	May get a reputation as a follower who is best suited doing the bidding of others
	May challenge or dismiss input from the wrong person	May over-promise as the result of being too eager to please
	May exceed latitude of authority in making decisions or taking action	Indecisiveness may slow progress by creating bottlenecks
Performance	Superiors may be uncomfortable with excessive independence	Superiors may tire of dependence or need for guidance
	Peers may question loyalty or trustworthiness	Peers may see a "yes person" incapable of independent action
	Direct reports may lack a role model for organizational citizenship	Direct reports may feel victimized by over-commitments
	Opponents may move into a void created by excessive independence or failure to stay in touch with senior players	Opponents may prey on eager-to-please attitude to accomplish work they want to avoid

Summary

The HDS is one of the most powerful assessment tools available to leaders and coaches. Its strength lies in providing a reputation-based taxonomy of information that will significantly enhance a leader's understanding of his or her performance risks and serve as a foundation for continuous improvement through focused development. In this chapter, we sought to expand your understanding of the 11 dysfunctional characteristics measured by the HDS and their potential impact on the reputation of a leader. In Chapter 4, we will use nine case studies to illustrate the many ways in which these dysfunctional behaviors can limit career success.

CHAPTER 4

Development Case Studies

Overview

The Leader Development Cycle (LDC) was designed as a simple heuristic that could easily be followed to make substantive changes to reputation, improve performance, and achieve successful career outcomes. A question remains as to how to convey the development content that leaders could employ when following the LDC that will result in substantive changes. The pure volume of development content available to leaders today is truly staggering. Some of it can be quite effective, some of it less effective, and a significant portion of it is a downright waste of time. The purpose of this chapter is to outline a finite number of case studies within which leaders could easily find circumstances that relate to their own situation. In subsequent chapters, we will use the case studies described in this chapter as the foundation for illustrating specific development content that leaders can employ to make substantive changes.

We decided that the best framework for designing the case studies was to use a combination of the three context factors (culture, manager, and role) with the 11 characteristics assessed by the Hogan Development Survey (HDS). The 11 characteristics can be organized according to three "global" factors of flawed interpersonal tendencies:

Moving Away (from people)—A tendency to put distance between oneself and others. This factor is comprised of five HDS scales including Excitable, Skeptical, Cautious, Reserved, and Leisurely.

Moving Against (people)—A tendency to exert influence over others. This factor is comprised of four HDS scales including Bold, Mischievous, Colorful, and Imaginative.

Moving Toward (people)—A tendency to curry favor from others, especially those in positions of power. This factor is comprised of two HDS scales including Diligent and Dutiful.

Using the three contextual factors arrayed against the three "global" HDS factors, we structured nine case studies that cover a broad spectrum of challenges often encountered by leaders in the workplace (See Table 2). Each case includes a description of the leader's situation before a significant change in the workplace, highlights of the leader's HDS profile, a description of the situational change, and potential consequences for the leader as a result of the change. The nine cases provide an efficient way to accurately portray a very wide range of leader behavior. In Part III, we take a scale-by-scale approach to illustrate the potential impact leader behavior can have on reputation and outline a comprehensive set of proven development tips and techniques that leaders can use to make the changes necessary to produce positive career outcomes.

HDS Factor	Contextual Factors		
	Culture	Manager	Role
Moving Away	**Case 1 (Low Cautious)** Rex, a risk taker, moves from a small company where he had autonomy to a much larger, more bureaucratic company. The acquiring company was not known for supporting risks, especially in sales.	**Case 2 (High Skeptical)** Phil, a skeptical logistics person working in a traditional logistics function, has been asked to report to a new head of logistics who has different ideas about the way the function should run.	**Case 3 (High Reserved)** Robert is an individual contributor who is very quiet and reserved. He has participated on project teams and is now being asked to be the leader of a project.
Moving Against	**Case 4 (High Mischievous)** Tanya is a crafty insurance professional. She is known for putting together big deals for corporate clients. Her success got her promoted to training manager, reporting to the regional VP.	**Case 5 (Low Bold)** Janis is a recently promoted customer service manager. She lacks self-confidence, but makes up for it with hard work and attention to detail. Her new manager is an ambitious high-potential leader.	**Case 6 (High Colorful)** Mark is a district account manager for a consumer products company. Mark's high profile style came under fire when the company expanded his role to include government accounts.
Moving Toward	**Case 7 (High Dutiful)** James is a marketing manager who worked for the same person in a family-owned business for more than ten years. When the company was sold, James's position was eliminated, forcing him to take a similar position in a technology start-up.	**Case 8 (Low Diligent)** Courtney just returned to the US from a new plant start-up assignment in Mexico. She was very successful managing a small team of start-up pros. Her new position is assistant operations manager in a manufacturing facility.	**Case 9 (High Diligent)** Kelly was promoted to CFO for a large clothing retailer. She was known as a detail person who put in long hours and made sure nothing ever fell through the cracks. In her new role, she manages all aspects of the finance function.

Table 2 Case Studies Categorized by Contextual Factors and HDS Factors

CASE 1—REX, VICE PRESIDENT OF SALES (LOW CAUTIOUS)

Situation

Rex is the vice president of sales for a small start-up company that specializes in the development and sales of natural vitamin supplements. The company has a solid regional presence with impressive growth numbers in a highly competitive market. In addition to the company-developed brand of supplements, Rex's sales team also represents several other brands that allow the company to offer a much broader range of products that complement their own brand. Rex has been with the company since the very early days of the start-up. He has a great deal of autonomy and is used to making lots of decisions about what brands the company represents and how they are represented to retail customers. Much of the company's growth can be attributed to his aggressive style and willingness to take chances on brands with little or no market presence in their region.

HDS Profile

Dimension	Score	Percentile	Description
Excitable	50		Rex is very self-confident to the point of being an arrogant leader (Bold—95%). He is quite willing to take risks (Cautious—10% and Mischievous—90%). He tends to work his own agenda (Leisurely—82%), and prefers to operate independently without a lot of close supervision (Dutiful—5%).
Skeptical	67		
Cautious	10		
Reserved	45		
Leisurely	82		
Bold	95		
Mischievous	90		
Colorful	75		
Imaginative	70		
Diligent	30		
Dutiful	5		

Situational Change

Six months ago, the company was acquired by a major producer of vitamin supplements. The acquiring company was well established, known for its strong brand recognition, and relied upon its size and market presence to drive sales. Rex was asked to stay on as vice president of sales and continue to build business for the company's natural brand of vitamin supplements. Rex continued to operate as he had in the past, relying on his aggressive style and willingness to take risks when the situation called for it. He paid little attention to the growing bureaucracy that was being imposed by the new parent company.

Situational Impact

The acquiring company in this case is described as large with strong brand recognition. It is likely that a company such as this would be somewhat bureaucratic with established boundaries for decision-making. Rex's entrepreneurial approach, including his tendency to follow his own agenda, take risks, and act independently, is likely to run counter to the prevailing culture of the parent company. The situation is further exacerbated by the fact that his decisions related to sales would be highly visible to others who are used to operating within the cultural guidelines associated with risk.

Case 2—Phil, Logistics Technician (High Skeptical)

Situation

Phil is the lead logistics technician for the western region of a national trucking company. He is known for his careful attention to detail and heavy-handed approach when it comes to cost control and routing options. He is proud of his ability to "sniff out" potential problems and call them to the attention of management before they create issues for the company. His current manager often relied upon him to detect problems and to deliver bad news to the field when the situation called for it. The field employees, on the other hand, viewed him as a "watchdog," always on the lookout for problems. They only approached him when necessary, and they knew that even relatively minor issues they might raise could be elevated to upper management and draw unwanted attention.

HDS Profile

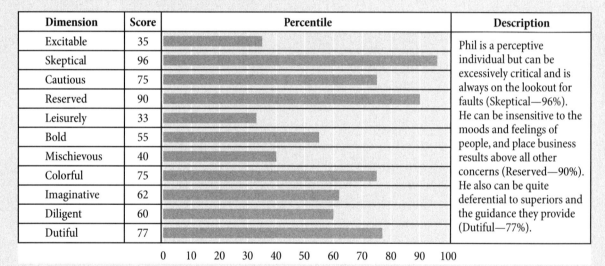

Dimension	Score	Percentile	Description
Excitable	35		Phil is a perceptive individual but can be excessively critical and is always on the lookout for faults (Skeptical—96%). He can be insensitive to the moods and feelings of people, and place business results above all other concerns (Reserved—90%). He also can be quite deferential to superiors and the guidance they provide (Dutiful—77%).
Skeptical	96		
Cautious	75		
Reserved	90		
Leisurely	33		
Bold	55		
Mischievous	40		
Colorful	75		
Imaginative	62		
Diligent	60		
Dutiful	77		

Situational Change

The head of logistics for whom Phil worked decided to leave and start his own logistics consulting firm. The CEO decided that this was an opportunity to bring in some new leadership talent and create more of a partnership between corporate and field. The new head of logistics began her tenure by touring the field and gathering input from employees including the regional logistics teams. During an offsite with the lead technicians, the head of logistics outlined her vision for the function and her plan for implementing it. Key among her plans was an insistence that the logistics function had to move away from the old "by the numbers" mentality and partner with the field employees much in the same way that the field employees partnered with their customers.

Situational Impact

Phil likely has two challenges that he will be faced with under the new leader. First, he clearly came out of the old "by the numbers" model where logistics was primarily a corporate "watchdog" function responsible for monitoring performance, monitoring costs, and enforcing route compliance. Second, it is quite likely that Phil's reputation would have preceded him in any employee-level interviews conducted by the new head of logistics. In other words, the head of logistics could have formed an early impression of Phil based on his reputation, and that impression would likely be in conflict with her vision for logistics to work in partnership with the field employees.

Case 3—Robert, Design Engineer (High Reserved)

Situation

Robert is a design engineer for a manufacturer of commercial aircraft electronic components. Since graduating from college, he has worked mainly as an individual contributor on a variety of project teams. He is known as a hard worker who attends closely to details. His team members often describe him as a quiet person who rarely speaks up in meetings or offers his owns ideas. They also describe him as a very dependable person whom they welcome as a team member because he always comes through in the clutch when the workload becomes demanding. His most recent assignment involved a high-profile project that was critical to the company's future success. Robert worked extensive overtime to see the project through and was seen by upper management as one of the "behind the scenes" guys who helped ensure the success of the project.

HDS Profile

Dimension	Score	Percentile	Description
Excitable	35		Robert is a hard worker who seems very calm and even-tempered under pressure. People view him as task focused with little interest in engaging with people (Reserved—98%). He tends to work long hours and is not bothered by the fact that his attention to detail spills over into work for others (Diligent—80%), which has earned him a reputation as a grinder who gets things done.
Skeptical	50		
Cautious	75		
Reserved	98		
Leisurely	80		
Bold	55		
Mischievous	40		
Colorful	30		
Imaginative	62		
Diligent	80		
Dutiful	30		

Situational Change

Robert's hard work and willingness to put in the hours needed to help ensure the success of his most recent project caught the attention of upper management. After considerable discussion, management concluded that Robert was ready to take on a project leadership role. The new project to which he was to be assigned involved the development of a new cabin security system. If successful, there was a high probability that the system would become a requirement for a wide array of commercial aircraft. The project team was slated to be cross-functional in nature and would even include external team members from the Transportation Security

Administration. The design-build timeline for the project looked to be demanding and well suited to Robert's no-nonsense, get-it-done approach.

Situational Impact

One of Robert's biggest challenges will be to moderate his quiet, reserved style and make sure his team members see him as approachable. The new role will also require him to be more proactive in his communications, given the cross-functional nature of the project and involvement of an external government agency. Finally, the project looks to be quite demanding, which seems well suited to Robert's hard working approach. However, he could easily slip into becoming an overly demanding leader with little regard for the toll it may take on his team members.

Case 4—Tanya, Insurance Professional (High Mischievous)

Situation

Tanya is a successful insurance professional for a medium-sized corporation. For years, the company relied on the entrepreneurial spirit of their insurance professionals for growth. In fact, Tanya's success in putting big deals together resulted in her promotion to training manager with the hope that she could impart her knowledge to up-and-coming pros. Tanya viewed the promotion as an opportunity to advance her own career and to teach young professionals how to get ahead in the business using her unique strategies for closing big deals. She knew the position would require her to teach the basic "blocking and tackling" aspects of the business; however, she felt her knowledge of how to stretch the envelope in putting together deals could be a real asset in developing new professionals.

HDS Profile

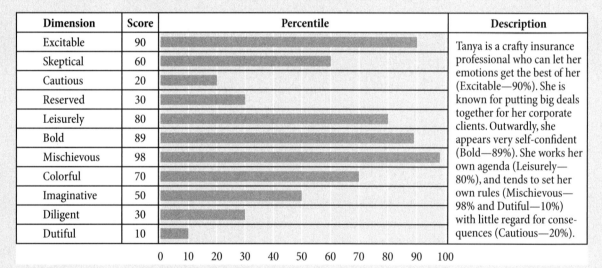

Dimension	Score	Percentile	Description
Excitable	90		Tanya is a crafty insurance professional who can let her emotions get the best of her (Excitable—90%). She is known for putting big deals together for her corporate clients. Outwardly, she appears very self-confident (Bold—89%). She works her own agenda (Leisurely—80%), and tends to set her own rules (Mischievous—98% and Dutiful—10%) with little regard for consequences (Cautious—20%).
Skeptical	60		
Cautious	20		
Reserved	30		
Leisurely	80		
Bold	89		
Mischievous	98		
Colorful	70		
Imaginative	50		
Diligent	30		
Dutiful	10		

Situational Change

The insurance industry has always come under scrutiny by government agencies. About the time Tanya was promoted to training manager, the company was inundated with a number of new government regulations. These regulations forced company leaders to embark on a culture-change initiative to ensure compliance with the new regulations. The initiative was viewed as critical because violations could result in heavy fines or worse. One of the most important components of the culture change initiative was to ensure new insurance professionals were well acquainted with the regulations and were scrupulous in their adherence to them in completing their jobs.

Situational Impact

Tanya's business approach prior to the new regulations was likely seen as simply stretching the envelope to meet customer needs. Her promotion resulted in her approach being put on stage in front of new professionals. The culture change initiative presents a significant challenge for Tanya. First, she will come under careful scrutiny because of the importance of the right message being conveyed to new professionals. Second, it is reasonable to assume that some aspects of her success formula could go beyond stretching the envelope and cross into areas that could challenge regulatory compliance. There are also risks associated with how Tanya will react to the regulatory constraints that were not in place when she accepted the position as training manager.

Case 5—Janis, Customer Service Manager (Low Bold)

Situation

Janis is a newly appointed customer service manager who works for a software company that sells and supports a variety of tax preparation software packages. Since joining the company, she worked closely with a regional manager who mentored her and was instrumental in getting her promoted from team member to team leader and, most recently, customer service manager. Janis is best known for being a very energetic person who has a knack for defusing difficult customer service situations. Customers consistently describe her as a positive person who did not overpromise and did a great job keeping them informed. Team members describe her as very conscientious and extremely loyal to the company. There were also rumblings that she sometimes did not stand up to people and could be easily manipulated.

HDS Profile

Dimension	Score	Percentile	Description
Excitable	60		Janis is a high-energy person who does not overpromise (Cautious—75%) and is very approachable (Reserved—15%). She lacks confidence (Bold—10%) but makes up for it through preparation and attention to detail (Diligent—85%). She is known for her loyalty and willingness to go the extra mile when it comes to protecting the reputation of the company and her manager (Dutiful—80%).
Skeptical	10		
Cautious	75		
Reserved	15		
Leisurely	20		
Bold	10		
Mischievous	40		
Colorful	30		
Imaginative	62		
Diligent	85		
Dutiful	80		

Situational Change

Janis's long-time regional manager was promoted shortly after her promotion to customer service manager. The new regional manager is viewed as hard charging, very confident, and charismatic. He is young for his position and is known for being very demanding of his team members. He is also known for being like "Teflon" in that he always seems to be in the right place when there is good news to be had and always seems to avoid blame or deflect bad news to those around him. Some have questioned his trustworthiness, but the results he achieves seem to override the negatives associated with how he achieves them.

Situational Impact

Janis's dutiful nature will likely make her an early favorite for the new regional manager. She will likely accept his demanding requests and will work very hard to see that they are achieved. The impact will likely be twofold. First, she may end up driving her team beyond acceptable limits, which could result in turnover. Second, her inability to push back could result in diminishing her own quality of life. The long-term career impact could be even more significant for her. If problems, even those beyond her control, should arise, it is likely the new regional manager could make her a target for the blame. Furthermore, her lack of self-confidence could be seen as weakness by the new regional manager, diminishing her prospects for future leadership opportunities.

Case 6—Mark, District Account Manager (High Colorful)

Situation

Mark is a district account manager for a consumer-product company. He has been with the company for more than 20 years and is regarded as a very loyal employee but a bit of a character. He has managed most of his accounts for years and is on a first-name basis with many of his customers. He tends to be a larger-than-life person who can take most of the oxygen out of a room. He is known for telling jokes and has a somewhat boorish interpersonal style. He can often exaggerate problem situations to elevate his own importance and likes to draw attention to his accomplishments, even those that are rather meager in their true importance. Those around him have grown accustomed to his style and have even learned to deal with his lack of attention to detail.

HDS Profile

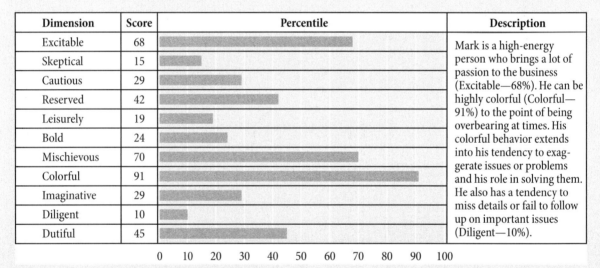

Dimension	Score	Percentile	Description
Excitable	68		Mark is a high-energy person who brings a lot of passion to the business (Excitable—68%). He can be highly colorful (Colorful—91%) to the point of being overbearing at times. His colorful behavior extends into his tendency to exaggerate issues or problems and his role in solving them. He also has a tendency to miss details or fail to follow up on important issues (Diligent—10%).
Skeptical	15		
Cautious	29		
Reserved	42		
Leisurely	19		
Bold	24		
Mischievous	70		
Colorful	91		
Imaginative	29		
Diligent	10		
Dutiful	45		

Situational Change

An economic downturn seriously impacted the company, creating the need for several changes. The first sign of trouble was when the company had to lay off 20 percent of the workforce. Mark survived the first round of layoffs because of his tenure in the company. The next major change involved the consolidation of government accounts with all other accounts. The consolidation significantly changed Mark's role by adding a number of large, new government accounts to those he was already managing. It was also a big change because of the type of customers he had to deal with on a day-to-day basis. Many were no-nonsense government employees who were used to doing business by the book and had little interest in relationship building.

Situational Impact

Mark's customers before the new accounts were added to his portfolio knew him quite well and had grown accustomed to his high-profile, colorful style. The accounts he took over were large government accounts with customers who had little interest in jokes or stories. They approached the business by the book. Mark's approach, using his colorful interpersonal style, is unlikely to be effective and may even alienate some. Plus, the transactional nature of the government accounts will require high attention to detail, which is not Mark's strength. The economic challenges faced by the company underscore the urgency for him to hit the ground running and avoid customer complaints.

Case 7—James, Marketing Manager (High Dutiful)

Situation

James held the position of marketing manager for 10 years in a relatively small family-owned technology business. He gained a lot of knowledge in his role because the owners pretty much relied on him to execute anything they needed from a marketing standpoint. His calm, even-tempered demeanor was perfect for the company because he never overreacted to requests by the owners regardless of how eccentric they might be. He also played a gatekeeper role by critically evaluating marketing requests from other parts of the organization and making very sure he had all the due diligence complete before bringing something to the owners. The owners really appreciated James because of his willingness do what they asked and, at the same time, keep what they viewed as distractions off the table.

HDS Profile

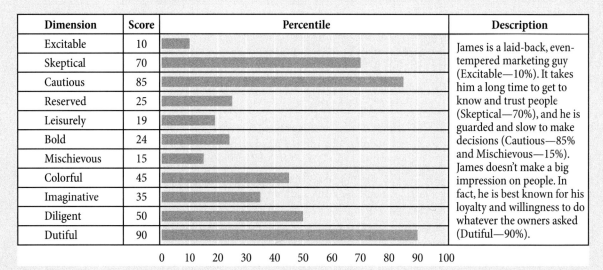

Dimension	Score	Percentile	Description
Excitable	10		James is a laid-back, even-tempered marketing guy (Excitable—10%). It takes him a long time to get to know and trust people (Skeptical—70%), and he is guarded and slow to make decisions (Cautious—85% and Mischievous—15%). James doesn't make a big impression on people. In fact, he is best known for his loyalty and willingness to do whatever the owners asked (Dutiful—90%).
Skeptical	70		
Cautious	85		
Reserved	25		
Leisurely	19		
Bold	24		
Mischievous	15		
Colorful	45		
Imaginative	35		
Diligent	50		
Dutiful	90		

Situational Change

The owners received a nice offer for the business from a well-established technology company and decided to accept it and take early retirement. The acquiring company had well-established staff functions, so several people were let go as the result of the acquisition, including James. The owners did help James find a new position with a local technology start-up company. It was a small company, but was growing very fast. New employees were often asked to wear multiple hats, and the fast-paced nature of the business forced people to make decisions without a lot of guidance or management support.

Situational Impact

Perhaps the biggest change for James was the fact that he was left to make a lot of important decisions on his own. Most of the people in the company knew very little about marketing, but they were more than willing to offer their thoughts and ideas. James's tendency to carefully analyze ideas and only make decisions when he has all the facts was likely not to be received well in this fast-paced environment. Furthermore, his lack of guidance contributed to his inability to make decisions, as he typically relied on the owners in his previous company to tell him what needed to get done. His early life in the new start-up company looked more like a data-collection exercise than a newly established marketing function in which steps were being taken to build a high-profile brand.

Case 8—Courtney, Assistant Operations Manager (Low Diligent)

Situation

Courtney has been viewed as a high-potential employee virtually since the day she joined this electronics-manufacturing company. She was placed on the fast track and given plenty of opportunities to develop her skills. In her last position, she was put in charge of a team of start-up professionals responsible for opening a new manufacturing facility in Mexico. The assignment was a good fit for her because she had a great deal of freedom to make decisions, and the folks working for her were equally independent and went about their jobs with little need for guidance. There were plenty of ups and downs, mostly due to government involvement. Courtney's ability to use her charm and influencing skills played an important role in keeping the project on track and getting the plant open on time.

HDS Profile

Dimension	Score	Percentile	Description
Excitable	30		Courtney is an energetic leader who is known for her confidence in taking on any challenge (Bold—95%). She tends to use her charm and charisma to get her way (Mischievous—90%). She also tends to grab high-profile assignments to keep herself in the limelight (Colorful—80%). Her superiors have put her on the fast track but have some concerns about her ability to be a team player.
Skeptical	50		
Cautious	20		
Reserved	25		
Leisurely	30		
Bold	95		
Mischievous	90		
Colorful	80		
Imaginative	85		
Diligent	5		
Dutiful	10		

Situational Change

Despite a strong track record and successful plant start-up, Courtney's superiors had lingering questions about her ability to be a team player. They decided to assign her to one of their best plant managers as assistant operations manager. Her new manager was the type of woman who never let things fall through the cracks. She worked long hours in her role as plant manager and was well known as a person who demanded the same from her team, but they always seemed to respond to her leadership style. Courtney's superiors viewed this move as an opportunity for her to learn from a seasoned professional, build her day-to-day management skills, and take some of the burden off the plant manager in keeping up with myriad operational details.

Situational Impact

The position of assistant operations manager is likely to be quite a challenge for Courtney. She is being asked to work closely with a seasoned leader who has a reputation for carefully managing the business. Her management responsibilities will be expanded to include not only a much larger team of people but responsibility for handling much of the burden for day-to-day operations. She will have to get work done through a lot of people while maintaining visibility to the details of the business. Her charismatic leadership style might be helpful in building relationships; however, it will not likely carry much weight with her new manager, who is focused on the performance of the plant.

Case 9—Kelly, Chief Financial Officer (High Diligent)

Situation

Kelly spent five years as the controller for a large clothing retailer. She managed the books with microscopic precision. She followed a set routine to close the books that took many hours of overtime but ensured that costs were fully accounted for down to the last penny. She had a reputation for being a bit cold interpersonally. More importantly, she could be quite probing or questioning of employees when it came to expenses or cost overruns. Employees didn't necessarily fear her. In fact, they admired how hard she worked and watched out for the company. Her interpersonal style did tend to get in the way of her building relationships. Even her team members treated interactions with her in a somewhat mechanical manner, almost like a financial transaction.

HDS Profile

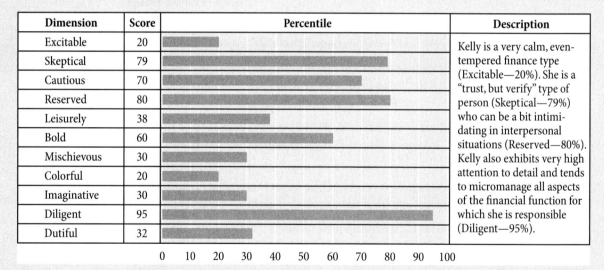

Dimension	Score	Percentile	Description
Excitable	20		Kelly is a very calm, even-tempered finance type (Excitable—20%). She is a "trust, but verify" type of person (Skeptical—79%) who can be a bit intimidating in interpersonal situations (Reserved—80%). Kelly also exhibits very high attention to detail and tends to micromanage all aspects of the financial function for which she is responsible (Diligent—95%).
Skeptical	79		
Cautious	70		
Reserved	80		
Leisurely	38		
Bold	60		
Mischievous	30		
Colorful	20		
Imaginative	30		
Diligent	95		
Dutiful	32		

Situational Change

Kelly's approach to the business was well suited for the role of controller. It required a high degree of attention to detail, did not suffer from her micromanaging tendencies, and didn't really require extensive relationship building. When the CFO passed away suddenly, it created a big gap in the company's leadership team. There was a lot of concern about putting Kelly in the role, but there was little choice given the needs of the business and the lack of adequate succession planning. When Kelly took over the role, her responsibilities expanded to all aspects of the finance function. Plus, she had to work closely with the other members of the leadership team to pull together the annual budget.

Situational Impact

Kelly was known well enough by members of the leadership team that her somewhat cold, argumentative interpersonal style didn't get in the way of their working with her. However, her new management responsibilities were a different matter. In the short term, keeping up was a matter of putting in more hours. Long term, it is likely that her tendency to micromanage everything is going to derail her with her team and cause her to burn out. Kelly will likely also struggle with her ability to contribute to the strategic aspects of the business. First, the vast amount of her time will be spent on details. Second, her low Imaginative and high Cautious thinking style may limit her big-picture perspective.

Summary

Organizing case studies by the three contextual factors (culture, manager, and role) and the "global" factors of the HDS provides an efficient way to present a broad range of challenges often faced by leaders in the workplace. These challenges, if not successfully addressed, will result in reputational scars that could impede performance and limit positive career outcomes. The cases were designed to give leaders an easy way to relate to the day-to-day challenges they often encounter in their own work situations. Furthermore, the cases studies present a straightforward way to organize development content presented in Part II that has been proven to be successful in addressing these challenges.

PART II

DEVELOPMENT TECHNIQUES FOR REPUTATION CHANGE

Chapter 5	Excitable	77
Chapter 6	Skeptical	91
Chapter 7	Cautious	107
Chapter 8	Reserved	123
Chapter 9	Leisurely	139
Chapter 10	Bold	157
Chapter 11	Mischievous	175
Chapter 12	Colorful	193
Chapter 13	Imaginative	209
Chapter 14	Diligent	225
Chapter 15	Dutiful	243

Chapter 5

Excitable

High Excitable: Controlling Your Emotions

It is emotions that make your life flow. They only become a problem when they go out of control.

Sadhguru

Detecting When It Is a Problem

High Excitable behaviors are easily observed in the workplace, and even one incident can have a devastating impact on a leader's reputation. Perhaps one of the best examples comes from the US political world involving a presidential candidate named Howard Dean. Mr. Dean had to deliver a concession speech following a third-place showing in an important primary election. He proceeded to go on stage in front of his supporters and explode into an emotional rant that culminated in screaming uninterpretable phrases, and he was red-faced and frothing at the mouth. Needless to say, Mr. Dean was not elected and has drifted into political obscurity.

It is rare for leaders not to be able to detect the fact they exhibit high Excitable behaviors. They see themselves getting overly emotional. They may even feel their emotionality at a visceral level. Admitting that these behaviors are having a negative impact on their reputation may be difficult, and controlling them, even more difficult. But these behaviors are easily observed and quickly accumulate to the detriment of the leader's reputation.

Tanya from Case 4—Tanya, insurance professional on page 62—provides a good example of an individual with a high Excitable profile. Tanya's highest derailer is her Mischievous score (98%), but the Excitable score is not far behind (90%). The following is Tanya's profile summary.

Tanya's Situational Summary				
Tanya was a successful insurance professional for a medium-sized corporation who was promoted into the role of training manager. The new role looked to be quite challenging because it required a new skillset to be successful, and the insurance industry as a whole was evolving into a highly regulated industry with many new government regulations. Tanya's new role as training manager could potentially be quite stressful given the job demands and industry changes.				
Dimension	**Score**	**Percentile**		**Description**
Excitable	90			Tanya is a crafty insurance professional who can let her emotions get the best of her (Excitable—90%). She is known for putting big deals together for her corporate clients. Outwardly, she appears very self-confident (Bold—89%). She works her own agenda (Leisurely—80%), and tends to set her own rules (Mischievous—98% and Dutiful—10%) with little regard for consequences (Cautious—20%).
Skeptical	60			
Cautious	20			
Reserved	30			
Leisurely	80			
Bold	89			
Mischievous	98			
Colorful	70			
Imaginative	50			
Diligent	30			
Dutiful	10			

Tanya's case is an interesting one in that her Mischievous score and the situational information presented in the case suggest that her Mischievous behaviors may present the more immediate concern from a development standpoint. However, Tanya is at a transition point in her career, having just received a promotion. High Excitable behaviors come under increasing scrutiny as a leader rises through increasingly more responsible positions. Furthermore, it is likely that future career roles for Tanya could involve people management responsibilities. It is likely that she will have more contact and greater need to rely upon her peers as her career progresses. At the very least, her high score on the Excitable scale suggests the need for probing regarding Excitable behaviors on the job. It may be the case that an early intervention could help her avoid any negative Excitable behaviors and the associated damage to her future reputation.

Sample Development Program (Case 4—Tanya)

Tanya's profile indicates an Excitable score of 90 percent. An examination of her subscale scores indicates that the Volatile subscale is elevated to the maximum level, while the Easily Disappointed and No Direction subscales are only moderately elevated. The case information presented about Tanya clearly indicates that Excitable behaviors may not be the top priority for her success in her current position. However, upon reflecting on Tanya's comments during feedback, it is clear that she has excitable moments related to her ability to control emotional outbursts and raising her voice to colleagues who do not agree with her as means of getting them to listen.

Reputation Change

In her new assignment, Tanya is rapidly gaining the reputation of a "hothead" due to her inability to control her emotions. Her ability to build and maintain relationships with her colleagues is being negatively impacted—the "buzz" is that she screams and has tantrums, and they do not want to interface with her. Further, her students are hesitant to ask questions because of her impatience, which does not encourage an open learning environment.

Given that Tanya has career potential and aspirations beyond her current role, she needs to turn these perceptions around swiftly before they become widespread. To progress, especially into roles where she will have more people management responsibilities, she needs to have a reputation of being calm and level-headed, making well-reasoned decisions, and encouraging new insurance professionals. To achieve this reputation change, development actions for Tanya should focus on her Excitable behaviors, emphasizing the behaviors associated with the Volatile subscale.

Development Actions for Tanya

The following are the proposed development actions for Tanya to take to drive a reputation of composure:

- Tanya should do a self-reflection exercise to identify incidents where she exhibited volatile behavior. The incidents should include a description of the situation and the details of what was said, including her affect and her perception of the impact she had on the others involved. What was the impact on her reputation?
- She should review the incidents of the self-reflection exercise to help her identify the themes, trigger points, and other cues that would help alert her to future situations that could cause an emotional moment.
- Tanya should develop a set of alternative behaviors that she can use to avoid such emotional moments, as follows:
  - Take a 10-to-15-minute walk before entering a situation that has a high probability of eliciting an emotional moment. Use the time to control breathing, and self-talk emotionally neutral statements that could be used to diffuse the situation.
  - Upon entering the situation, have in place a behavioral reminder to use neutral self-talk statements that were practiced during the walk.

- (Optional) Forewarn those who may be in the meeting or interaction that this is an issue that she is passionate about or has strong feelings regarding it.
- (Optional) Follow up with those who were a part of the meeting or interaction to determine if she was appropriately passionate without excessive emotions.

- Tanya should maintain a journal cataloging incidents that could have elicited or did elicit an emotional moment on her part and what the reputational impact was. This will assist her in tracking her progress as she practices her new behaviors.

Evaluating Your Need for Change

The following behavioral questions should be considered in conjunction with your high Excitable score when evaluating the need for a change in your behavior. A "yes" response to three or fewer items suggests that there is no imminent need for behavioral changes. A "yes" response to four to six items suggests that a high score on the Excitable scale should be a watch-out for you. A "yes" response to more than six items suggests that you should take active steps toward making behavioral changes.

Do you:

1. Quickly get visibly angry when frustrated or annoyed by the actions of others?   Yes   No   Not Sure

2. Demonstrate emotional outbursts, such as yelling at employees, vendors, or customers?   Yes   No   Not Sure

3. Appear to fuel the emotions in a situation by failing to exert emotional control?   Yes   No   Not Sure

4. Appear to be on an emotional roller coaster with highs and lows associated with various colleagues?   Yes   No   Not Sure

5. Get easily disappointed or disenchanted with employees who do not live up to expectations?   Yes   No   Not Sure

6. Regularly convey disappointment in others through emotional reactions?   Yes   No   Not Sure

7. Express an excessive amount of emotional regret regarding the way challenging situations are handled?   Yes   No   Not Sure

8. Make it difficult for others to determine your values or beliefs because of emotional highs and lows? **Yes   No   Not Sure**

9. Create directional uncertainty because of unpredictable emotional reactions? **Yes   No   Not Sure**

These items should be considered as behavioral indicators. Similar or associated behaviors to any of those listed that you exhibit likely suggest a "yes" response. They provide additional support that you may be at risk for the negative reputational consequences associated with those scoring high on the Excitable scale, such as Tanya.

Development Tactics

Development tactics cover a range of approaches and resources that have been found useful in addressing high Excitable behaviors. These tactics are typically used in combination to form a custom plan suited to the specific learning needs of a leader. The tactics are divided into four categories: (1) thought-provoking questions, (2) exercises to improve performance, (3) tips and techniques to improve performance, and (4) support resources that can be consulted to gain additional insights in addressing high Excitable behaviors.

Thought-Provoking Questions

- What can you do to pause in a situation and consider your impact on others?
- How do you build a long-term view of success and key milestones?
- How can you be selective about sharing emotional responses?
- Reflect back on observations of a high Excitable leader and ask, "Would you want to work with this person?"
- How do you handle situations when your emotions have gotten the best of you?

Exercises

- Assess situations where you have dealt with stress effectively and have not dealt with it effectively.
- Practice pausing and breathing to create a calmer emotional state.
- Give a colleague permission to issue a volatility alert.
- Keep track of the cues that seem to trigger an emotional response.

- Evaluate a situation prior to becoming involved in terms of how an emotional response by you might be triggered and how you plan to handle it.

Tips and Techniques

- Prepare for potentially stressful situations by anticipating challenges ahead and doing what-if planning.
- Preview your Outlook calendar to flag potentially stressful events, and plan ahead regarding how the events should be handled.
- Strengthen your awareness of the emotional style associated with a high Excitable score, and understand the emotional styles of others who pose a challenge.
- Develop a visual cue to think "calm and peaceful" that can be incorporated into a routine used as preparation for stressful events.
- Debrief stressful events with a trusted colleague, and evaluate the triggers and responses that were elicited.

Support Resources

Bradberry, T. (2014, February). How successful people stay calm. *Forbes.* **Retrieved from http://www.forbes.com/sites/travisbradberry/2014/02/06/how-successful-people-stay-calm/**

Bradberry, author of a best-selling book on emotional intelligence and cofounder of an organization that serves 75 percent of Fortune 500 companies, describes tactics successful people use when faced with stressful situations.

Coutu, D. (2002, May). How resilience works. *Harvard Business Review.* **Retrieved from https://hbr.org/2002/05/how-resilience-works**

Harvard Business Review senior editor Diane Coutu discusses why resilience is currently a "hot topic" in the business world, the unexpected relationship between resilience and optimism, resilience's building blocks, and what resilience looks like in today's world.

Daft, R. L. (2010). *The executive and the elephant: A leader's guide for building inner excellence.* **San Francisco, CA: John Wiley & Sons.**

Leadership expert Daft posits that, despite having clear intentions, leaders often fall prey to their instincts. His book offers real-life examples and case studies to help readers find balance between their intentions and their instincts.

Gordon, J. (2011). *The seed: Finding purpose and happiness in life and work.* **Hoboken, NJ: John Wiley & Sons.**

Wall Street Journal best-selling author Jon Gordon uses an engaging parable to inspire and guide people through the process of finding meaning in and sparking passion for their work.

Harvard Business Review (2014). *HBR guide to managing stress at work.* Boston, MA: HBR Press.

HBR's guide teaches readers how to channel tension productively, avert stress-inducing circumstances, set realistic expectations, manage anxiety when it inevitably arises, and bounce back after succumbing to stress and pressure.

McGonigal, K. (2013). How to make stress your friend [Video file]. Retrieved from http://www.ted.com/talks/kelly_mcgonigal_how_to_make_stress_your_friend

Based on research suggesting that stress is detrimental only if people believe the preceding is true, psychologist Kelly McGonigal urges listeners to see stress as beneficial and introduces them to an underacknowledged mechanism for stress reduction—reaching out to others.

Seldman, M., & Seldman, J. (2008). *Executive stamina: How to optimize time, energy, and productivity to achieve peak performance.* Hoboken, NJ: John Wiley & Sons.

Gleaned from top executive coaches and world-class athletes' training tactics, this book offers overextended executives readily applicable tips and tools to help optimize their career potential, sustain physical health, and live true to their personal values.

Summary

Keep Doing

Act with passion, energy, and enthusiasm.

Stop Doing

Lose emotional control, allowing emotions to run away, yelling.

Start Doing

Recognize and handle situations that cause frustration and emotional moments.

High Excitable behaviors are extremely visible to all constituencies who are a part of a leader's work environment. A leader who demonstrates these behaviors can quickly develop a reputation for lacking executive maturity, presence, and the ability to handle workplace pressure. These behaviors can be difficult to control. They stem from what has been called the "caveman brain" and require discipline and significant effort on the part of the leader to prevent them from creating reputational damage. Development actions that involve an active Self-Monitoring program and the substitution of appropriate alternative behaviors can correct or even prevent their negative reputational consequences.

Low Excitable: Generating Passion

If you are tuned out of your own emotions, you will be poor at reading them in other people.

Daniel Goleman

Detecting When It Is a Problem

Low Excitable behaviors are typically difficult to observe in the workplace and are often mistaken for other characteristics. For example, it is not uncommon for a low Excitable person to be mistaken for an introvert or even someone who is arrogant or above it all emotionally. People use the emotional responses of their leaders as a barometer of the seriousness of a situation. When there is an absence of an emotional response or the leader has a flat affect, people tend to fill in the emotional gap with their own take on the situation. It is difficult to cite a memorable example of low Excitable behaviors because they are anything but memorable. One high-profile example that illustrates low Excitable is Prince Charles. He is often described in his public appearances as coming off as intelligent, aloof, and a bit awkward. He is almost never described as inspirational or able to motivate others through his passion. In fact, it is often discussed in the tabloids that Prince Charles may be passed over in favor of Prince William as the heir to the British throne. While there is a panoply of reasons offered as to why something that flies against a tradition that goes back centuries may occur, one cannot help but speculate that Prince Charles's inability to be inspirational could be a contributing factor. A flat affect and the inability to inspire others are the hallmark behaviors that can impact the career of a low Excitable leader.

James from Case 7—James, marketing manager on page 68—provides a good example of a low Excitable profile. James's highest derailer is his Dutiful score (90%), but his Excitable score is very low (10%) and worth examining in terms of his long-term leadership potential. The following is James's profile summary.

	James's Situational Summary			
\multicolumn{5}{l}{James was the marketing manager for a small family-owned business that was sold to a well-established technology company. After the sale, James moved on to a small, fast-moving start-up technology company. He had clear challenges with his ability to get things moving in the new company. His low Excitable score tended to exacerbate the problem because he seemed to lack passion and urgency around the challenges confronting him in a fast-moving start-up company.}				
Dimension	Score	Percentile		Description
Excitable	10			James is a laid-back, even-tempered marketing guy (Excitable—10%). It takes him a long time to get to know and trust people (Skeptical—70%), and he is guarded and slow to make decisions (Cautious—85% and Mischievous—15%). James doesn't make a big impression on people. In fact, he is best known for his loyalty and willingness to do whatever the owners asked (Dutiful—90%).
Skeptical	70			
Cautious	85			
Reserved	25			
Leisurely	19			
Bold	24			
Mischievous	15			
Colorful	45			
Imaginative	35			
Diligent	50			
Dutiful	90			

Notice the descriptive language associated with James's profile. He is described as "laid-back" and "does not make a big impression on people." These are not the kind of descriptions that are commonly associated with an effective leader, especially one in a high-profile function like marketing. James may be very competent and could achieve a degree of success based on his competence. However, his inability to summon his emotions and inspire others with what has often been called "fire in the belly" could be a limiting factor in his future career success. He also runs the risk of displaying what others may perceive as a lack of urgency because of his laid-back emotional style. Start-up companies, especially those in a highly competitive industry like technology, tend to be populated with people who enjoy a fast-paced lifestyle. James may actually enjoy the pace, but his emotional demeanor conveys otherwise.

Sample Development Program (Case 7—James)

James's profile indicates an Excitable score of 10 percent. An examination of his subscale scores indicates that all three—Volatile, Easily Disappointed, and No Direction—are depressed. The case information presented about James indicates that Dutiful (90%) may be a more immediate development priority. However, his reputation for being "laid back" and failing to "leave a big impression on people" indicates that his long-term success as a leader will be impacted by his low Excitable score.

Reputation Change

James needs to quickly dispel his reputation as "laid back" and "not leaving a big impression on people," especially now that he is in a fast-paced environment. In order to succeed in launching the new brand, it is critical that he not be tagged with these descriptors. He needs to be seen as a leader who is enthusiastic about the brand and who can get others excited about it and the future of the marketing organization. While he might not ever be described as a "dynamo," he can certainly acquire a reputation of a committed, influential leader who is passionate in a lower-key way.

Development Actions for James

James's situation offers a fairly low-risk environment for addressing the low Excitable aspect of his profile. The company is small, fast moving, and likely forgiving as long as there is a perception that James is making progress. Given that his early days in the organization were spent collecting information from people who do not have a great familiarity with marketing, it would make good sense for James to craft a presentation for the troops outlining the vision and direction for marketing. It would give James the opportunity to build content based on his technical background, present an opportunity to make sure he is aligned with his manager, and challenge his low Excitable demeanor to deliver a passionate statement about the direction of marketing. The following are the proposed steps for this aspect of James's development initiative:

- James should craft a draft presentation about the direction he wants to take marketing, based on the information he has gathered and his technical competence.

- He should review the presentation on two levels. First, does it contain content that he truly believes in? Second, are the logic and flow of the presentation sound?

- He should gain support from his manager and then prepare for the delivery of his message:

  - Once the draft is in solid form, James should set up a meeting with his manager to do a preliminary review. Prior to the meeting with his manager, he should complete several test-runs on the presentation and even ask a trusted colleague to role-play his manager.

  - James needs to leave the meeting with any modifications to the presentation and a commitment from his manager to create a forum for James to present it to the troops.

  - Assuming modifications to the presentation have been made and presentation to the troops is set, James should begin working on his delivery.

- James should practice in front of a mirror and observe the emotions he is displaying so he can deliver the presentation in an inspiring manner.
- James should follow up with several meeting participants to gather feedback regarding the presentation from both a content and delivery standpoint.
- He should establish a follow-up plan that offers him opportunities to update the troops and that further reinforces the lessons learned during his initial presentation.

Evaluating Your Need for Change

The following behavioral questions should be considered in conjunction with your low Excitable score when evaluating the need for a change in your behavior. A "yes" response to three or fewer items suggests that there is no imminent need for behavioral changes. A "yes" response to four to six items suggests that a low score on the Excitable scale should be a watch-out for you. A "yes" response to more than six items suggests that you should take active steps toward making behavioral changes.

Do you:

1. Remain calm or subdued even when the situation calls for an emotional reaction?   **Yes No Not Sure**

2. Show little to no emotional reaction even when others create an obvious annoyance?   **Yes No Not Sure**

3. Demonstrate little to no emotional reaction regardless of the situation or circumstances?   **Yes No Not Sure**

4. Appear to lack any emotional reaction even when clearly disappointed by the performance of others?   **Yes No Not Sure**

5. Rarely or never seem disappointed or disenchanted with employees who fail to live up to expectations?   **Yes No Not Sure**

6. Avoid conveying any disappointment with others through emotional reactions or demeanor?   **Yes No Not Sure**

7. Express little to no emotional regret when challenging situations are not handled effectively?   **Yes No Not Sure**

8. Demonstrate such a lack of emotion that core principles and beliefs are very difficult to read by others?   **Yes No Not Sure**

9. Create directional uncertainty because of a lack of emotional reaction or even passion? Yes   No   Not Sure

These items should be considered as behavioral indicators. Similar or associated behaviors to any of those listed that you exhibit likely suggest a "yes" response. They provide additional support that you may be at risk for the negative reputational consequences associated with those scoring low on the Excitable scale, such as James.

Development Tactics

Development tactics cover a range of approaches and resources that have been found useful in addressing low Excitable behaviors. These tactics are typically used in combination to form a custom plan suited to the specific learning needs of a leader. The tactics are divided into four categories: (1) thought-provoking questions, (2) exercises to improve performance, (3) tips and techniques to improve performance, and (4) support resources that can be consulted to gain additional insights in addressing low Excitable behaviors.

Thought-Provoking Questions

- What emotional cues in others do you find most helpful in reading a situation?
- What do you find most difficult when trying to bring your emotions into a situation?
- What are some of the cues you might consider to help you detect how you feel about a situation or an issue?
- How would you go about circling back with people to make sure they know your position on critical issues?
- How will adding more emotional range to the way you address groups help your career?

Exercises

- Identify the situations in which you think you need to utilize more emotional range in order to successfully navigate them.
- Describe leaders who communicate emotions effectively, including what emotions they convey.
- Practice verbalizing descriptive language for communications with your team members or other key stakeholders.
- Exercise your emotional range in front of a safe audience prior to rolling it out in a critical situation.

- After a key presentation, ask for feedback from key stakeholders on your effectiveness in conveying emotions.

Tips and Techniques

- Review the career implications of using greater emotional range in critical situations.
- Identify situations, issues, or people who do elicit emotional peaks from you (as small as they may be) and determine what they have in common.
- Develop a list of situations, from easy to hard, where emotional range can be practiced without negative reputational impact.
- Develop an outline illustrating your as-is emotional range with a to-be emotional range.
- Identify a colleague to provide you with an emotional mirror in practice situations leading up to a critical talk or speech.

Support Resources

Chamorro-Premuzic, T. (2014). *Confidence: Overcoming low self-esteem, insecurity, and self-doubt.* **New York, NY: Penguin.**

Chamorro-Premuzic argues that, contrary to popular belief, confidence is capable of thwarting achievement, employability, and likability. Among other topics, this book discusses the silver linings of low confidence, teaches readers how to identify when to feign self-assurance (and how to do so effectively), and offers tactics for improving physical and emotional health.

Goleman, D., Boyatzis, R., McKee, A., & Finkelstein, S. (2015). *HBR's 10 must reads on emotional intelligence.* **Boston, MA: HBR Press.**

Ten thoughtfully selected articles written and identified by experts in the field of emotional intelligence.

Gordon, J. (2007). *The energy bus: 10 rules to fuel your life, work, and team with positive energy.* **Hoboken, NJ: John Wiley & Sons.**

Gordon takes readers on a thought-provoking and inspirational ride, sharing 10 tactics for approaching work and life with the type of optimistic, forward thinking that facilitates true accomplishment both professionally and personally.

Sanborn, M., & Maxwell, J. C. (2004). *The Fred factor: How passion in your work and life can turn the ordinary into the extraordinary.* **Colorado Springs, CO: WaterBook.**

Sanborn and Maxwell summarize four principles intended to "release fresh energy, enthusiasm, and creativity" in readers' careers and lives.

Schneider, B. (2007). *Energy leadership: Transforming your workplace and life from the core.* Hoboken, NJ: John Wiley & Sons.

Renowned coach Bruce Schneider teaches readers how to understand and harness their most valuable personal resource—energy.

Toastmasters International (https://www.toastmasters.org/)

Toastmasters International is a global network of clubs devoted to helping members improve their communication and leadership skills.

Summary

Keep Doing

Maintain a calm, even-tempered demeanor when others lose control of their emotions.

Stop Doing

Respond to others in ways that they may infer a lack of urgency or "fire in the belly."

Start Doing

Practice bringing passion, energy, and enthusiasm to public speeches or presentations.

Low Excitable behaviors are often difficult to detect, and it is even more difficult to determine if they are having a negative impact on a leader's reputation. Often, a leader only finds out that these behaviors might be a problem when a promotion has been missed or a plum opportunity has been offered to someone else. It can be difficult for a leader to change his or her reputation once it includes labels like "laid back" or "no fire in the belly," but it is not impossible. Furthermore, once a low Excitable leader learns to use emotions selectively and with sincerity, the impact on others can be quite significant because of the contrast with the leader's natural tendencies.

CHAPTER 6

SKEPTICAL

HIGH SKEPTICAL: STAYING POSITIVE

If you are going to be rude, cynical, negatively-sarcastic or pessimistic, your life options are going to be very limited.

Bryant McGill

Detecting When It Is a Problem

Leaders with high Skeptical scores are generally perceptive, but they look at others' actions through a lens of distrust. These leaders question the motives behind others' actions and assume the worst. They are highly critical, do not easily build trust, and expect to be mistreated. The collaborative relationships required in today's heavily matrixed organizations suffer with high Skeptical leaders. These leaders are unlikely to forget or forgive a wrong and will hold these memories ever-present.

The North Korean dictator Kim Jong-Un serves as a good illustration of a leader who does not trust. This wariness holds Kim Jong-Un back from even considering international alliances that otherwise might be in the best interests of his country. In certain environments and circumstances, this highly skeptical approach may be seen as being savvy. However, in most environments and circumstances, this potential derailer can get in the way of building productive, sustainable relationships and can have even broader consequences, as with Kim Jong-Un.

Phil from Case 2—Phil, logistics technician on page 58—provides a good example of a high Skeptical profile. Phil's HDS results indicate two high-risk behaviors: Skeptical (96%) (being excessively critical and on the lookout for faults) and Reserved (90%) (being insensitive to the moods and feelings of people and placing business results above all other concerns). The following is Phil's profile summary:

Phil's Situational Summary				
Phil is a lead logistics technician for a national trucking company. Phil's approach to his job generally has been one of a watchdog who tries to identify problems and deliver bad news. A new incoming leader for whom he will be working in the future has a decidedly different view of how the function should run. The leader believes technicians should take more of a partnership approach with field employees, treating them as internal customers.				
Dimension	**Score**	**Percentile**		**Description**
Excitable	35			Phil is a perceptive individual but can be excessively critical and is always on the lookout for faults (Skeptical—96%). He can be insensitive to the moods and feelings of people and place business results above all other concerns (Reserved—90%). He also can be quite deferential to superiors and the guidance they provide (Dutiful—77%).
Skeptical	96			
Cautious	75			
Reserved	90			
Leisurely	33			
Bold	55			
Mischievous	40			
Colorful	75			
Imaginative	62			
Diligent	60			
Dutiful	77			
		0 10 20 30 40 50 60 70 80 90 100		

Under the prior leadership in logistics, Phil's highly skeptical behavior might have been encouraged. Phil was expected to be alert for problems and function as a watchdog. However, his environment has shifted with the change in leadership. The new head of logistics is taking an approach that engages other departments and builds partnering relationships. Trust is often at the core of such relationships and partnerships. High Skeptical leaders do not trust readily and hold negative expectations of others. While these behaviors may have been valued by the previous leader of Phil's organization, the new leader is seeking to establish a culture centered on partnerships between corporate and field. It will be challenging for Phil to shift his reputation and interactions with others as his new manager will expect. Phil will need to repair existing relationships and establish new partnerships. With the added challenge of his high Reserved score, Phil is likely to find it difficult to build relationships in general, and his high Skeptical behaviors may hinder his ability to pivot to a different approach.

Sample Development Program (Case 2—Phil)

Phil's profile indicates a Skeptical score of 96 percent. The subscale scores associated with this—Cynical, Mistrusting, and Grudges—are all elevated to the maximum level. In the past, Phil's Skeptical scale score and the associated behaviors were rewarded. His previous boss appreciated that Phil could anticipate every potential problem and deliver bad news. However, as the situation shifted and Phil's boss was replaced, the goals for Phil's role also shifted. The associated Skeptical behaviors made it challenging for Phil to adjust to the new priorities and style of a different boss, one who values collaboration and partnering.

Reputation Change

To be successful in his new role, Phil will need to change his reputation from one of being a confrontational watchdog and rule enforcer to one of a collaborative resource who supports the field. Given his new boss's focus on cooperation and partnering, he will have a difficult time winning her trust and support until she starts receiving feedback from his field interfaces about his ability to work with them and collaboratively add value. This reputation change is critical for Phil long-term as well, if he hopes to move into a field role at some point. The field leaders will never give him a position in their organizations as long as he has the reputation of being a "headquarters Nazi."

Development Actions for Phil

Phil will need to change the way he approaches his role and, just as important, will need to repair and redefine existing relationships. Phil's high Reserved score will make engaging in these new behaviors even more challenging.

- As a starting point, Phil should think about what it will take to be successful with his new boss. Phil should outline the priorities of his role so they align with his new boss's priorities. He should look at the role as a vacant position, and ask himself the question, "What attributes would I look for in a person to fill this role?" Phil needs to recognize that his role has changed significantly and is essentially a new position. He should ask himself, "What will I need to do to meet the challenges of the role?"

- He should identify the strengths and capabilities he brings to this redefined role that will support his success. He should reflect on how he will demonstrate these attributes and how he intends to build trust with his new boss.

- Phil needs to list stakeholders with whom he needs to rebuild relationships because of past negative encounters. He should create a plan to connect with each of them, apologizing if necessary, and articulating his desire to build a positive relationship.

- Phil should focus on thinking positively about others and their intentions and capabilities. Using the list he created above, he should reflect on the value he can get from each one. Phil should push himself to identify at least one point of added value for each person.
- In his dealings with the field, he should intentionally shift his emphasis from what might be wrong to what is right. He should develop questions that can lead others to see issues on their own and make adjustments before there is a problem.
- Phil should take a moment to pause in tense situations and ask, "Is this a battle worth fighting? Is it important to be right in this instance?"

Evaluating Your Need for Change

The following behavioral questions should be considered in conjunction with your high Skeptical score when evaluating the need for a change in your behavior. A "yes" response to three or fewer items suggests that there is no imminent need for behavioral changes. A "yes" response to four to six items suggests that a high score on the Skeptical scale should be a watch-out for you. A "yes" response to more than six items suggests that you should take active steps toward making behavioral changes.

Do you:

1. Have difficulty accepting a compliment without questioning the motives?	Yes	No	Not Sure
2. Assume people have questionable or suspicious motives when they offer to do a favor?	Yes	No	Not Sure
3. Regularly question what management is up to or planning?	Yes	No	Not Sure
4. Express distrust for coworkers even when there is no reason to think they are untrustworthy?	Yes	No	Not Sure
5. Indicate that people will cheat you if given the opportunity?	Yes	No	Not Sure
6. Not take feedback due to a lack of trust for those offering ideas or input?	Yes	No	Not Sure
7. Have a hard time forgiving people even for minor issues?	Yes	No	Not Sure

8. Express concerns that most people are only motivated by their own self-interests?	Yes No Not Sure	
9. Write people off or suggest that some people should never be forgiven?	Yes No Not Sure	

These items should be considered as behavioral indicators. Similar or associated behaviors to any of those listed that you exhibit likely suggest a "yes" response. They provide additional support that you may be at risk for the negative reputational consequences associated with those scoring high on the Skeptical scale, such as Phil.

Development Tactics

Development tactics cover a range of approaches and resources that have been found useful in addressing high Skeptical behaviors. These tactics are typically used in combination to form a custom plan suited to the specific learning needs of a leader. The tactics are divided into four categories: (1) thought-provoking questions, (2) exercises to improve performance, (3) tips and techniques to improve performance, and (4) support resources that can be consulted to gain additional insights in addressing high Skeptical behaviors.

Thought-Provoking Questions

- In what ways has being highly skeptical helped you? In what circumstances has it interfered with your ability to achieve a result or build a relationship?
- How could being less skeptical positively impact your overall effectiveness as a leader? How could it enhance your career?
- What specific behaviors associated with being highly skeptical would be most important for you to stop or dial back? What new behaviors would be most important to start?
- What might you gain by assuming a positive intent on the part of others? What do you risk?
- How can you allow space for others to vet their ideas without being dismissed?

Exercises

- Practice reframing a challenging scenario by retelling the story, assuming the colleague's positive intent.
- Identify the value and contributions of someone with whom you have difficulty.

- Create two lists: List 1 should be a list of people you trust and also who are important to your success and your team's success. List 2 should be a list of people you do not trust and who are important to your success and your team's success. Discuss who from list 2 needs to be on list 1. Develop an action plan to engage in small experiments to build trust gradually (e.g., pick one person a month from the second list and work to establish a relationship and move that person to the first list).

- Think back to why you hold a grudge against an important stakeholder. Determine what it would take to build a functional working relationship with the individual over time.

- Identify and deliver at least one positive or uplifting statement you could make to a coworker each day.

Tips and Techniques

- Identify a situation where you can assume positive intent, and record observations of outcomes.
- Role-play giving balanced, motivational feedback to a colleague, team, and so on.
- Recognize when a conversation is about to start or evolve into an argument. Practice pausing and asking yourself, "Is this a battle worth fighting?"
- Make a list of the positive attributes key stakeholders bring to the table when completing tasks or assignments.
- Identify a specific relationship that has been damaged due to a trust issue. Put a strategy in place for rebuilding trust with the individual over time.

Support Resources

Brown, B. (2010, June). The power of vulnerability [Video file]. Retrieved from http://www.ted.com/talks/brene_brown_on_vulnerability?language=en

Brené Brown, researcher and expert on the topic of human connection, discusses what true vulnerability is and why it should be fostered and celebrated instead of avoided and disdained.

Caruso, D. R., & Salovey, P. (2004). *The emotionally intelligent manager: How to develop and use the four key emotional skills of leadership.* **San Francisco, CA: Jossey-Bass.**

Caruso and Salovey challenge the notion that emotions do not have a place in the workplace, arguing that emotions are fundamental to our intelligence as well as our thinking and reasoning capabilities. The authors teach readers how to quantify, learn, and hone each component of their hierarchy of emotional skills.

Covey, S. M. R. (2006). *The speed of trust: The one thing that changes everything.* New York, NY: Simon & Schuster.

Covey asserts that trust is the linchpin of the new global economy and demonstrates that trust—and the speed at which it can be developed with employees, clients, and constituents—is a defining factor within successful, high-performance organizations.

Ferrazzi, K. (2009). *Who's got your back: The breakthrough program to build deep, trusting relationships that create success—and won't let you fail.* New York, NY: Broadway Books.

Best-selling author, consultant, and coach Ferrazzi provides a convincing argument why one cannot "win" alone and offers a step-by-step guide for lowering one's guard, using "sparring" as a productive tool, and building deeper and more trusting relationships.

Hill, L. A., & Lineback, K. (2011). *Being the boss: The 3 imperatives for becoming a great leader.* Boston, MA: Harvard Business Review Press.

Hill and Lineback explain why and how your reputation impacts the people you manage, the quality of their work, their loyalty and commitment, and their willingness to make personal sacrifices for the good of their teams and organizations.

The Arbinger Institute. (2010). *Leadership and self-deception: Getting out of the box.* San Francisco, CA: Berrett-Koehler.

The Arbinger Institute argues that self-deception determines one's experience in every aspect of life. The extent to which it does the preceding and, in particular, the extent to which it is the central issue in leadership, is the subject of this best-selling book.

SUMMARY

> ### *Keep Doing*
>
> Analyze and try to understand the motives and intentions of others.
>
> ### *Stop Doing*
>
> Approach the world in a negative, cynical, glass-half-empty fashion.
>
> ### *Start Doing*
>
> Look for the positive aspects in people and situations.

High Skeptical behaviors can hinder leaders from being effective and progressing in their careers. Highly skeptical individuals generally are seen as negative and do not build a foundation of positive relationships, resulting in difficulty building followership, alliances, and collaboration—all of which are required for long-term career success. For high Skeptical leaders to change these behaviors, they must shift their belief system about people or, at the very least, work to see people through a different lens—a lens that is not as tainted by mistrust and an expectation that others are out to do them wrong. This can be challenging because high Skeptical leaders' natural tendency is to look at the world and other people from a glass-half-empty perspective. It takes considerable effort for these leaders to go beyond behavior change and make a change in their belief system, which is essential for long-term career success.

Low Skeptical: Trust, but Verify

I am a kind of paranoid in reverse. I suspect people of trying to make me happy.

J. D. Salinger

Detecting When It Is a Problem

Low Skeptical behaviors may not be readily evident early in a leader's tenure and may, in fact, result in a leader's being seen as open, approachable, and willing to see the best in everyone. Gandhi might be an example of a low Skeptical individual. Gandhi was known for his trusting nature and proclivity to see the positive in each individual and every situation. While Gandhi may have been an inspiration to many, one might wonder how successful his outlook would have been inside a Fortune 500 company. Leaders in organizations must be able to navigate the political environment. While they need not be overly cynical or paranoid, they do need to evaluate the range of consequences in situations rather than assume the best outcome or that all involved have the noblest of motives. Being overly naïve can result in missing potential problems, being taken advantage of, and not being as aware of the undercurrents of the organization as necessary for a savvy leader. Additionally, leaders with low Skeptical scores may have difficulty accurately assessing team members, seeing only the best in individuals who may or may not be performing effectively. Over time, these leaders can develop a reputation for being poor at evaluating talent or unwilling to address performance problems.

Mark from Case 6—Mark, district account manager on page 66—provides a good example of a low Skeptical profile. The following is Mark's profile summary:

Mark's Situational Summary			
Mark is a long-tenured district account manager for a consumer products company. A significant change in his account porfolio brought a number of new government accounts under his control. These customers were no-nonsense type customers who had little interest in his affable nature and tendency to exaggerate to garner attention.			
Dimension	**Score**	**Percentile**	**Description**
Excitable	68		Mark is a high-energy person who brings a lot of passion to the business (Excitable—68%). He can be highly colorful (Colorful—91%) to the point of being overbearing at times. His colorful behavior extends into his tendency to exaggerate issues or problems and his role in solving them. He also has a tendency to miss details or fail to follow up on important issues (Diligent—10%).
Skeptical	15		
Cautious	29		
Reserved	42		
Leisurely	19		
Bold	24		
Mischievous	70		
Colorful	91		
Imaginative	29		
Diligent	10		
Dutiful	45		

Mark provides an example of the pitfalls of being a low Skeptical leader. Over the course of his career, Mark built trusting relationships with his clients. They knew him well, knew what to expect from him, and tolerated his high Colorful behavior. His organization viewed Mark as a loyal employee, and Mark trusted and supported the leadership team. When the company revenues began dropping, lay-offs commenced. Mark seemed unaware of the impact of these developments. He survived the initial round of cuts, but then his role was changed, and he was asked to assume responsibility for government accounts. Mark's low Skeptical score may present some challenges in his new circumstances. Mark may be too ready to assume that his new customers will be transparent, and he may not be aware of the politics of working with the government bureaucracy. He is likely to approach and interact with his new customers in exactly the same way he dealt with his previous customers and not see the downside of one-size-fits-all approaches. Additionally, Mark seems to have missed the cues about the urgency behind the recent changes in his organization. The leadership team might have supported him in the past while he produced the requisite bottom-line results. But now, Mark needs to carefully consider how best to navigate the new political landscape of his organization. Assuming that the leadership will continue to support him may be naïve. Mark may be in danger of being included in the next round of layoffs.

Sample Development Program (Case 6—Mark)

Mark's Skeptical scale indicates a score of 15 percent. An examination of his sub-scale scores indicates that Cynical and Mistrusting are at the very low end of the scale. The case information presented about Mark indicates that his addressing his low Skeptical score may not be the top priority for his success in his current position. However, for Mark to continue in his role, be successful, and help his company sustain their business, he will need to shift some of his low Skeptical behaviors.

Reputation Change

Mark has a reputation for being a "glass half-full" kind of guy to a fault—always optimistic about outcomes and looking for the best in people, even when he should have a more realistic perspective. He is trusting to the point of being naïve, including accepting excuses from his team when they miss commitments, and this will not serve him well with his new demanding government clients and in the new downsized environment. He will need to be more vigilant for political behavior and for hidden agendas. He will also need to realize how critical it is for him and his team to succeed, or he might be part of the next round of lay-offs. It is crucial that he hold his team accountable for results. He needs to garner a reputation for being a "nice guy," but also as one who is street smart and who is not going to accept excuses and situations at face value.

Development Actions for Mark

Based on prior results, Mark has demonstrated sales capability, and it is likely that his organization is looking to him to contribute significantly to revenue production. The following are the proposed steps for Mark to take:

1. Mark should reflect on how his low Skeptical behaviors have supported his success and when they have created difficulties for him in achieving his goals.

2. He should describe how he views other individuals when engaging in a relationship. Ask himself what might be important to the individual that Mark may not see or be aware of. Mark can practice with different scenarios to ascertain what might be important to know besides what is right on the surface of an interaction.

3. Mark should look ahead and assess what it takes to be successful in his organization—what might be obvious and what might not be obvious? What has changed now that the organization has downsized and his clients are government agencies?

4. Mark should build a list of key organizational decision makers and assess the state of his relationships with each. What sort of reputation does he have with each of them? From this assessment, Mark can design an action plan to enhance needed support and move the needle on his reputation.

5. Mark should identify someone who demonstrates the concept of "trust but verify" and consider how he might best employ this approach.

Evaluating Your Need for Change

The following behavioral questions should be considered in conjunction your low Skeptical score when evaluating the need for a change in your behavior. A "yes" response to three or fewer items suggests that there is no imminent need for behavioral changes. A "yes" response to four to six items suggests that a low score on the Skeptical scale should be a watch-out for you. A "yes" response to more than six items suggests that you should take active steps toward making behavioral changes.

Do you:

1. Appear overly optimistic even when the situation suggests othewise?   **Yes   No   Not Sure**

2. Accept people at face value without ever questioning their motives?   **Yes   No   Not Sure**

3. Ignore or deny the existence of politics in the workplace?	Yes	No	Not Sure
4. Appear to trust people even when their behavior suggests that they have ulterior motives?	Yes	No	Not Sure
5. Seem to get taken advantage of by others?	Yes	No	Not Sure
6. Appear to be naïve when it comes to the motives of others?	Yes	No	Not Sure
7. Forgive people even when they have done nothing to warrant forgiveness?	Yes	No	Not Sure
8. Fail to recognize when people are only out for their own self-interests?	Yes	No	Not Sure
9. Take people at their word even when their past actions suggest otherwise?	Yes	No	Not Sure

These items should be considered as behavioral indicators. Similar or associated behaviors to any of those listed that you exhibit likely suggest a "yes" response. They provide additional support that you may be at risk for the negative reputational consequences associated with those scoring low on the Skeptical scale, such as Mark.

Development Tactics

Development tactics cover a range of approaches and resources that have been found useful in addressing low Skeptical behaviors. These tactics are typically used in combination to form a custom plan suited to the specific learning needs of a leader. The tactics are divided into four categories: (1) thought-provoking questions, (2) exercises to improve performance, (3) tips and techniques to improve performance, and (4) support resources that can be consulted to gain additional insights in addressing low Skeptical behaviors.

Thought-Provoking Questions

- Describe a decision or action that did not turn out positively that could have had a better outcome if you had asked more questions ahead of time. If you had asked more questions, how would the outcome have been more positive? What will you do differently next time?
- Using what you learned from the preceding bulleted item, identify an upcoming project where probing more deeply upfront will have a positive impact the outcome. What questions will you pose?

- How do you know when you can trust someone, and how do you verify that?
- What words come to mind when we talk about "influencing" or "political savvy"?
- How do you know when someone has earned your trust? How do you know when someone has earned your distrust?

Exercises

- Think about a leader who effectively demonstrates the concept of "trust, but verify." What do you admire about this leader's approach?
- List some bullet points that describe critical feedback. List some bullet points that describe the impact on the team and team members when this type of feedback is not provided.
- Design a set of questions that elicit information needed to evaluate and check on projects and identify potential roadblocks to success (for example, "Are you sure you can do this?" or "Is there enough time?").
- Develop a "political savvy" map listing key influencers and indicating their potential impact on your career, along with the level of support you believe you receive from them.
- Develop a personal set of what-if questions that you can easily use to enhance your situational understanding as opportunities arise.

Tips and Techniques

- Select an upcoming project or assignment. Develop a set of questions that can be used to gain an appropriate level of situational understanding. Include with the questions the names of the stakeholders from whom input is needed on the project or assignment. After you have had an opportunity to use the questions, think about what information you obtained through the questions and what impact the information had on your situational understanding.
- Role-play a negotiation scenario in which you need to achieve a balanced outcome or a win-win solution.
- Role-play a performance review in which you have to deliver negative feedback and set appropriate expectations for an improvement in performance.
- Identify a situation where critical feedback would be valuable. Create and implement a plan to provide that feedback.
- Identify an individual in the organization who makes effective use of political skills or demonstrates political savvy. Define the political behaviors demonstrated by this individual and how you might incorporate similar behaviors to achieve a political advantage.

Support Resources

Browne, M. N., & Keeley, S. M. (2014). *Asking the right questions* (11th ed.) [Kindle edition]. Retrieved from Amazon.com

Browne and Keeley's concise book provides readers actionable guidance for enhancing critical thinking skills and identifying inconsistencies.

Connors, R., & Smith, T. (2011). *How did that happen?: Holding people accountable for results the positive, principled way.* New York, NY: Penguin.

Experts on workplace accountability and authors of the best-selling book *The Oz Principle*, Connors and Smith tackle the next crucial step everyone and anyone (e.g., managers, supervisors, CEOs, or individual contributors) can take in *How Did That Happen?*—instilling greater accountability in all the people you depend upon.

DeLuca, J. R. (2002). *Political savvy: Systematic approaches to leadership behind the scenes.* Berwyn, PA: EBG Publications.

DeLuca describes tactics employed by ethical leaders, helps readers identify their own political styles, and offers an efficient and actionable guide to navigating murky political waters.

Grimshaw, J., & Baron, G. (2010). *Leadership without excuses: How to create accountability and high-performance.* New York, NY: McGraw Hill.

Grimshaw and Baron detail how leaders can help generally good (but less-than-fully accountable) employees drastically decrease their use of excuses and markedly improve their performance.

Hanson, T., & Hanson, B. Z. (2007). *Who will do what by when? How to improve performance, accountability and trust with integrity.* Tampa, FL: Power Publications.

True to their book's title, Hanson and Hanson present a holistic system for improving trust, accountability, and performance within the context of an engaging parable.

Marquardt, M. J. (2014). *Leading with questions: How leaders find the right solutions by knowing what to ask.* San Francisco, CA: Jossey-Bass.

Marquardt describes how asking the right questions can encourage participation and teamwork, foster forward thinking, empower people, build relationships, and solve problems. Both directly and indirectly via interviews with thirty esteemed leaders, Marquardt's book helps readers determine which questions can spark solutions to their most challenging problems.

Maxwell, J. C. (2014). *Good leaders ask great questions: Your foundation for successful leadership.* New York, NY: Hachette.

Maxwell makes a strong case for the power of questions and why questioning should not be underutilized. He explains how questions can have a marked impact on leadership and discusses the questions leaders should be asking their teams.

Summary

> ### *Keep Doing*
>
> Be open to seeing the positive in people and building trust-based relationships.
>
> ### *Stop Doing*
>
> Naïvely make the assumption that all is well in every circumstance.
>
> ### *Start Doing*
>
> Practice looking below the surface and probing to consider alternative possibilities.

The risks associated with a low Skeptical score often emerge over time. The negative consequences of low Skeptical behaviors tend to have a cumulative effect. As time passes, a low Skeptical leader is more and more often labeled as less effective. To combat this reputational damage, a leader can develop the self-awareness necessary to create a repertoire of alternative approaches and behaviors. This often requires a leader to recognize that these behaviors, while appearing negative or even questioning others' trustworthiness, often have a positive outcome. Furthermore, a leader needs to learn that developing political or organizational savvy can be accomplished without becoming deceitful or untrustworthy.

CHAPTER 7

CAUTIOUS

HIGH CAUTIOUS: LEVERAGING RISK

Cautious, careful people, always casting about to preserve their reputations ... can never effect a reform.

Susan B. Anthony

Detecting When It Is a Problem

High Cautious behaviors are common in the corporate world and may even be encouraged by leaders in corporate cultures that value accuracy, compliance, top-down decision-making, and the avoidance of mistakes.

Individuals with elevated Cautious scores are likely to appear timid, unassertive, indecisive, and lacking in confidence. These high Cautious behaviors can impact people's perceptions of the leaders' competence, credibility, and overall leadership presence. Team members at all levels—including their bosses—are likely to be frustrated with the inability of high Cautious leaders to make timely decisions as well as their inability to take a firm stand when needed.

One recent example of a high Cautious individual involves former Japanese Prime Minister Yukio Hatoyama. Hailing from a Kennedy-like Japanese political family—and having served in a variety of government roles as a career politician—Hatoyama would have seemed to possess the perfect background for the top leadership role in his country's government. In fact, he was swept into office in September 2009 with an unprecedented majority of the vote. However, he resigned his office in disgrace in June 2010, barely nine months into his term.

What was the cause of his demise? In a nutshell, it was his indecisiveness as a leader, along with changing his initial opinions on key issues when faced with any kind of opposition or setbacks. Early decisions were often reconsidered and then changed. Hatoyama was seen as being a flip-flopper on key domestic issues. Soon, the voting public lost faith in his credibility as a leader.

People want leaders who are capable of making tough decisions and who then lead them forward. People will often forgive leaders who make the occasional mistake, but they insist on leaders who are decisive. Hatoyama failed to appreciate the importance of decisiveness in determining the credibility of a leader.

While Prime Minister Hatoyama provides an international, high-profile example of high Cautious behavior, what form does this behavior take in day-to-day corporate settings? James from Case 7—James, marketing manager on page 68—provides a good example of a high Cautious profile. James's highest score on the HDS is on the Dutiful scale (90%), but his score on the Cautious scale is close behind at 85 percent. Taken together, these elevations underscore a lack of decisiveness, an unwillingness to take a stand, overall unassertiveness, and an elevated need to require affirmation or support from others before moving forward. The following is James's profile summary.

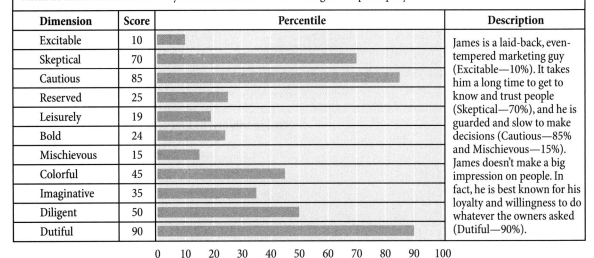

As detailed in the situational information above, James's elevations on both the Cautious and Dutiful scales are likely to be problematic in his new role with the fast-paced technology company that is in start-up mode. While these elevations may not have been major concerns in his previous company, where his meticulous nature and emphasis on avoiding mistakes were actually rewarded, his inability to make quick decisions and make strong recommendations will likely result in negative outcomes in his new role.

Sample Development Program (Case 7—James)

James is clearly in a situation of "what got you here won't get you there," and he definitely needs to modify his behaviors. However, because he is new to the organization and no one has any history with him, he has an opportunity to intentionally craft his reputation with his new stakeholders.

Reputation Change

In his former organization, James was known as a person who implemented whatever the owners decided. When he did make a decision on his own, it was only after long, sometimes painful, contemplation, and then, only with the concurrence of the owners. In the new organization, James needs to be seen as an assertive leader who has a vision for where he wants to take both the brand and the marketing department. He needs to be seen as decisive and energetic about the direction he is proposing. There are already some "rumbles" among a few of his stakeholders who think he is indecisive and not very dynamic, so James needs to take immediate action before this reputation takes hold.

Development Actions for James

An analysis of James's subscale scores shows maximum elevations on the Fearful and Unassertive subscales with no elevation on the Avoidant subscale. Therefore, James's reticence to make key decisions in his role with the new company is not due to general unease when interacting with his new coworkers but is, instead, due to his fear of making mistakes and his overall unassertiveness. The case information shows that a lack of specific guidance from the new leadership team greatly contributed to James's lack of decisiveness. As such, James should focus on clarifying his role, including identification of issues that he is expected to handle on his own. He should also pursue actions that will help him build confidence and establish himself as a solid marketing leader among his colleagues. The following steps will be beneficial in this situation:

- James should outline areas where he can take on a leadership role, including being more assertive and more decisive.
- James should list the current areas where he is facing key decisions and then suggest a course of action for each.

- James needs to meet with his manager to review the information gleaned from steps 1 and 2 and jointly decide on a course of action for each.
- James should ask his manager to outline additional areas where James can be more decisive, including support his manager is willing to provide when decisions need to be made.
- James needs to ask his manager to explain his or her approach to risk taking and dealing with mistakes. James is now part of a newer and fast-growing organization, and chances are the corporate culture is more forgiving of mistakes. He can gain clarity on this in a discussion with his manager.
- James should compile a list of his major successes, with a particular emphasis on those situations where he had unique insights or where he demonstrated decisiveness. James should review this list regularly as a way of increasing his self-confidence about his decision-making abilities.

Evaluating Your Need for Change

The following behavioral questions should be considered in conjunction with your high Cautious score when evaluating the need for a change in your behavior. A "yes" response to three or fewer items suggests that there is no imminent need for behavioral changes. A "yes" response to four to six items suggests that a high score on the Cautious scale should be a watch-out for you. A "yes" response to more than six items suggests that you should take active steps toward making behavioral changes.

Do you:

1.	Have a hard time expressing opinions that are unpopular or out of the mainstream?	Yes	No	Not Sure
2.	Have difficulty expressing views in front of strangers or unfamiliar groups?	Yes	No	Not Sure
3.	Seem reluctant to ask others for favors or support even when it is clearly needed?	Yes	No	Not Sure
4.	Worry about making a mistake or hesitate in taking action when the risk of a mistake exists?	Yes	No	Not Sure
5.	Lack self-confidence or vacillate when the time for a decision is due (or overdue)?	Yes	No	Not Sure
6.	Use excessive data collection or ask employees for additional legwork in order to avoid making a decision?	Yes	No	Not Sure

7. Fail to take a stand or voice an opinion when there is disagreement or controversy regarding a decision?   **Yes   No   Not Sure**

8. Seem to take a backseat when important decisions are being discussed or being made?   **Yes   No   Not Sure**

9. Easily back down when an opinion is challenged or contrary views are expressed?   **Yes   No   Not Sure**

These items should be considered as behavioral indicators. Similar or associated behaviors to any of those listed that you exhibit likely suggest a "yes" response. They provide additional support that you may be at risk for the negative reputational consequences associated with those scoring high on the Cautious scale, such as James.

Development Tactics

Development tactics cover a range of approaches and resources that have been found useful in addressing high Cautious behaviors. These tactics are typically used in combination to form a custom plan suited to the specific learning needs of a leader. The tactics are divided into four categories: (1) thought-provoking questions, (2) exercises to improve performance, (3) tips and techniques to improve performance, and (4) support resources that can be consulted to gain additional insights in addressing high Cautious behaviors.

Thought-Provoking Questions

- What steps do you take when assessing risk? Are you more likely to focus on the negative aspects resulting from unsuccessful change or focus more on the positive impact from change?
- What areas have been described by your leadership team and other key stakeholders as areas in need of change?
- Are your manager and your organization in general receptive to change? Does your corporate culture facilitate or inhibit risk taking?
- How can you best identify areas where change is needed? What types of change are important to you, and what positive outcomes could you see from such changes?
- Do others see you as a decisive leader? Why or why not?
- Do you have a clear understanding of where your decision-making authority starts and where it stops? Do you know the decisions that you have the authority to make versus those decisions your manager wants to review before action is taken?

- How do you handle situations where you need to make a quick decision when facts or data are not available?
- Do you always need to get a second—or third—opinion before moving forward with a decision?

Exercises

- Reflect on past successes. Make a list of the decisions you made that turned out to be correct and the special insights that you brought to these decisions. Use this list to build confidence in your decision-making abilities.
- Prioritize and set deadlines. Identify three to four critical decisions that you need to make, and then set deadlines for when you will make them. Use these deadlines as a way of limiting the amount of time that you spend on data gathering and analysis.
- Identify and articulate your worst-case scenario. What is the worst outcome that can occur if you make an incorrect decision? Sometimes articulating a worst-case scenario can allow for a more realistic assessment of the negatives associated with an incorrect decision.
- Identify two to three areas where you can display a higher level of assertiveness in your current role. List specific behaviors that you will engage in to help with assertiveness and get feedback from colleagues on whether they see improvement in your assertiveness.
- Identify a meeting situation in which you would normally be reluctant to express your opinion. Ahead of time, outline a specific position or opinion that you believe needs to be expressed and discussed. Follow your outline and assert yourself in the meeting. Then, after the meeting, ask a trusted source for feedback about your performance.

Tips and Techniques

- Understand there are costs associated with either delaying or not making a decision. These may involve opportunity costs as well as a cost to your reputation and perceived competence by others.
- Ensure you have not overestimated the negative consequences associated with an incorrect decision.
- Ensure there is a clear understanding between you and your manager of where your decision-making authority starts and where it stops. With your manager, identify a few areas where you will take a more active and decisive role.

- Realize that enhanced learning and experience can come with decisions that turn out to be incorrect. Take steps to ensure your manager will be supportive of decisions even if they should turn out to be incorrect.
- Identify a mentor or role model who can provide informal feedback on key decisions and take steps to ensure you use this information to supplement decision-making efforts.

Support Resources

Farber, S. (2004). *Radical leap: A personal lesson in extreme leadership.* Poway, CA: Mission Boulevard.

Hailed as one of the "100 Best Business Books of All Time," Farber's book describes a leadership model to aspire to—one that does not frighten leaders into shunning risks, avoiding mistakes at all costs, or, despite good intentions, paying lip service to employee input.

George, M. L., & Wilson, S. A. (2004). *Conquering complexity in your business: How Wal-Mart, Toyota, and other top companies are breaking through the ceiling on profits and growth.* New York, NY: McGraw Hill.

Six Sigma and Lean production experts, George and Wilson make a convincing case that every business harbors unnecessary cost-inflating and profit-draining complexity and offer methods for increasing efficiency, cutting costs, and improving resource use in corporate environments.

Heath, R. (2009). *Celebrating failure: The power of taking risks, making mistakes, and thinking big.* Pompton Plains, NY: Career Press.

Heath offers readers tactics they can employ to reframe failure as a valuable learning tool and convincingly argues that "positive failures" can be springboards to beneficial change and success.

Jiang, J. (2015). *Rejection proof: How I beat fear and became invincible through 100 days of rejection.* New York, NY: Penguin.

Jiang offers practical lessons learned during his "100 days of rejection experiment," including secrets of successful requests, strategies for picking targets, how to determine when an initial "no" can be transformed into a "yes," techniques for handling rejection, and confidence-building strategies.

Klein, M., & Napier, R. (2003). *The courage to act: 5 factors of courage to transform business.* Palo Alto, CA: Davies-Black.

Based on fieldwork conducted across four continents, Klein and Napier offer a simple yet elegant model for gauging, promoting, teaching, and embodying courage. Readers will benefit from a thorough description of the factors needed to effectively manage ambiguity, face adversity, capitalize on fleeting opportunities, and work through conflict.

Patterson, R. J. (2014). *The assertiveness workbook: How to express your ideas and stand up for yourself at work and in relationships.* Oakland, CA: New Harbinger.

Patterson's highly rated workbook explains how to establish and sustain personal boundaries without becoming unapproachable and offers readily applicable cognitive behavioral techniques capable of fostering increased assertiveness.

Tichy, N. M., & Bennis, W. G. (2009). *Judgment: How winning leaders make great calls.* New York, NY: Penguin.

Tichy and Bennis, consultants and advisors to prominent CEOs, offer a framework for making tough calls when stakes, pressure, and ambiguity are high. Their book teaches readers how to identify pivotal moments during the decision-making process, determine when decisive action is vital, and how to effectively execute and move forward once key decisions have been made.

SUMMARY

Keep Doing

Review plans and proposals thoughtfully for feasibility and unnecessary risks.

Stop Doing

Hold up progress due to indecisiveness and a lack of assertiveness.

Start Doing

Provide suggestions and solutions instead of simply raising objections.

High Cautious behaviors are readily observable, and leaders who exhibit these behaviors are often passed over for promotions or surpassed by peers who are more action oriented and dynamic. For a leader to accomplish a reputation change in this area involves identifying and structuring situations where he or she can be more assertive and more decisive. Success often begets success, and once a high Cautious leader begins making progress in this area, future progress will rapidly follow. An integral step for a high Cautious leader who wants to change his or her reputation is to gain the support of his or her manager. Further, it is important for the leader to assess the degree to which the corporate culture supports risk and change. It is more difficult for a high Cautious leader to enact behavior change if the organizational dynamics do not support risk taking or change. However, once the boundaries or limits are known, the high Cautious leader can stretch his or her behavior to make the most of decision-making opportunities.

Low Cautious: Becoming Prudent

If you don't invest in risk management, it doesn't matter what business you're in, it's a risky business.

Gary Cohn

Detecting When It Is a Problem

Low Cautious behaviors—including making rapid decisions without an appropriate level of data gathering, analysis, or reflection—are not only difficult to detect but may be encouraged by corporate cultures that reward action-oriented and decisive behavior.

Low Cautious leaders often escape being held accountable for the outcome of their decisions. The rapidity with which individuals change roles in organizations—let alone the speed with which people change organizations—may mean that low Cautious leaders are long gone by the time the ramifications of their decisions become apparent. The leader-like behaviors that these individuals display (action-orientation, assertiveness, decisiveness, etc.) are frequently remembered, but the actual outcomes of their decisions are often given scant attention.

When low Cautious leaders' behaviors are recognized, the damage to their reputations can be disastrous. They might be labeled as a "loose cannon" or "not a team player," resulting in a loss of credibility and impacting relationships.

One historical example of a leader who probably would have had a low Cautious score is Captain Edward Smith of the *RMS Titanic*. As all movie lovers and history buffs are aware, the *Titanic* was a luxury ocean liner that sank on its inaugural voyage after hitting an iceberg. Captain Smith, who was making his final scheduled voyage as a captain before retirement, was at the helm of the fastest and most luxurious ship of its time. In the hubris of the day, the construction of the ship led it to be labeled as being "unsinkable." It is speculated that Smith's motivation to not just beat, but smash, the existing time record for a trans-Atlantic crossing led him to ignore iceberg warnings and run the *Titanic*'s engines at an accelerated rate. With the ship having lifeboats for only one third of the passengers she carried, over 1,500 people lost their lives when she sank on April 15, 1912.

While not as dramatic a tale as Captain Smith of the *RMS Titanic,* Rex from Case 1—Rex, vice president on page 56—provides a good example of a low Cautious profile. The following is Rex's profile summary.

PART II Development Techniques for Reputation Change

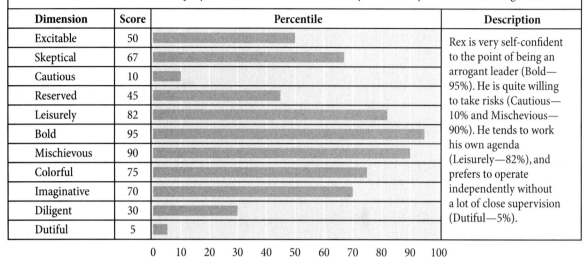

	Rex's Situational Summary		
	Rex worked in a small company as vice president of sales. In his role, he had considerable autonomy and freedom to make decisions. The company was acquired by a much larger, well-established company with rules, processes, and procedures that often accompany a large bureaucracy. Rex's willingness to take risks and make fast, independent decisions runs counter to the culture that exists in the new company. This issue could be exacerbated by his tendency to follow his own agenda.		
Dimension	**Score**	**Percentile**	**Description**
Excitable	50		Rex is very self-confident to the point of being an arrogant leader (Bold—95%). He is quite willing to take risks (Cautious—10% and Mischievous—90%). He tends to work his own agenda (Leisurely—82%), and prefers to operate independently without a lot of close supervision (Dutiful—5%).
Skeptical	67		
Cautious	10		
Reserved	45		
Leisurely	82		
Bold	95		
Mischievous	90		
Colorful	75		
Imaginative	70		
Diligent	30		
Dutiful	5		

Rex has a combination of scores (low Cautious and low Dutiful, and high Mischievous and high Leisurely) that will exacerbate both his tendency to make quick decisions and his tendency to be very independent and resistant to supervision or control. These characteristics are likely to be troublesome in his new work environment with its emphasis on agreed-upon processes and standardized operations.

Sample Development Program (Case 1—Rex)

An analysis of Rex's Cautious subscale scores indicates lower scores in all three areas—Avoidant, Fearful, and Unassertive. Therefore, Rex is very eager to participate in meetings and have an impact, he is not afraid of making mistakes, and he is very comfortable being assertive. Each of these behaviors was previously rewarded in his sales role in his old organization.

Reputation Change

Rex's reputation of being independent, decisive, and sometimes even "playing it fast and loose" has carried over to the new organization. While his colleagues who worked with him for years in the old organization know him well and chalk some of his rogue actions up to "that's just Rex," his newer colleagues think he is not a team player and that he disregards rules and procedures that are in place for a reason. They think he is impulsive and takes risks unnecessarily, sometimes even against their advice. Rex needs to repair his reputation immediately, or he will be at risk of derailing in the new organization's culture. To succeed, he needs to build trust, especially with his new colleagues, and build a reputation of a prudent risk taker who, while still action oriented, weighs the options and acts in a more measured, structured way.

Development Actions for Rex

Rex needs to identify some situations and decision-making opportunities where he can display more measured behaviors in the new corporate culture. Some possible steps to accomplish this are as follows:

- Rex should clearly outline the areas where he has the autonomy to make independent decisions versus those areas that need additional levels of discussion or approval before acting.
- Rex needs to learn more about the corporate culture of the acquiring organization. He should find a mentor or role model who can meet regularly with him and give him insights into key cultural issues and who can provide feedback to him on his interactions with others.
- Rex needs to understand the operations of the acquiring company, including its rules, policies, procedures, and modes of operation. This knowledge should help him work more effectively in the new corporate culture.
- Rex should think about his comfort level with analytics and data and whether he has the ability to recognize when additional fact finding and analysis are needed before making a decision.
- He should identify strategies that can help when he encounters roadblocks or setbacks. He should learn to develop alternatives to simply acting independently and making his own decisions.
- Rex should actively participate in planning meetings and progress report meetings. He should make sure he stays updated with the current status of projects and other company efforts.
- Rex should identify key individuals who can give him real-time feedback on how he is coming across to others in meetings, with particular emphasis on situations where he has come across as being too assertive, domineering, or impulsive.
- Rex should review key decisions he is making and alternative courses of action that he might take. He should include a postmortem of the decisions that he makes, with a critical eye on whether he could have involved others, whether he could have made more effective use of available data and other information available.

Evaluating Your Need for Change

The following behavioral questions should be considered in conjunction with your low Cautious score when evaluating the need for a change in your behavior. A "yes" response to three or fewer items suggests that there is no imminent need for behavioral changes. A "yes" response to four to six items suggests that a low score on the Cautious scale should be a watch-out for you. A "yes" response to more than six items suggests that you should take active steps toward making behavioral changes.

Do you:

1. Express an opinion even when it is unpopular or politically unwise?   Yes   No   Not Sure

2. Willingly express views regardless of the people present or the potential for negative consequences?   Yes   No   Not Sure

3. Comfortably make requests or ask for favors from people known only casually?   Yes   No   Not Sure

4. Rarely express concern about or reflect on past mistakes?   Yes   No   Not Sure

5. Demonstrate excessive confidence in decisions you have made or in your decision-making ability in general?   Yes   No   Not Sure

6. Make decisions even when it is clear that additional data or input from others would be helpful?   Yes   No   Not Sure

7. Take rigid stands on issues even without data to support the positions taken on issues?   Yes   No   Not Sure

8. Seem to get out in front with an opinion even when the issue or decision is controversial?   Yes   No   Not Sure

9. Fail to back down on an opinion even when faced with data or evidence suggesting it may be wrong?   Yes   No   Not Sure

    These items should be considered as behavioral indicators. Similar or associated behaviors to any of those listed that you exhibit likely suggest a "yes" response. They provide additional support that you may be at risk for the negative reputational consequences associated with those scoring low on the Cautious scale, such as Rex.

Development Tactics

Development tactics cover a range of approaches and resources that have been found useful in addressing low Cautious behaviors. These tactics are typically used in combination to form a custom plan suited to the specific learning needs of a leader. The tactics are divided into four categories: (1) thought-provoking questions, (2) exercises to improve performance, (3) tips and techniques to improve performance, and (4) support resources that can be consulted to gain additional insights in addressing low Cautious behaviors.

Thought-Provoking Questions

- List the major decisions you made that have been successes and then list those that were not successes. For the unsuccessful decisions, would you have made a different decision had you spent more time researching and evaluating this issue? Why or why not?
- On average, have your independent decisions turned out to be effective and correct? List examples to justify your answer.
- How has your decision-making style affected others in the organization and your relationships with others in the organization?
- How do you determine which decisions you have the authority to handle on your own as opposed to those that require input or approval from your manager?
- Is your decision-making style collaborative and inclusive? Do you actively incorporate the ideas and viewpoints of others when making decisions?
- What decisions do you wish that you could redo? How would your decision—and the process you undertook to make it—be different the second time around?
- How do you determine when to be assertive and push for results versus adopting a more subtle approach? Provide examples of when you have been successful with both styles.

Exercises

- Do a postmortem on a decision that did not go well and identify any additional data you should have gathered (and coworkers whom you should have involved) when making this decision.
- Identify some role models in your organization who are decisive but who also demonstrate high levels of collaboration and coordination with others when making decisions. Spend time with these individuals and gain insights from them on how you can improve in this area.

- Faced with a key decision, make a list of the key stakeholders involved in the decision and make a concerted effort to communicate and coordinate with them during the decision-making process.
- Take the time to list the pros and cons of the different courses of action you are considering. Find a person whose judgment you trust and use him or her as a sounding board for the decisions you are considering.
- Make sure that you are comfortable with analytics and data. If this is not an area of strength for you, find a coworker who can assist in this area. Make sure that you make appropriate use of data and information when making decisions.
- Maintain a journal covering the decisions that you think are critical in your job or career. Because outcomes often take time to determine, update your decisions with information about outcomes as it comes available.

Tips and Techniques

- Make sure you understand the impact of any decisions that have not been well thought out or that have been incomplete. Make sure you understand the impact that these decisions have had on coworkers and the organization overall.
- Enlist your manager in your efforts, including obtaining a clear picture on what decisions you are empowered to make individually versus those requiring additional input or approval from your manager.
- Make sure you have access to, and an understanding of, the data and information that are available when making key decisions.
- Ensure that you recognize when there is a need to gather additional information and research issues more fully before making a decision.
- Find internal people who can serve as a sounding board and help you make more effective decisions.
- Find sources to provide real-time feedback regarding your behavior in meetings, such as whether you are being too assertive, dominating discussions, being too impulsive, and so on.
- Practice different decision-making styles (such as, decisive, flexible, hierarchic, integrative, etc.) under safe circumstances to increase your range of decision-making styles and comfort in using them.

Support Resources

Bartkus, V. O., & Conlon, E. (2008). *Getting it right: Notre Dame on leadership and judgment.* San Francisco, CA: Jossey-Bass.

The authors present a problem-solving framework that has served as the basis of Notre Dame's business education and has been tested in corporate settings. The model encompasses three overarching themes: discovering solutions, moving from analysis to action, and driving solutions through the organization.

Bazerman, M. H., & Moore, D. A. (2008). *Judgment in managerial decision making* (7th ed.). Hoboken, NJ: John Wiley & Sons.

Bazerman and Moore examine judgment in a variety of organizational contexts, describe practical strategies for changing and improving readers' decision-making tactics, and offer abundant examples and hands-on decision-making exercises.

Brousseau, K. R., Driver, M. J., Hourihan, G., & Larsson, R. (2006, February). The seasoned executive's decision-making style. *Harvard Business Review.* Retrieved from https://hbr.org/2006/02/the-seasoned-executives-decision-making-style

Brousseau and his colleagues describe the decision-making styles of leaders, how the styles are best applied at various levels of the management hierarchy, and how the styles must evolve as individuals move up the corporate ladder to ensure continued career success.

Hoch, S. J., & Kunreuther, H. (2001). *Wharton on making decisions.* New York, NY: John Wiley & Sons.

Based on a compilation of perspectives on decision-making from leading researchers at The Wharton School, Hoch and Kunreuther describe how to apply the latest approaches in decision-making from four angles: personal, managerial, negotiator, and consumer.

Lowy, A., & Hood, P. (2010). *The power of the 2 × 2 matrix: Using 2 × 2 thinking to solve business problems and make better decisions.* San Francisco, CA: Jossey-Bass.

Based on an examination of hundreds of the most effective and original business minds, Lowy and Hood describe how 2 × 2 matrices can be used within essentially any scenario to deeply (but efficiently) analyze situations and identify the best possible course of action.

Nutt, P. C. (2002). *Why decisions fail: Avoiding the blunders and traps that lead to debacles.* San Francisco, CA: Berrett-Koehler.

Nutt analyzes fifteen notoriously bad decisions, describes how these mistakes could have been avoided, and explains how to improve organizational decision-making tactics to avoid similar failures.

Sundheim, D. (2013). *Taking smart risks: How sharp leaders win when the stakes are high.* New York, NY: McGraw-Hill.

Sundheim reconceptualizes risk, suggesting that instead of fearing risk, leaders should be more fearful of what could be lost if "good" risks are not pursued. *Taking Smart Risks* helps readers identify, anticipate, and pursue the type of intelligent, savvy risks capable of moving organizations forward.

Tassler, N. (2009). *The impulse factor: An innovative approach to better decision making.* New York, NY: Simon & Schuster.

Tasler, a researcher and director at the pioneering think tank TalentSmart, guides readers through a process of analyzing their decision-making styles, helps readers understand why they make the choices that they do, and offers tools designed to help readers maximize their unique decision-making styles.

Summary

Keep Doing

Be open and receptive to both change and new ideas.

Stop Doing

Overlook the risks associated with decisions, and minimize concerns raised by others.

Start Doing

Ensure due diligence when evaluating the positive and negative aspects of risk.

Low Cautious behaviors may be rewarded in the short term, but they usually catch up with an individual over time. For a leader to change behavior in this area takes time and commitment as this quick-decision mode is often a highly ingrained behavior. There may also be the added challenge of reputation repair if the leader has accumulated a history of making bad decisions. In addition, the leader needs to address the degree to which his or her low Cautious behaviors have been rewarded. If the organization currently rewards low Cautious behaviors, the leader needs to be aware of the impact of these rewards on his or her behaviors. Long-term career success rarely follows individuals who exhibit low Cautious behaviors even when they are rewarded. Leaders who are aware that existing reward structures may be fueling their low Cautious behaviors can also recognize that as their careers evolve and their decisions have greater impact, their mistakes will not be easily forgotten, and rewards can disappear in hurry.

CHAPTER 8

RESERVED

HIGH RESERVED: ENSURING YOUR APPROACHABILITY

Our emotions need to be as educated as our intellect. It is important to know how to feel, how to respond, and how to let life in so that it can touch you.

Jim Rohn

Detecting When It Is a Problem

High Reserved behaviors are not readily apparent in the workplace and often go unnoticed for long periods of time, especially in tough or low social environments. As such, these behaviors can be difficult for others to describe and name. The reason for this is because high Reserved behaviors are as much about what leaders *are not* doing as what they *are* doing. For example, classic high Reserved behaviors, such as pulling back, being cold and aloof, or being uncommunicative, are often described by others as making them feel awkward, disconnected, or nervous. Others may also suggest that these leaders appear to lack warmth, compassion, or a sense of social connection. In other words, interacting with high Reserved leaders causes others to feel a level of discomfort and to sense that something is missing in these individuals.

High Reserved leaders may exhibit overt behaviors that are problematic, such as being tactless, socially clumsy, or blunt. These behaviors add to the inability of these individuals to build social relationships or establish social networks, which are fundamental skills for successful performance in senior-level positions. Development for high Reserved individuals includes their dialing down high Reserved behaviors while adding more effective social skills that will improve their ability to form and maintain connections with others. High Reserved individuals with self-awareness and average social skills perform better than those with low self-awareness and poorly developed social skills. Therefore, it is critically important to address the behaviors high Reserved leaders are demonstrating as well as those they are not demonstrating.

One example of a fictional high Reserved individual is the infamous Michael Corleone from Mario Puzo's best-selling *Godfather* novels and *The Godfather* film trilogy. Michael's reserved behavior is apparent in comments such as "never hate your enemies, it affects your judgment" and "never let anyone know what you're thinking," as well as in his brutal actions, such as dispassionately arranging the murder of his brother Fredo (among many others). While throughout the movies Michael has his passionate moments, his cold, logical toughness is his defining characteristic. While most high Reserved individuals are not as callous as Michael Corleone, descriptors such as dispassionate, ruthless, cold, and calculating certainly can apply.

Robert from Case 3—Robert, design engineer on page 60—provides a good example of a high Reserved profile. Robert's highest derailer is his Reserved score (98%), but his Leisurely and Diligent scores (both 80%) may add to his reputation as a tough, stubborn man of few words and high expectations. The following is Robert's profile summary.

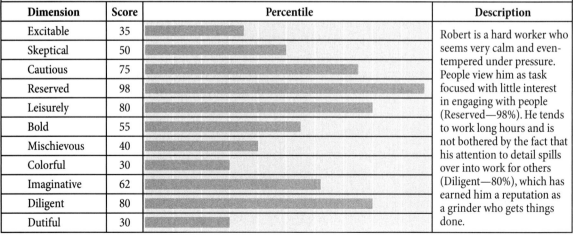

Robert's Situational Summary
Robert is a design engineer for a manufacturer of commercial aircraft electronic components. He has worked primarily as an individual contributor and was known for getting things done. His hard work resulted in a promotion to project leader on a cross-functional team. His new role will be highly demanding and require effective leadership skills that will be a challenge for his quiet, reserved nature, and tendency to fade into the background in social situations.

Dimension	Score	Percentile	Description
Excitable	35		Robert is a hard worker who seems very calm and even-tempered under pressure. People view him as task focused with little interest in engaging with people (Reserved—98%). He tends to work long hours and is not bothered by the fact that his attention to detail spills over into work for others (Diligent—80%), which has earned him a reputation as a grinder who gets things done.
Skeptical	50		
Cautious	75		
Reserved	98		
Leisurely	80		
Bold	55		
Mischievous	40		
Colorful	30		
Imaginative	62		
Diligent	80		
Dutiful	30		

The foregoing description highlights the challenge that will face Robert in his new role as project leader. As a design engineer, Robert was only responsible for his own work, and the social interaction component of his job was likely quite minimal. As a leader, the social interaction demands on Robert will increase significantly. In fact, the biggest challenge may not come from managing his direct team members, as they will have ample opportunity to become accustomed to his interpersonal style. It may come from the cross-functional aspects of his new role and the networking that will likely be necessary. This new emphasis on social connections will put Robert in the position of having to initiate social interactions to build relationships and to use a range of social skills to persuade and influence constituents who will be essential to the success of the project. Putting his head down and relying on his hard work, attention to detail, and high standards will not be enough for him to succeed.

Sample Development Program (Case 3—Robert)

Robert's profile indicates a Reserved score of 98 percent and a Diligent score of 80 percent. An examination of his subscale scores indicates that all three subscales (Introverted, Unsocial, and Tough) are elevated. The case information clearly indicates that Robert's detail orientation and diligence have helped him advance to where he is and that his quiet reserved nature has not hindered him. In the new role, however, these former strengths could quickly become liabilities as he will be required to motivate and inspire a cross-functional team to deliver top-notch, accurate results while staying out of the weeds himself and without overworking the team.

Reputation Change

Robert is known as a quiet, hard-working, individual who sets very high standards. While not unfriendly, he has the reputation for being an introvert who is happier working on his projects than interacting with people. In his new role of project leader, his reputation needs to change to one of a leader rather than an individual contributor. He needs to be seen as a good communicator who gains buy-in from his constituent groups, who keeps them informed, and who advocates for the project with the rest of the organization. Further, since the project is high profile and cross-functional, he needs to be more visible and more vocal throughout the organization.

Development Actions for Robert

Given his profile, there is a high risk for Robert to communicate too little and try to do too much of the work himself. Robert should first understand the need for a behavioral shift and then learn the necessary skills to proactively communicate with his team, create and communicate a compelling vision and strategy for the project, set clear expectations with his team (to maximize the likelihood that they will meet his high standards), and create a system for coordinating work and managing the project to include a feedback loop to monitor his team's engagement and energy level. The following are suggestions for Robert's development:

- Robert should perform an analysis of the best ways to get the work done and how to create a vision and strategy for the project.
- He should identify challenges associated with his personality and work style in this Situational Context. He needs to understand that he cannot do all the work himself and that he will need to lead others in order for the project to be successful.
- He should create a plan to meet each member of the new team for the purpose of identifying what each member can contribute and the ways in which the team might work together. This task may require some basic social-skill building on Robert's part.
- Robert needs to create and implement a plan for communicating his vision and strategy. He should reflect on why it is important for his team to know the vision and strategy and regularly communicate and reinforce his vision and strategy with all the stakeholders and people working on the project. It would be worthwhile for Robert to explore if there are others who can help him communicate his messages about the strategy.
- Given Robert's track record of working independently, he should reflect on the benefits of having the team collaboratively set the goals and tactics for implementing his strategy.
- Robert needs to meet with each member of his team to identify individual responsibilities and communicate his expectations. He should set up regular meetings during which the team can communicate progress.
- To combat his higher Diligent score (and the potential for him to become a micromanager), Robert should set up a dashboard to monitor progress. He should create checkpoints to determine when he needs to get involved in team problems. This will help him make conscious decisions about when to let his team members handle things.

Evaluating Your Need for Change

The following behavioral questions should be considered in conjunction with your high Reserved score when evaluating the need for a change in your behavior. A "yes" response to three or fewer items suggests that there is no imminent need for behavioral changes. A "yes" response to four to six items suggests that a high score on the Reserved scale should be a watch-out for you. A "yes" response to more than six items suggests that you should take active steps toward making behavioral changes.

Do you:

1. Often work behind closed doors or in locations that ensure social contact is kept to a minimum? **Yes   No   Not Sure**

2. Have difficulty interacting with strangers, casual acquaintances, or unfamiliar colleagues? **Yes   No   Not Sure**

3. Appear to be too socially guarded or maintain social barriers that limit approachability? **Yes   No   Not Sure**

4. Interact with few friends, colleagues, or associates at work? **Yes   No   Not Sure**

5. Put up interpersonal barriers to keep people out or put people off? **Yes   No   Not Sure**

6. Appear to lack social skills, or come off as awkward in social situations? **Yes   No   Not Sure**

7. Act indifferent to the plight or problems of others? **Yes   No   Not Sure**

8. Tend to treat employees as replaceable parts in a machine rather than as people? **Yes   No   Not Sure**

9. Seem to be unconcerned about reputational issues, especially those related to interpersonal skills? **Yes   No   Not Sure**

These items should be considered as behavioral indicators. Similar or associated behaviors to any of those listed that you exhibit likely suggest a "yes" response. They provide additional support that you may be at risk for the negative reputational consequences associated with those scoring high on the Reserved scale, such as Robert.

Development Tactics

Development tactics include a range of approaches that have been found useful in addressing high Reserved behaviors. These tactics are typically used in combination to form a custom plan suited to the specific learning needs of the leader. The tactics are divided into four categories: (1) thought-provoking questions, (2) exercises to improve performance, (3) tips and techniques to improve performance, and (4) support resources that can be consulted to gain additional insights in addressing high Reserved behaviors.

Thought-Provoking Questions

- Why would it be helpful for you to engage others to garner support and build alliances?
- In what circumstances have specific high Reserved behaviors worked for you?
- What's the potential risk of not engaging with others?
- What can you do to occasionally share genuine emotional responses?
- Is there any benefit to just chatting and interacting with others?
- How do you build trust? Are there any relationships that might benefit you or your work if you could build trust with others? How might you do this?
- How did you build your closest relationships, and how do people get into your inner circle? What aspects of this can be applied to work relationships?
- What would it take for you to accept that feelings are important and that other people can be hurt easily?

Exercises

- Learn the key elements of EQ and how to apply them to specific relationships.
- Develop your personal time-out message that you can use to gracefully exit social situations that have become tiresome.
- Establish specific quiet times during the course of the workday in which others know you are not to be interrupted.
- Establish a set of quiet time activities that you can engage in after situations involving extensive interactions.
- Identify situations in your past where others have exploited your toughness (such as asking you to fire someone, lead a downsizing, deliver bad news, etc.) and become vigilant regarding those types of situations in the future.

Tips and Techniques

- Build a stakeholder matrix and then decide how to engage each stakeholder.
- Build access points for others, such as office hours or proactive social engagements.
- Videotape yourself to help identify behaviors and body language that others might describe as smug and aloof.
- Take time after meetings to check with others to gauge the overall message that was communicated (e.g., ask them what they heard).

- Practice asking others about themselves, and reflect privately on what was learned. How might this information inform the way you build trust with and communicate with others?
- Think continuously about why connecting with others is important and the ways in which a lack of connection with others can be detrimental.
- Approach behavior change in terms of baby steps because of your propensity to withdraw or disengage.

Support Resources

Cain, S. (2013). *Quiet: The power of introverts in a world that can't stop talking.* New York, NY: Crown.

Cain discusses the "Extrovert Ideal," how it has contributed to the devaluation of introverted qualities, and the risk we as a society take when we underestimate what introverts have to offer. *Quiet* highlights groundbreaking achievements of introverts from past and present and likely will leave readers seeing themselves and other introverts in a different light.

Carnegie, D. (2010). *How to win friends and influence people.* New York, NY: Simon & Schuster.

This business classic has helped countless now-celebrated figures achieve success, both professionally and personally, for over 60 years.

Conant, D., & Norgaard, M. (2011). *TouchPoints: Creating powerful leadership connections in the smallest of moments.* San Francisco, CA: Jossey-Bass.

Based on Conant's tenure as CEO of Campbell Soup Company and Norgaard's extensive consulting experience, the authors make a convincing case for the argument that a leader's impact and legacy are created via hundreds of interactions that, in the moment, seem inconsequential.

Cuddy, A. J. C., Kohut, M., & Neffinger, J. (2013, July–August). "Connect, then lead." *Harvard Business Review.* Retrieved from https://hbr.org/2013/07/connect-then-lead

One of HBR's 10 must-reads on emotional intelligence.

Dotlich, D. L., & Cairo, P. C. (2003). *Why CEO's fail: The 11 behaviors that can derail your climb to the top and how to manage them.* San Francisco, CA: Jossey-Bass.

The authors alternate high profile cases with compelling examples from their coaching practice. The Aloofness chapter offers coaching tactics for Reserved tendencies.

Ferrazzi, K. (2014). *Never eat alone, expanded and updated: And other secrets to success, one relationship at a time.* New York, NY: Crown Business.

After distinguishing genuine relationship building from "networking," this bestselling business classic describes the specific steps (as well as the mentality) needed to make meaningful connections, both in general and in the digital realm.

Fishbein, M. (2013). *How to build an awesome professional network: (Meet new people and build relationships with business networking)* [Kindle edition]. Retrieved from Amazon.com

Based on extensive research and his own personal experience, Fishbein thoroughly but succinctly offers practical and actionable tips that will help readers develop and sustain relationships with people capable of facilitating career and business growth.

SUMMARY

Keep Doing

Show steadiness when others are becoming emotional and overwrought.

Stop Doing

Tune other people out, and ignore their concerns.

Start Doing

Check for understanding after important interactions or meetings.

High Reserved behaviors involve pulling away and disconnecting from others. The internal motive for pulling away varies across leaders and may range from a need for solitude to gather thoughts, to emotional parsimony, to pleasure in watching others squirm or attempt to connect with them. The Reserved subscales of Introverted, Unsocial, and Tough are important in helping determine how others are likely to see the high Reserved behaviors. While high Reserved behaviors may sometimes assist individual contributors to be productive in tough environments and with high workloads, these behaviors become problematic when these individuals are expected to lead and develop others.

Development should include social-skill building as well as becoming more comfortable in being with others. High Reserved leaders should recognize that the goal is not to take away all private time or solitary work but rather to determine where and when these behaviors are not in their best interests.

Low Reserved: Taking Tough Stands

When you care about someone more than they deserve, you get hurt more than you deserve.

Unknown

Detecting When It Is a Problem

If high Reserved behaviors are not readily apparent in the workplace, low Reserved behaviors are even less obvious. Low Reserved leaders are frequently described as friendly, warm, engaging (and engaged), and interpersonally skilled. The problems that these leaders encounter are associated with their lack of awareness or ability to emotionally, socially, or even physically pull back when situations are overheated, toxic, or politically detrimental. Their social boundaries are poorly defined, which often results in excessive concern for the feelings of others and a strong level of discomfort with conflict. In the workplace, these individuals miss cues about the intentions of others, have a difficult time saying "no," and often do not stand up for themselves. They can appear to others as naïve and are quite vulnerable to being manipulated.

A great example of a low Reserved individual can be found in the first film of *The Godfather* trilogy. During the wedding scene at the opening of the movie, Johnny Fontane (a singer and actor) goes before Don Corleone and pleads for help in dealing with a mean movie producer. Johnny Fontane appeared weak, soft, and very conflict averse. Don Corleone, annoyed with Johnny Fontane's low Reserved behaviors, slapped him around and demanded that he toughen up. It was clear from the interaction that Don Corleone had lost respect for Johnny Fontane because of his inability to stand up for himself. While workplace situations may not be as dramatic, loss of respect is potentially a real consequence of low Reserved behaviors.

Janis from Case 5—Janis, on page 64—provides a good example of a low Reserved profile. The following is Janis's profile summary:

Janis's Situational Summary
Janis is a newly promoted customer service manager who works for a software company. Her long-time regional manager was recently promoted, and her new manager is described as young, hard-charging, and very demanding. Janis is very conscientious and works hard to keep everybody happy. Her new manager will likely test her ability to push back, or she will find herself challenged to keep up with his demands. Her lack of self-confidence will also be readily apparent to her new manager.

Dimension	Score	Percentile	Description
Excitable	60		Janis is a high-energy person who does not over-promise (Cautious—75%) and is very approachable (Reserved—15%). She lacks confidence (Bold—10%) but makes up for it through preparation and attention to detail (Diligent—85%). She is known for her loyalty and willingness to go the extra mile when it comes to protecting the reputation of the company and her manager (Dutiful—80%).
Skeptical	10		
Cautious	75		
Reserved	15		
Leisurely	20		
Bold	10		
Mischievous	40		
Colorful	30		
Imaginative	62		
Diligent	85		
Dutiful	80		

Janis's case is an interesting one in that her Reserved score is at the 15th percentile, but her Skeptical score is even lower, at the 10th percentile. These two scores together suggest that Janis could be quite naïve about the intentions of others and organizational politics. She will have difficulty delivering tough messages or correcting problematic behavior of others. She might also overexpose herself to others socially and emotionally, allowing others to know too much too quickly about her.

Combining these behaviors with her tendency to overwork to please others (high Diligent) and her intense loyalty (high Dutiful), a profile emerges of a very vulnerable leader. It suggests that Janis will be easy prey for those who may not have her best interests at heart or who use politics to advance their own agendas. She will not push back even if work requests are unreasonable, she will not notice when she is being used to gain a political advantage, and she will not raise concerns even when she observes (or is asked to participate in) behaviors that stretch the limits of good business ethics.

Sample Development Program (Case 5—Janis)

Janis has a Reserved score of 15 percent. Her subscale scores indicate that she is low on the Introverted and Tough subscales. Further, she is low on the Skeptical, Leisurely, and Bold scales, and she has elevations on the Cautious, Diligent, and Dutiful scales. In combination, these scales portray an individual who is warm, engaging, friendly, and hardworking. More problematic characteristics include the likelihood that she is conflict avoidant, people pleasing, and overly soft in tough situations. Additionally, the combination of these scores suggests she is naïve about both organizational politics and the downside of overexposure.

Reputation Change

Janis is known as a really nice person who is always cooperative, rarely says "no," and is very supportive of her manager. Her team loves her, but they realize that they can miss commitments without her becoming angry or confrontational; she merely does the work herself to pick up the slack. In her new environment, with a manager who is such a hard-charger, Janis needs dispel her reputation of being a pushover. She needs to keep the reputation of being hardworking and collaborative, but she needs to add to it the ability to stand up for herself, to push back when needed, and to be tough when the situation calls for it.

Development Actions for Janis

The following steps are recommended for Janis's development:

- Janis needs to understand that while her energy, positivity, conscientiousness, and ability to diffuse difficult customer service issues are all positive in many situations, the landscape (including the management) has changed. She now needs a new set of strategies and a new repertoire of behaviors.
- She needs to understand that the new landscape calls for firm limits with her new manager about the workload for herself and her team and for careful consideration of what she discloses to the new manager.
- Janis should think about ways she can redirect her social skills into "targeted charisma" to project a confident presence to her new manager, to her peers, and to her direct reports.
- Given her low score on the Leisurely scale, Janis may need to clearly define her own mission and objectives so that her new charismatic and driven regional manager does not usurp her agenda.
- Janis needs to recognize that projecting a confident image and clear agenda will help her negotiate her workload, thus protecting her team and her work-life balance. Further, she should realize that a confident person is less likely to become a target for blame and more likely to be considered for promotion in the future.
- Janis needs to reflect on her criteria for trusting others. This may lead to the need for her to better read the intentions of others.

Evaluating Your Need for Change

The following behavioral questions should be considered in conjunction with your low Reserved score when evaluating the need for a change in your behavior. A "yes" response to three or fewer items suggests that there is no imminent need for behavioral changes. A "yes" response to four to six items suggests that a low score on the

Reserved scale should be a watch-out for you. A "yes" response to more than six items suggests that you should take active steps toward making behavioral changes.

Do you:

1. Openly welcome discussions or interactions even when they disrupt work that is under way? Yes No Not Sure
2. Exhibit too much ease and comfort when interacting with strangers? Yes No Not Sure
3. Prefer to work in meetings or in group situations compared to working alone to accomplish tasks? Yes No Not Sure
4. Rely excessively upon a network of colleagues or associates to discuss routine business issues? Yes No Not Sure
5. Open up to the point that others may become too familiar with personal information unrelated to work? Yes No Not Sure
6. Lack the verbal and bodily cues to signal others to back off? Yes No Not Sure
7. Exhibit an excess of concern over and involvement in the plight or problems of others? Yes No Not Sure
8. Delay or fail to make difficult people calls because the individual involved may be negatively impacted? Yes No Not Sure
9. Display an excess of concern regarding reputational information or the perceptions of others? Yes No Not Sure

These items should be considered as behavioral indicators. Similar or associated behaviors to any of those listed that you exhibit likely suggest a "yes" response. They provide additional support that you may be at risk for the negative reputational consequences associated with those scoring low on the Reserved scale, such as Janis.

Development Tactics

Development tactics cover a range of approaches and resources that have been found useful in addressing low Reserved behaviors. These tactics are typically used in combination to form a custom plan suited to the specific learning needs of a leader. The tactics are divided into four categories: (1) thought-provoking questions, (2) exercises to improve performance, (3) tips and techniques to improve performance, and (4) support resources that can be consulted to gain additional insights in addressing low Reserved behaviors.

Thought-Provoking Questions

- Do you think it is possible for leaders to be overexposed and for others to know too much about them, their thought process, their vulnerabilities, and their feelings? What is the risk?
- How do you think your prosocial behavior (such as putting others ahead of your own interests, helping others, extending kindness, etc.) is sometimes abused by others?
- What do you think are some of the benefits to others when you give them direct feedback?
- How do you think others would describe your executive presence as a leader?
- How has your inability to say "no" affected your work-life balance?
- Are there any negative implications when you withhold critical feedback?
- What is the value of giving positive or negative feedback in the moment?
- Does it ever decrease your power (or do you ever lose respect from others) when you are overly engaged and friendly with others?
- Do you ever pay a personal price when others have access to you all the time?

Exercises

- Practice setting parameters about when and for how long you are available to be interrupted.
- Describe a team member who would benefit from feedback. Consider the adverse impact on this individual by delaying the feedback or not giving it at all.
- Develop a script for an upcoming interaction that you anticipate will be difficult. During the interaction, follow the script. After the interaction, evaluate how it went and what was achieved.
- Create an incremental plan to increase communication about expectations and disappointments and to share feedback.
- Practice saying "no" in a way that shows self-respect and respect for others.

Tips and Techniques

- Engage in rigorous calendar management that leaves time for reflection, thinking strategically, and business planning.
- Develop a list of acceptable high Reserved behaviors that serve to increase your executive presence. Develop an implementation plan to incorporate these behaviors into regular use to build a more commanding executive presence.

- Practice giving difficult feedback through role-play.
- Role-play a difficult negotiation in which tough stands are required, as well as saying "no" in response to unreasonable demands.
- If you do not have socially fulfilling connections outside of work, devise a plan to build a greater network of friends and acquaintances outside of work. That is, make sure that you are not meeting all of your social and emotional needs at work.
- Review incidents in your past where you accepted work assignments or commitments that should have been turned down or at least modified to something more reasonable. Discuss how these incidents came about and how they could have been handled differently to achieve a more reasonable outcome.
- Strengthen your awareness of politics within the organization and develop a plan to manage those politics.

Support Resources

Brandon, R., & Seldman, M. (2004). *Survival of the savvy: High-integrity political tactics for career and company success.* **New York, NY: Free Press.**

Two of the nation's most successful corporate leadership consultants reveal their proven, systematic program for using the power of "high-integrity" politics to achieve career success, maximize team impact, and protect the company's reputation and bottom line.

Fisher, R., Ury, W., & Patton, B. (1992). *Getting to yes: Negotiating agreement without giving in.* **New York, NY: Penguin.**

Getting to Yes has a 30-year history of helping people negotiate smarter and more strategically. Based on the work of the Harvard Negotiation Project, *Getting to Yes* offers readers an established and systematic strategy for achieving mutually satisfactory agreements regardless of the circumstances at hand.

Patterson, K., Grenny, J., McMillan, R., & Switzler, A. (2011). *Crucial conversations: Tools for talking when stakes are high.* **New York, NY: McGraw-Hill.**

This best-selling book offers readers concrete and actionable advice about how to communicate when circumstances are less than ideal: when the stakes are high, all parties are on different pages, and emotions are heightened.

Rosenberg, M. B. (2003). *Nonviolent communication, a language of compassion.* **Encinitas, CA: PuddleDancer Press.**

Rosenberg offers an easy-to-implement model for communicating non-aggressively, compassionately, and in a manner that "fosters respect, attentiveness, and empathy."

Stone, D., Patton, B., & Heen, S. (2010). *Difficult conversations: How to discuss what matters most.* New York, NY: Penguin.

Based on 15 years of research at the Harvard Negotiation Project, *Difficult Conversations* walks readers through a step-by-step, proven approach to having less-than-welcome conversations with "less stress and more success."

Ury, W. (2007). *The power of a positive no: Save the deal save the relationship and still say no.* New York, NY: Bantam Dell.

Saying "no" the right way is critical because, according to Ury, "no" is quite possibly the most powerful word in our language. Based on his acclaimed Harvard University course for leaders and executives, Ury offers readers specific and actionable advice about how to effectively say "no" in any situation, defend their interests, resist challenges, and ultimately reach the target—"yes."

Summary

Keep Doing

Use positive social skills and the ability to connect productively with others.

Stop Doing

Allow others to abuse your time or have unlimited access to you.

Start Doing

Project confidence in setting boundaries with others and saying "no" when necessary.

Reserved behaviors are all about social, emotional, and even physical connections with others. A low Reserved score predicts friendly, warm, and engaging behaviors that are often beneficial in building relationships, developing others, and creating team cohesion. Unfortunately, these same behaviors when overdone can become problematic for the leader and the organization. Subscales help determine how and where the more troublesome low Reserved behaviors are likely to create problems. Contextual elements can help gauge how big a problem these behaviors are likely to create. Low Reserved behaviors are most likely to become problematic in environments or situations that require social and emotional toughness. They are also more likely to be problematic when a low Reserved individual, lauded for his or her warmth and social skills and for being a good team player, becomes a leader who needs to develop firmer social boundaries. In cases of this type, open door policies and displaying overly chummy behaviors can drain the leader's time and energy, lead to overexposure, and reduce the executive presence necessary to appear leader-like.

CHAPTER 9

LEISURELY

HIGH LEISURELY: MAINTAINING YOUR COMMITMENTS

Sometimes you don't realize you're drowning, when you're trying to be everyone else's anchor.

Unknown

Detecting When It Is a Problem

The impact of high Leisurely behavior is not immediately apparent. A leader may initially be perceived as capable, cooperative, and friendly. As time passes, however, and stresses intensify, cracks may appear in the façade. High Leisurely leaders do what they want, when they want, rather than meet the expectations of their managers and the organization. They consistently say one thing and do another—even after verbally agreeing to deliver exactly what the manager needs. Time and time again, they follow their own agenda, leaving a trail of unmet commitments in their wake. The pattern eventually becomes obvious. Trust is lost; credibility is compromised.

The disconnect that high Leisurely leaders create with the larger organization has repercussions for all of the leaders' stakeholders. But the biggest impact is on their direct reports, who are left without a connection to the work of the larger organization. This disconnect is exacerbated by the tendency of high Leisurely leaders to be uncommunicative. They keep their agendas to themselves and cut off questions with monosyllabic answers. They seem unwilling or unable to share information. So not only do high Leisurely leaders operate outside the objectives of the larger organization, but they also leave their followers without any communication about the larger organizational goals. Further, high Leisurely leaders do not like to be hurried or interrupted and become irritated or aggressive if requests persist, creating yet another barrier to effective communication.

Another characteristic of high Leisurely leaders is passive aggression, or the indirect expression of hostility. The list of passive-aggressive behaviors is too long to recount here, but among the more obvious behavioral signs are:

- Not doing what they say they will.
- Procrastinating.
- Unwillingness to confront others.
- Blaming others for situational outcomes.
- Lacking empathy for the urgency of others.

George W. Bush (43) is an example of a high Leisurely leader. In the book *Decision Times,* he alludes to several missteps during his presidency. However, in spite of his role as president, he expresses no accountability for these. Rather, he named those who influenced his decisions as the ones with sole responsibility for those decisions. High Leisurely behaviors were also evident in his decisions about the Iraq war. Despite enormous pressure to change his war strategy and move in a different direction, he held steadfastly to his own agenda. An important aspect of high Leisurely leaders is that they firmly believe in their own agenda despite the prevailing zeitgeist.

The high Leisurely leader's manager needs to be alert for signs of any missed deadlines and miscommunications and deal with them as soon as possible to mitigate the negative impact the high Leisurely leader may have on the organization. At the same time, the manager also needs to be aware that the high Leisurely leader may be both stubborn and hard to coach.

Rex from Case 1—Rex, vice president of sales on page 56—provides an illustration of a high Leisurely profile.

Rex's Situational Summary
Rex worked in a small company as vice president of sales. In his role, he had considerable autonomy and freedom to make decisions. The company was acquired by a much larger, well-established company with rules, processes, and procedures that often accompany a large bureaucracy. Rex's willingness to take risks and make fast, independent decisions runs counter to the culture that exists in the new company. This issue could be exacerbated by his tendency to follow his own agenda.

Dimension	Score	Percentile	Description
Excitable	50		Rex is very self-confident to the point of being an arrogant leader (Bold—95%). He is quite willing to take risks (Cautious—10% and Mischievous—90%). He tends to work his own agenda (Leisurely—82%), and prefers to operate independently without a lot of close supervision (Dutiful—5%).
Skeptical	67		
Cautious	10		
Reserved	45		
Leisurely	82		
Bold	95		
Mischievous	90		
Colorful	75		
Imaginative	70		
Diligent	30		
Dutiful	5		

Rex's profile is reminiscent of the lone-cowboy syndrome—a man who lives life on his own terms and by his own rules. This maverick mentality is an asset in a small start-up but is more of a liability in a larger organization with a well-established code of conduct and brand. Now that he is part of such an organization, Rex will have to make significant adjustments to his modus operandi and consciously work to change his reputation of being a loner.

Sample Development Program (Case 1—Rex)

In his development initiative, Rex should focus on his high Leisurely behaviors, specifically his tendency to ignore rules, procedures, and processes. This rebellious behavior will not be acceptable in a more bureaucratic organization.

Reputation Change

Prior to the acquisition, while Rex was considered a maverick, he was also known as the "golden boy" because so much of the company's growth was due to his autonomous decisions that were wildly successful. Now, however, in the new environment, he is rapidly gaining the reputation of ignoring rules, and in many cases, even thumbing his nose at the new senior leaders and continuing to work his own agenda. Because he is the VP of sales, his behaviors are very visible, and the C-suite leaders and board are concerned that he is setting a bad example for his sales force. He has lost their trust and the trust of his colleagues, and he must rebuild it to succeed in the new environment. He needs to change his reputation to being someone who, while an independent thinker, is a trusted team player who puts the company's and brand's welfare ahead of his own.

Development Actions for Rex

Two of the Leisurely subscales were elevated for Rex, so development actions need to address his Passive Aggressive and Irritated subscales. His feelings of Unappreciated were not elevated. These are Rex's priorities:

- Rebuilding trust and credibility.
- Accepting his role as an organizational citizen, which includes doing what he says he will (acting in alignment with the rest of the organization), openly communicating his perspectives, and building relationships with stakeholders.

The first step in modifying behavior is accepting feedback. Given that Rex tends to discount feedback, learning to take feedback seriously is of utmost importance. Rex should identify those people in the organization whose opinions he respects and whose opinions are driving his reputation and include them in a multi-rater assessment process. Certainly, Rex should ask his manager to be a part of this. Rex needs to hear about as many critical incidents and the repercussions of these incidents as possible, so he cannot deny the feedback.

Rex's development should address his Passive Aggressive behavior (specifically doing what he says he will) and his Irritated behavior (finding alternative ways of dealing with interruptions).

Passive Aggressive

Rex does want to maintain smooth relationships with stakeholders. Once he accepts the feedback that his stakeholders do not trust him, his motivation for change will most likely be activated. These steps should be taken:

- He should recognize that one of the most important trust builders is doing what he says he will.
- He needs to realize that accepting a role as a leader in an organization indicates that he is willing to act in alignment with that organization. His new position does not mean that he cannot have a different perspective, but it does imply that he will be willing to openly express his perspective and will ultimately act in accordance with the organization's point of view.
- Rex should learn to recognize when his body language and his words are incongruent. This incongruity can erode trust and make Rex seem that he is giving lip service to change as opposed to expressing wholehearted commitment to change.

- Rex needs to consider carefully before he agrees with any request whether or not he really intends to comply. If he is not in agreement, he needs to say so.
- Rex should find a trusted colleague who will role-play a high-stakes situation with him. Rex can practice saying "no" in a way that is not likely to be offensive to his stakeholders.
- Rex needs to remember that consistently doing what he says he will is the only way to rebuild trust.
- Rex should schedule a meeting with each one of his stakeholders to make amends for his past behavior. These meetings should be carefully planned to rebuild trust.

Irritated

Behavioral Approach: From a purely behavioral perspective, this issue is much more easily changed than "doing what you say you will." It involves planning ahead and scheduling time for interruptions and times when there will be no interruptions except for emergencies. Medical doctors and other professionals sometimes schedule calling times for their clients when they plan to make themselves available as needed and other times when office hours or project work takes precedence. Rex can employ these same techniques.

Mind Management Approach: In conjunction with dealing with the behavioral aspects of this issue, Rex should also approach it from a mind management perspective:

- Rex needs to identify the thoughts that he is thinking when he is interrupted that directly affect his mood and cause him to be irritated. For example, is he thinking, "Doesn't this person realize how important my work is?" or "This person should not be interrupting me or wasting my time!"?
- Rex should reframe the situation once he identifies these unrealistic or dysfunctional thoughts. Reframing is a way to help Rex look at a situation from a variety of perspectives and learn to substitute different emotional reactions to the situation. For the first example above, he might substitute "There is no way that person knows the importance of what I am working on," and for the second example the substitution, "I am sure this must be urgent for this person to be interrupting me."
- Rex needs to practice reframing so that it becomes a useful tool. He might keep a journal and record any time he becomes irritated, frustrated, impatient, or upset, what his thoughts were at the time, and how he might reframe the situation.
- Rex should set realistic expectations for controlling his tendency to become irritated. He should initially use the reframing process with minor emotional upsets. Once success is achieved here, he can start slowly using

reframing with more difficult emotional situations. He should start with situations where there is a high probability of success.

Unappreciated

Although the Unappreciated subscale was not elevated for Rex, as he works diligently on changing his behavior, he may start to feel unappreciated, especially if no one notices his progress. Rex's manager will probably make positive comments. However, other people probably will not as most people are quite self-involved. One strategy that may prove useful is for Rex to let trusted associates know about the behavioral changes he is trying to make. This information increases the probability that they will notice the changes.

Evaluating Your Need for Change

The following behavioral questions should be considered in conjunction with your high Leisurely score when evaluating the need for a change in your behavior. A "yes" response to three or fewer items suggests that there is no imminent need for behavioral changes. A "yes" response to four to six items suggests that a high score on the Leisurely scale should be a watch-out for you. A "yes" response to more than six items suggests that you should take active steps toward making behavioral changes.

Do you:

1. Put off or delay completing tasks that are viewed as less important than personal agenda items?   **Yes   No   Not Sure**

2. Appear to suppress anger even when it is obvious that a request creates an annoyance?   **Yes   No   Not Sure**

3. Often agree to a course of action, even when you have no intention of taking action, just to avoid a conflict?   **Yes   No   Not Sure**

4. Appear to be "put upon" when others ask for help or assistance?   **Yes   No   Not Sure**

5. Express discontent with the way others express or fail to express gratitude that you think you deserve?   **Yes   No   Not Sure**

6. Leave the impression that personal agenda items should supersede the agenda items of others, even superiors?   **Yes   No   Not Sure**

7. Come across as insincere or even annoyed when others ask for help or assistance?   **Yes   No   Not Sure**

8. Get annoyed when your personal agenda is challenged by those wanting to go in a different direction?   **Yes   No   Not Sure**

9. View interruptions or distractions, regardless of how important, as unnecessary and annoying?   **Yes   No   Not Sure**

These items should be considered as behavioral indicators. Similar or associated behaviors to any of those listed that you exhibit likely suggest a "yes" response. They provide additional support that you may be at risk for the negative reputational consequences associated with those scoring high on the Leisurely scale, such as Rex.

Development Tactics

Development tactics cover a range of approaches and resources that have been found useful in addressing high Leisurely behaviors. These tactics are typically used in combination to form a custom plan suited to the specific learning needs of a leader. The tactics are divided into four categories: (1) thought-provoking questions, (2) exercises to improve performance, (3) tips and techniques to improve performance, and (4) support resources that can be consulted to gain additional insights in addressing high Leisurely behaviors.

Thought-Provoking Questions

- What situations cause you to be stubborn or to procrastinate? How do these behaviors impact your effectiveness? What do you think they are doing to your reputation?
- How often do you make commitments and then not meet them? What situations are more likely to result in this happening? Does this ever create problems for your credibility?
- What situations make you feel as if people do not value your contributions? Do you feel underappreciated? Do you have any ideas about how to get the recognition you think you deserve?
- Under what circumstances do you question the competence of others? Direct reports? Peers? Bosses? How do you handle this? How could you handle it more effectively?
- What impact are high Leisurely behaviors having on your career?

Exercises

- Scan the organization and identify others who exhibit high Leisurely behaviors. List the consequences or negative impact of these behaviors and how the problems they created could have been averted.
- Generate a list of questions that are designed to understand rather than to undermine the directions or agendas of others.
- Identify a trusted colleague in the organization, and ask the colleague to help track your high Leisurely behaviors including the *tells* that indicate irritation.
- Schedule project review meetings with your manager to ensure that expectations are clearly communicated and agendas are aligned.
- Identify examples when you should have spoken up when you disagreed or when things were not going according to your agenda. List some alternative ways these situations could have been handled to avoid people thinking you were in agreement when you really were not.

Tips and Techniques

- Work with your manager to gain a clear understanding of your manager's priorities and objectives. Identify where alignment and misalignment between your and your manager's priorities exist. In those areas where they are misaligned, meet with your manager to determine an acceptable way forward.
- Generate two lists. One list includes commitments that you have met in the last six months, and the other list includes commitments that have not been met. What distinguishes the lists from one another? Are there any consistent patterns or themes?
- Learn how to pause and think before making a commitment. Consider if making a particular commitment is something you really want to do. It is better to refuse right away than to disappoint the person to whom you have made a commitment that you do not keep.
- Do you have trouble saying no? Look around for a role model who is able to say no smoothly and without giving offense. Also, it is important to differentiate between a trivial request and an urgent request.
- Understand the *tells* you exhibit when irritated. They are important, as others pick up on them.

Support Resources

Braiker, H. B. (2002). *The disease to please: Curing the people-pleasing syndrome.* New York, NY: McGraw Hill.

After discussing why people pleasing is more than just a "benign problem," Braiker offers readers a self-assessment, describes the roots of people-pleasing tendencies, and provides simple, subtle, and easy-to-implement tips for breaking free of the "Disease-to-Please Triangle."

Brandt, B., & Rothschild, B. (2013). *Keys to eliminating passive aggressiveness.* New York, NY: W. W. Norton & Company.

Brandt and Rothschild discuss the often benign roots of communication labeled as passive-aggressive and teach readers how to subtly change their communication tactics so that they come across as assertive, transparent, and constructive.

Butler, G., & Hope, T. (2007). *Managing your mind: The mental fitness guide.* New York, NY: Oxford University Press.

Based on time-tested management advice and proven clinical psychology tactics such as Cognitive-Behavior Therapy, Butler and Hope describe how readers can develop the "mental fitness" necessary to be fulfilled and productive, both personally and professionally.

Cooper, R. (2014). *Difficult people: Ultimate dealing with difficult people guide!* [Kindle edition]. Retrieved from Amazon.com

Difficult People helps readers discover how to effectively and constructively interact with challenging people in professional and nonprofessional settings. Among many other topics, Cooper discusses the roots and precursors of people's behavior, how to respond to passive aggression, and how to quickly and effectively defuse conflict.

Runion, M. (2010). *Speak strong: Say what you MEAN. MEAN what you say. Don't be MEAN when you say it.* New York, NY: Morgan James.

Filled with real-life examples and practical, actionable advice, *Speak Strong* teaches readers how to find their voices, express their true sentiments, create boundaries, set and maintain higher communication standards, and overcome less-than-constructive communication tendencies, among many other valuable lessons.

Simon, G. K. (2010). *In sheep's clothing: Understanding and dealing with manipulative people.* Little Rock, AR: A. J. Christopher & Company.

Simon's succinct but example-laden book helps readers understand what they can do to decrease the odds that they are targets for manipulators and offers easy-to-implement tactics readers can employ when interacting with controlling or manipulative people.

SUMMARY

Keep Doing

Foster positive relationships by using effective social skills.

Stop Doing

Make commitments that may not be met.

Start Doing

Be candid regarding agenda disagreements or conflicts.

The negative impact of high Leisurely behaviors is sometimes hard to recognize because it may take a while for repercussions to occur. Managers who repeatedly experience high Leisurely behaviors on the part of a subordinate will, over time, recognize the signals and lose trust in the person. High Leisurely leaders need to recognize that they might tend to feel misunderstood and, as a result, may be quite stubborn and resistant to feedback. Further, they need to understand that they often do not recognize the negative impact of their behavior on others. Consequently, they need to become more aware. While high Leisurely behaviors may be well entrenched, they are not impossible for a motivated leader to change.

Low Leisurely: Establishing a Personal Agenda

Lack of direction, not lack of time is the problem. We all have twenty-four hour days.

Zig Ziglar

Detecting When It Is a Problem

Low Leisurely leaders only want to please and have no personal agenda. They are people pleasers and completely "other-directed." Low Leisurely leaders are easy to spot. One or two interactions and coworkers have them pegged.

Low Leisurely leaders are patient when interrupted, regardless of whether the interruption is trivial or urgent. They will agree to anything, which often leads to overload. But no problem, they will trudge through, almost always deliver on time, and exceed the requestor's expectations. They are overly cooperative and put others' needs before their own. Because they do this, they seldom delegate and are always willing to step in and help an overwhelmed colleague, manager, or direct report.

Good examples of low Leisurely leaders can be found among one's past or present colleagues. They accept whatever level of performance their staffs deliver, never setting "stretch" goals or expecting improvements in performance. They find it difficult to correct average or low-performing direct reports, or to encourage and urge high performers to excel. They are overly focused on whether or not their direct reports like them and tend to accept the status quo and overly value and praise mediocre results.

Reality TV offers copious examples of low Leisurely scores in action. Watch any of the shows with multiple participants, such as *Celebrity Apprentice* or *Survivor*, and note that there is always at least one person who is overly agreeable and looks to others for leadership.

Janis from Case 5—Janis, customer service manager on page 64—provides a good example of a low Leisurely profile. The following is Janis's profile summary.

\multicolumn{4}{c}{Janis's Situational Summary}

Janis is a newly promoted customer service manager who works for a software company. Her long-time regional manager was recently promoted, and her new manager is described as young, hard-charging, and very demanding. Janis is very conscientious and works hard to keep everybody happy. Her new manager will likely test her ability to push back, or she will find herself challenged to keep up with his demands. Her lack of self-confidence will also be readily apparent to her new manager.

Dimension	Score	Percentile	Description
Excitable	60		Janis is a high-energy person who does not over-promise (Cautious—75%) and is very approachable (Reserved—15%). She lacks confidence (Bold—10%) but makes up for it through preparation and attention to detail (Diligent—85%). She is known for her loyalty and willingness to go the extra mile when it comes to protecting the reputation of the company and her manager (Dutiful—80%).
Skeptical	10		
Cautious	75		
Reserved	15		
Leisurely	20		
Bold	10		
Mischievous	40		
Colorful	30		
Imaginative	62		
Diligent	85		
Dutiful	80		

With a new ambitious and demanding manager, Janis's low Leisurely score (20%) may prove to be problematic. As a low Leisurely leader, Janis's desire to please is likely to result in her accepting a workload that is unrealistic. Further, she will probably neither feel nor express frustration or irritation at such demands. As always, she will put her own needs behind the needs of her manager and the organization. Given her new manager's tendency to place blame on others for any failure to deliver, Janis may find herself in a precarious position.

Janis's other scores increase the likelihood of an undesirable career outcome. Her Dutiful score (80%) indicates a person who tries hard to do what she is expected to do. Given Janis's high Cautious score (75%), she wants these expectations to be spelled out in minute detail. Because they seldom are, Janis is often indecisive and resistant to change. Her high Diligent score suggests that she is attentive to detail and that she will provide others with structure and direction, but she may be reluctant to delegate. With a hard-charging new manager, these characteristics will not be valued.

While Janis has numerous strengths, including her attention to detail and her loyalty (Dutiful), she lacks initiative and leadership energy, as indicated by her low Bold, Mischievous, Colorful, and Imaginative scores. She also may be overly trusting, given her low Skeptical score, which is not an asset for leaders. This lack of potential for leadership is exacerbated by her low Leisurely score, indicating that she has no agenda of her own. For Janis, this lack of an agenda may become a major obstacle to her career success.

Sample Development Program (Case 5—Janis)

Janis's Leisurely score is 20 percent, and in combination with the scale scores discussed above, could quickly derail her with her new manager.

Reputation Change

While being known as a pleaser, Janis also has the reputation of being hard-working, unselfish, cooperative, and always willing to help others. This served her well in the old environment because her manager was not the type to take advantage of Janis's good nature. Her new hard-charging manager, however, is already taking advantage of her by overloading her and her team with work. His initial impression of her that she just does not know how to say "no" is being reinforced on a daily basis as she continues to do more for him without indicating that her plate is full or that she has an agenda of her own that he is hijacking. He is the primary stakeholder with whom she needs to change her reputation to one of a conscientious and loyal direct report who also stands up for herself and her team and who pushes back when necessary. If she does not establish some boundaries, and soon, her reputation as a pushover or a "yes person" who cannot think for herself could spread throughout the organization. Further, her team could see her as not advocating for them and also feel whiplashed due to changing priorities.

Development Actions for Janis

An examination of Janis's three subscale scores indicates that her Passive Aggressive and Irritated scores were low, while her Unappreciated score was not low. Because Janis works tirelessly at pleasing others, this is not surprising. Initially, Janis needs to pay more attention to her low Passive Aggressive and Irritated scores. Once she gets more in touch with her emotions, her Unappreciated score may turn out to warrant consideration as well. The following are suggested development approaches for the subscales.

Passive Aggressive

- Janis should imagine she were her more successful twin sister. Is her twin more assertive? Does her twin take stands and push back more than Janis does?
- Janis should solicit behavioral feedback from key stakeholders as to what they see as her strengths and areas for development, especially as related to standing up for herself and her team and setting boundaries.
- Janis should anticipate situations that are likely to occur and plan how she will behave. The goal is for her to begin to act in a manner that is consistent

with her needs but not offensive to others. In other words, she will start learning how to handle situations in an assertive manner.

- Janis should ask a trusted colleague to observe her in her day-to-day interactions in order to help her fine-tune her behaviors and to brainstorm alternatives to interactions with others who do not meet her expectations.

Irritated

Janis is always willing to turn her attention to the needs of others, even when their needs interfere with her own needs. When interrupted, Janis should start to think of herself first and what might be sacrificed if she allows the interruption. If the interruption will result in an inconvenience to her, she needs to communicate this in a firm but tactful manner. Role-playing interruptions with a trusted colleague will help her learn to do this. Saying "no" in this situation is a great opportunity for Janis to practice setting limits and boundaries so that she is not as vulnerable to the whims of others.

Unappreciated

As Janis begins saying "no" to others, they may respond by withdrawing from her to some degree. Furthermore, the extent to which others express their appreciation may also decline as she begins to stand up for herself. As she becomes more and more aware of her own feelings and acts accordingly, she will recognize the changes in the behavior of others and may start to feel less appreciated. She needs to anticipate this reaction and think about mechanisms to deal with it.

Evaluating Your Need for Change

The following behavioral questions should be considered in conjunction with your low Leisurely score when evaluating the need for a change in your behavior. A "yes" response to three or fewer items suggests that there is no imminent need for behavioral changes. A "yes" response to four to six items suggests that a low score on the Leisurely scale should be a watch-out for you. A "yes" response to more than six items suggests that you should take active steps toward making behavioral changes.

Do you:

1. Agree to unrealistic timeframes for requests regularly, with little or no push back?	Yes	No	Not Sure
2. Put your own agenda aside or have it supplanted completely in fulfilling the requests of others?	Yes	No	Not Sure

3. Comply with requests, even when they appear to run counter to your own views or beliefs? **Yes No Not Sure**

4. Maintain a demeanor of gratitude even when requests are unreasonable? **Yes No Not Sure**

5. Appear excessively appreciative in situations where such emotions are inappropriate or should be tempered? **Yes No Not Sure**

6. Happily acquiesce to the agenda of others without offering any challenge or resistance? **Yes No Not Sure**

7. Appear excessively compliant or agreeable when others make requests? **Yes No Not Sure**

8. Suppress negative emotions even in situations that would test the patience of most people? **Yes No Not Sure**

9. Accommodate interruptions or distractions, regardless of how trivial, without showing signs of irritation? **Yes No Not Sure**

These items should be considered as behavioral indicators. Similar or associated behaviors to any of those listed that you exhibit likely suggest a "yes" response. They provide additional support that you may be at risk for the negative reputational consequences associated with those scoring low on the Leisurely scale, such as Janis.

Development Tactics

Development tactics cover a range of approaches and resources that have been found useful in addressing low Leisurely behaviors. These tactics are typically used in combination to form a custom plan suited to the specific learning needs of a leader. The tactics are divided into four categories: (1) thought-provoking questions, (2) exercises to improve performance, (3) tips and techniques to improve performance, and (4) support resources that can be consulted to gain additional insights in addressing low Leisurely behaviors.

Thought-Provoking Questions

- What is most important to you at work? What reputation would you like to have? Is there anything you would like to do differently?
- When is it important to take a stand? How do you express this?
- How do you set limits with colleagues? How and when do you say "no"?

- When there is a difference of opinion with a colleague, how do you resolve the situation?
- Do you find yourself doing the work of others or doing more than your fair share? How can you push back to avoid this circumstance in the future?

Exercises

- Identify and observe colleagues who are good role models for assertiveness.
- Generate a list of appropriate phrases that can be used when encountering situations that provide an opportunity for assertiveness.
- Describe the characteristics you admire in great leaders, and compare those characteristics with your areas of strength and weakness.
- Identify situations in which other leaders use their emotions effectively to achieve their goals and objectives. How does that compare with the way you use your emotions?
- Are your contributions to the organization being noticed or recognized? How could you go about raising awareness regarding the value you bring to the table?

Tips and Techniques

- Role-play expressing a definitive opinion to peers. As your development progresses, you should role-play refusing a request constructively, expressing disagreement, resolving a dispute, and providing feedback to a direct report.
- Develop a personal statement describing values, needs, and wants, and then discuss the statement. As the next step, craft a description of what you want to stand for as a leader in the organization.
- Keep in mind that low Leisurely leaders are inveterate people pleasers, and be aware of this in your interactions with others.
- Look for your in-the-moment low Leisurely behaviors, and think about how you could have modified them to be more effective as a leader.
- Look for opportunities to remind yourself that assertiveness requires appropriate body language, which makes points clearer and more effective.
- Remember to "practice, practice, practice" assertive behaviors.

Support Resources

Breitman, P., & Hatch, C. (2001). *How to say no without feeling guilty: And say yes to more time, more joy, and what matters most to you.* **New York, NY: Broadway Books.**

Based on the premise that anyone can learn how to say "no" with self-assurance, grace, and kindness, Breitman and Hatch teach readers five simple techniques that make saying "no" easier and less guilt-inducing regardless of the circumstances.

Chamorro-Premuzic, T. (2014). *Confidence: Overcoming low self-esteem, insecurity, and self-doubt.* **New York, NY: Penguin.**

Chamorro-Premuzic argues that, contrary to popular belief, confidence is capable of thwarting achievement, employability, and likability. Among other topics, this book discusses the silver linings of low confidence, teaches readers how to identify when to feign self-assurance (and how to do so effectively), and tactics for improving physical and emotional health.

Craig, N., George, B., & Snook, S. (2015). *The discover your true north fieldbook: A personal guide to finding your authentic leadership* **[Kindle edition]. Retrieved from Amazon.com**

Based on the best-selling book *True North,* this workbook walks leaders through a series of exercises that help them identify their leadership objectives and facilitate the development of authentic leadership skills.

Klaus, P. (2004). *Brag!: The art of tooting your own horn without blowing it.* **New York, NY: Warner Business.**

Renowned communication expert Klaus offers readers a "subtle but effective" plan for selling themselves without seeming self-promoting or overeager to impress.

Murphy, J. (2011). *Assertiveness: Stand up for yourself and still win the respect of others* **[Kindle edition]. Retrieved from Amazon.com**

Based on a list of principles she calls the "Bill of Rights of Assertiveness," Murphy helps readers understand how to be assertive without crossing the line to aggressiveness and offers numerous examples and exercises designed to help readers practice being assertive in a variety of contexts.

Patterson, R. J. (2014). *The assertiveness workbook: How to express your ideas and stand up for yourself at work and in relationships.* **Oakland, CA: New Harbinger.**

Patterson's highly rated workbook explains how to establish and sustain personal boundaries without becoming unapproachable and offers readily applicable cognitive behavioral techniques capable of fostering increased assertiveness.

Smith, M. J. (2000). *When I say "No," I feel guilty* (Vol. 2). N.p.: A Train Press.

This classic assertiveness training book offers readers immediately implementable tips for saying "no" without guilt or regret, staying calm when people are trying to push their buttons, and standing up for themselves and their best interests.

Summary

Keep Doing

Maintain positive and agreeable attitudes and behaviors.

Stop Doing

Say "yes" to every request no matter how daunting or unrealistic.

Start Doing

Use more assertive behavior when appropriate.

Low Leisurely leaders are people pleasers. They are unassertive and can be easily manipulated. It can be challenging for a leader to change his or her reputation once colleagues have concluded that the leader is a pushover and wishy-washy. A motivated leader can undergo a dramatic transformation and achieve an enhanced reputation by consciously developing greater assertiveness. The most challenging aspect of reshaping the reputation of a low Leisurely leader is establishing a toughminded attitude to build an agenda and stick with it. The natural tendency to revert to pleasing others is powerful. Low Leisurely behaviors can be quite career limiting in a world that values strong-willed leadership. These behaviors may not get an individual fired, but they certainly can contribute to the individual's being passed over.

CHAPTER 10

BOLD

HIGH BOLD: MANAGING YOUR OVERCONFIDENCE

No persons are more frequently wrong, than those who will not admit they are wrong.

François de La Rochefoucauld

Detecting When It Is a Problem

Individuals who have high scores on the Bold scale are typically described by others as being arrogant, being overconfident, acting in an entitled way, and seeing themselves as being destined for greatness. This pattern becomes a problem when the behavior starts breeding resentment in others or drives the individual to engage in reckless activities. High Bold behavior can be a serious problem if it becomes so extreme that it borders on delusional and is impervious to a reality check.

Moderate elevations on the Bold scale can sometimes be useful. Most leaders of organizations need to have at least a moderate degree of self-confidence in order to assume positions of leadership and convey confidence to the people who must follow them. The optimal point for the Bold characteristic depends on the situation or challenge that must be faced. What constitutes confident, decisive leadership behavior in one situation or organizational culture may appear unrealistic or reckless in another context.

A good example of a high Bold individual is the World War II general George Patton. Patton languished for over 16 years as a major in the US Army prior to the war and was even briefly demoted back to captain. An early evaluation of Patton stated that "he would be invaluable in a time of war, but is a disturbing element in time of peace." He failed to be selected for Command and General Staff School, which was a prerequisite for advancement. When war broke out, though, his unusual combination of self-confidence, ambition, and excitability catapulted him into a generalship. Eventually, he became a four-star general, but during his tenure as general, he came perilously close to being drummed out of the service and was sidelined from several important battles owing to his arrogance, competitiveness, and lack of interpersonal sensitivity. By the end of the war, Patton was once again in danger of derailing his career owing to a series of incidents. Eventually fate intervened, and he was killed in a peacetime accident, so we will never know if he would have been able to make the transition back to a world not at war.

One of the distinguishing features of individuals with high Bold behaviors is that they are impervious to negative feedback or events. Donald Trump, the well-known businessman who was elected president of the United States, could be a poster child for this phenomenon. Although he has had many successful business ventures over his career, he has also had many failures, which he seems unwilling to acknowledge. Several years ago, *Time* magazine documented his many failed business ventures, which included Trump Airlines, Trump Vodka, Trump Mortgages, a Trump Monopoly game, various Trump casinos, and several bankruptcies. When asked about why he was filing for bankruptcy for a third time in a New Jersey bankruptcy court, he responded, "I don't like the B word." His high Bold behaviors continued throughout his presidential campaign.

What makes this profile especially difficult from a development standpoint is that people who are high on the Bold scale are often very successful and do, in fact, gain status among their peers. If we think about life's challenges as getting along, getting ahead, and making sense out of life, high Bold people often do quite well, at least at the getting ahead part.

Rex from Case 1—Rex, vice president of sales on page 56—is a good example of a high Bold individual whose situation has recently changed dramatically. Factors that previously made him successful may now conspire to derail him. The following is Rex's profile summary.

Rex's Situational Summary

Rex worked in a small company as vice president of sales. In his role, he had considerable autonomy and freedom to make decisions. The company was acquired by a much larger, well-established company with rules, processes, and procedures that often accompany a large bureaucracy. Rex's willingness to take risks and make fast, independent decisions runs counter to the culture that exists in the new company. This issue could be exacerbated by his tendency to follow his own agenda.

Dimension	Score	Percentile	Description
Excitable	50		Rex is very self-confident to the point of being an arrogant leader (Bold—95%). He is quite willing to take risks (Cautious—10% and Mischievous—90%). He tends to work his own agenda (Leisurely—82%), and prefers to operate independently without a lot of close supervision (Dutiful—5%).
Skeptical	67		
Cautious	10		
Reserved	45		
Leisurely	82		
Bold	95		
Mischievous	90		
Colorful	75		
Imaginative	70		
Diligent	30		
Dutiful	5		

In addition to his high Bold scores, Rex's profile displays several extreme scores that could spell trouble for him in the workplace. A score of 90 percent on the Mischievous scale indicates someone with a proclivity to test the limits and chafe under bureaucratic rules and regulations. His elevated score on the Leisurely scale might also predict that he will be stubborn about accommodating rules with which he does not agree. Exceedingly low scores on the Cautious and Dutiful scales also would predict someone who may act impulsively and not be good at following orders.

As we saw with Patton, in the right set of circumstances a high Bold pattern can drive ambitious, energetic leadership. For Rex, as vice president of sales for a small company, this high Bold pattern contributed to a large part of the company's growth. But six months ago, the Situational Context for Rex changed when the company was acquired by a larger and more bureaucratic organization. The autonomy he previously enjoyed is likely to be greatly restrained. Rex was a major contributor to the growth of his organization before it was acquired, so he may have feelings of entitlement that are not entirely unjustified. He has continued to operate in an aggressive and risk-taking manner that will not be a good fit with the new organization. His extremely high Bold score, coupled with elevations on the Leisurely and Mischievous scales, will increase the likelihood that he will run afoul of the new, more bureaucratic culture.

Sample Development Program (Case 1—Rex)

An analysis of Rex's subscales (Entitled, Overconfidence, and Fantasized Talent) suggests that he is particularly elevated in the Overconfidence subscale. This will especially derail him in the new bureaucratic organization that eschews the autonomy that he has displayed and been rewarded for in the past. Further, his tendency to overestimate his and his team's abilities and to over-commit might be seen as recklessness and arrogance by the new organization.

Reputation Change

In the new environment, Rex is rapidly garnering the reputation of a loose cannon who sets unrealistic goals and overcommits, sometimes against the expressed direction of his manager (the CEO) and colleagues. He ignores policies and processes if they are inconvenient for him. Further, he is seen as arrogant and out for himself. To succeed in the more bureaucratic environment, he needs to do reputation repair immediately, especially with the CEO and board, as they have been known to fire people whom they see as mavericks. Rex needs to make a concerted effort to change his reputation to someone who, while a confident leader and an independent thinker, is a team player who readily accepts input from his manager and colleagues. He needs to be known for respecting authority without being a "yes man," for setting stretch yet realistic goals, and for putting the company and brand ahead of his self-interests.

Development Actions for Rex

- In Rex's development program, he should particularly target reining in his tendency to set unrealistic goals for himself or his team. Further, Rex should practice sharing credit when things go well and refrain from blaming others when things go badly, as these behaviors are contributing to his reputation of being out for himself.
- Rex should take time to acknowledge his past contributions to the former organization, which allowed it to grow and eventually be purchased.
- He should engage in a "motivated abilities exercise," (i.e., those times and accomplishments when he was not only successful but felt that he was using his abilities to their fullest).
- He should identify the times when he overcommitted or set goals that turned out to be beyond his or his team's abilities. How could he have assessed his and the team's capabilities more accurately?
- Rex needs to identify his direct reports' key strengths and capabilities, and likewise, the areas where they struggle. In the past, has he fully considered these when he committed to a deliverable?
- Rex should make a list of his key business goals. Are the goals realistic given his and his team's abilities? If not, what can he do to develop his team members so that they can succeed?

- Rex needs to think about what he will need to do differently as a leader in the new organization. What does the organization value? How can he modify his behaviors to be successful? What are the organization's priorities? Are his goals in alignment?

- Rex should think about how he can dispel his reputation for being out for himself—that is, developing and mentoring others and being recognized for his guidance, sharing credit with his team rather than taking it all for himself, and shouldering blame when projects hit a snag.

- Rex should ask key stakeholders to provide feedback about any changes they see in his behavior, especially regarding setting more realistic goals for himself and his team, sharing credit when appropriate, and shouldering blame when appropriate.

Evaluating Your Need for Change

The following behavioral questions should be considered in conjunction with your high Bold score when evaluating the need for a change in your behavior. A "yes" response to three or fewer items suggests that there is no imminent need for behavioral changes. A "yes" response to four to six items suggests that a high score on the Bold scale should be a watch-out for you. A "yes" response to more than six items suggests that you should take active steps toward making behavioral changes.

Do you:

1. Appear to take liberties beyond those approved or appropriately sanctioned?	Yes No Not Sure	
2. Insist on a level of respect that is beyond that which has been earned?	Yes No Not Sure	
3. Express disdain or even refuse to accept assignments considered more appropriate for those of lesser status?	Yes No Not Sure	
4. Display arrogance when it comes to the probability of success, regardless of the challenge?	Yes No Not Sure	
5. Always accept the credit, but never accept the blame?	Yes No Not Sure	
6. Lack humility when it comes to abilities or accomplishments?	Yes No Not Sure	

7. Proclaim unusual talent and the greatness that will result from it?	Yes	No	Not Sure
8. Have an inflated self-image when it comes to skills or abilities?	Yes	No	Not Sure
9. Complain about personal talents that are underutilized or that career opportunities should be more forthcoming?	Yes	No	Not Sure

These items should be considered as behavioral indicators. Similar or associated behaviors to any of those listed that you exhibit likely suggest a "yes" response. They provide additional support that you may be at risk for the negative reputational consequences associated with those scoring high on the Bold scale, such as Rex.

Development Tactics

Development tactics cover a range of approaches and resources that have been found useful in addressing high Bold behaviors. These tactics are typically used in combination to form a custom plan suited to the specific learning needs of a leader. The tactics are divided into four categories: (1) thought-provoking questions, (2) exercises to improve performance, (3) tips and techniques to improve performance, and (4) support resources that can be consulted to gain additional insights in addressing high Bold behaviors.

Thought-Provoking Questions

- How can you ensure that others will perform to your expectations?
- What steps can you take to increase the likelihood of others' success?
- If others fail, how will that reflect on you?
- What might go wrong that is beyond your control?
- As the leader and developer of the team, how will recognizing the contribution of the team reflect positively on you as well?
- How can you be successful in a way that gets the support and recognition of your peers and manager?
- If you are entitled to special privileges or considerations, how are your colleagues likely to react?
- From whom should you get input in order to build commitment to your agenda?
- How can you leverage your confidence to inspire others most effectively?

- How can you drive your agenda in such a way that others do not feel dominated?
- How can you create win-win situations in your dealings with others?
- Because everyone has blind spots, whom can you select as a truth teller to give you feedback about how you come across to others?
- What could derail you from achieving the goals and recognition you feel you deserve?
- What is the best way you can show the humility a true leader would display?
- Which of your special abilities can you use to get others to cooperate, collaborate, or follow you?

Exercises

- Discuss where people have failed implementing your plans before. With hindsight, how could you have ensured success?
- Discuss your experience setting goals that might ensure success in the future.
- Role-play having a discussion with someone about how to best ensure success for your ideas.
- Anticipate resistance you might get from others about a project and prepare arguments you can present about "What's in it for them?"
- Role-play how you might engage your team in a discussion of "What could go wrong?" on a project.
- List two or three ways you can best fulfill your role as an inspirational leader for the team and set them up for success.

Tips and Techniques

- Engage in what-if planning.
- Rehearse how you will give people constructive feedback if things do not go well.
- Rehearse how you will give people pats on the back if things go well.
- Identify the ways that using positive reinforcement with others can build commitment to and enthusiasm for you.
- Think about how admitting to some vulnerabilities or uncertainties may make you more appreciated as a leader.
- Observe how the best leaders spread credit for success around to others but put failures on their own shoulders.

Support Resources

Bolton, R. (1986). *People skills: How to assert yourself, listen to others, and resolve conflicts.* New York, NY: Simon & Schuster.

In this communication skills handbook, Bolton describes the twelve most common barriers to effective communication and teaches readers how to better listen, assert themselves, resolve conflicts, and find mutually agreeable compromises.

Burg, B. (2011). *The art of persuasion: Winning without intimidation.* Mechanicsburg, PA: Tremendous Life Books.

Based on an in-depth examination of some of the most influential people across history, best-selling author Burg distills and shares key principles of persuasion in clear and, often, entertaining terms.

Burg, B., & Mann, J. D. (2011). *It's not about you: A little story about what matters most in business.* New York, NY: Penguin.

Using the form of an engaging parable, best-selling authors Burg and Mann help readers understand the power of subtle influence tactics.

Connors, R., & Smith, T. (2011). *How did that happen? Holding people accountable for results the positive, principled way.* New York, NY: Penguin.

Experts on workplace accountability and authors of the best-selling book *The Oz Principle,* Connors and Smith tackle the next crucial step everyone and anyone (e.g., managers, supervisors, CEOs, or individual contributors) can take in *How Did That Happen?*—instilling greater accountability in all the people you depend upon.

Dotlich, D. L., & Cairo, P. C. (2003). *Why CEO's fail: The 11 behaviors that can derail your climb to the top and how to manage them.* San Francisco, CA: Jossey-Bass.

The authors alternate high profile cases with compelling examples from their coaching practices. The Arrogance chapter addresses coaching tactics for Bold.

Hunter, J. C. (2006). *The servant leadership training course: Achieving success through character, bravery, and influence* [Kindle edition]. Retrieved from Amazon.com

The acclaimed author of the best-selling book *The Servant* teaches listeners about the servant leadership tactics employed in over one-third of Fortune Magazine's "100 Best Companies to Work For."

Salvador, T. (2013). The listening bias [Video file]. Retrieved from http://www.ted.com/watch/ted-institute/ted-intel/tony-salvador-the-listening-bias

Salvador shares tactics for becoming a better listener; for example, doing away with preconceptions, allowing vulnerability, and challenging the fear of hearing unwelcome messages.

Summary

Keep Doing

Be a role model for a positive attitude toward challenges and problems.

Stop Doing

Overpromise, and blame others when a plan or project fails.

Start Doing

Share credit with your staff for successes and missions accomplished.

Leaders who are high on the Bold scale exhibit a constellation of behaviors that can include confidence, ambition, high levels of energy, dominance, competitiveness, entitlement, arrogance, impulsivity, and self-promotion. High Bold leaders can find development quite challenging because they are often unwilling or unable to see the destructive aspects of their behavior. Thus, at least initially, they should focus on using appropriate behaviors that will lead to the success and recognition these leaders feel they deserve. Additionally, by building self-reflective questions into their repertoire, these leaders may eventually gain a better understanding of the consequences of high Bold behaviors.

Low Bold: Strengthening Your Resolve

Too many people overvalue what they are not and undervalue what they are.

Malcolm Forbes

Detecting When It Is a Problem

It is always harder to observe something that is not happening than something that is happening. Individuals who are high on the Bold scale normally stand out to others. Individuals who are low on this scale usually do not stand out from the crowd in any noticeable way. People who score low on this scale are often described as modest, lacking in self-confidence, laid back, restrained, reluctant to lead, non-confrontational, and self-effacing. They often are the good, reliable workers who follow orders and do not make waves. Prominent examples of low Bold people are hard to come by because, almost by definition, they are followers, not leaders. They are more likely to take orders than to give them, particularly if they are also high on scales such as Diligent or Dutiful. When low Bold people also have a high Cautious score, the fear of failure can paralyze them from taking action.

Like so many potential derailing tendencies, the Situational Context can play a significant role in determining the degree to which low Bold behaviors impact an individual's career. For example, low Bold individuals may thrive in subordinate roles but derail when they are thrust into leadership positions that require confidence, independent thinking, and action.

A good example of a low Bold leader is General George McClellan during the American Civil War. McClellan had been a successful general in peacetime, but the demands of the job changed when the North and South went to war. While McClellan played an important role in raising a well-trained and organized army for the Union, his extreme unwillingness to take bold action by engaging in battle brought the North perilously close to losing the war in the first year of the conflict. McClellan's timid, restrained style in battle hampered him greatly in a fast-moving battlefield environment. He chronically overestimated the strength of enemy units and was reluctant to engage the enemy troops unless he was almost certain of victory. Eventually, President Lincoln had to replace him with another general, Ulysses S Grant, who was a bolder, decisive leader willing to take risks. It is also worth noting that Grant was frequently accused of being overly bold and reckless.

Janis from Case 5—Janis, customer service manager on page 64—provides a good example of someone who has a low Bold profile combined with higher potential derailers in her Diligent and Dutiful scores. The following is Janis's profile summary:

Janis's Situational Summary				
Janis is a newly promoted customer service manager who works for a software company. Her long-time regional manager was recently promoted, and her new manager is described as young, hard-charging, and very demanding. Janis is very conscientious and works hard to keep everybody happy. Her new manager will likely test her ability to push back, or she will find herself challenged to keep up with his demands. Her lack of self-confidence will also be readily apparent to her new manager.			
Dimension	**Score**	**Percentile**	**Description**
Excitable	60		Janis is a high-energy person who does not over-promise (Cautious—75%) and is very approachable (Reserved—15%). She lacks confidence (Bold—10%) but makes up for it through preparation and attention to detail (Diligent—85%). She is known for her loyalty and willingness to go the extra mile when it comes to protecting the reputation of the company and her manager (Dutiful—80%).
Skeptical	10		
Cautious	75		
Reserved	15		
Leisurely	20		
Bold	10		
Mischievous	40		
Colorful	30		
Imaginative	62		
Diligent	85		
Dutiful	80		

Janis's situation has changed recently. She has a new boss, and she is now in a new position of authority. Until now, the biggest criticism of Janis was that she was not assertive enough in some situations. For the most part, however, her high scores on service-related scales, such as Diligent and Dutiful, may have contributed to her being well liked and successful in a customer service job where defusing unhappy customers was critical. But now, she has a new boss in addition to a new job. Her new boss is described as charismatic, confident, and hard-charging. He also seems to have a knack for avoiding responsibility when bad things happen. We can imagine that, in the beginning, the new boss will appreciate Janis's careful planning, attention to detail, loyalty, and conscientiousness. But over the longer term, his hard-charging style is likely to be incompatible with Janis's more conservative way of working. She also would likely make a good target for taking the blame when bad things happen because of her reluctance to push back. In other words, she could end up being the new manager's whipping boy.

Sample Development Program (Case 5—Janis)

Janis is not only low on the Bold scale, she also scores high on several other combinations of scales that might portend future conflict with her manager. Her elevated score on the Diligent scale (85%) predicts that she will work very hard for her new boss, and because he is a hard-charger, this pair will be a good fit, at least initially. Her score of 80 percent on the Dutiful scale predicts that she will be a loyal direct report and eager to please.

But the fact that she is also elevated on the Cautious scale may mean that her hard-charging boss will eventually find her conscientiousness and attention to detail too slow and plodding for his style. Her low Bold score makes it unlikely that she will push back, and her Dutiful and Cautious scores predict that she will have difficulty saying no to him. She may push her team of people beyond their limit in an attempt to please the new boss, but it is just as likely that she will diminish the quality of her personal life by taking too much on herself.

This is probably not a scenario that will be sustainable over the long run. Things inevitably fall through the cracks, and when they do, Janis's new boss, who is described as "Teflon," will probably deflect the blame to someone else. Janis's low Bold score makes her a prime target.

Reputation Change

In her former job with her former manager, Janis had the reputation of being a hard worker who always went above and beyond the call of duty to support the team. She was not known to be dynamic and assertive, but it was not problematic in her situation, especially since her customers loved her. With her new hard-charging manager and in her new leadership role, she needs to gain a reputation as a confident leader who is in charge, who speaks up for herself and her team, and who is not shy about expressing her opinions. Otherwise, her new boss will run all over her, and both she and her team will suffer.

Development Actions for Janis

Janis's scores on all the Bold subscales (Entitled, Overconfidence, and Fantasized Talent) were low, so her development needs to address low Bold behaviors in general and include the following steps:

- Janis needs to ramp up assertiveness to a more reasonable level. She needs to fully understand that if she does not, her prospects for future leadership opportunities will be greatly diminished.
- Janis needs to review the successes she has had in her career in order to bolster themes normally found in a high Bold profile, such as becoming more confident, recognizing her particular talents, and feeling comfortable and entitled to some credibility in the organization where she has been successful for years.

- Janis needs to practice saying "no" to unreasonable requests; however, she will probably need to build up to this in gradual steps because it is unlikely she can be assertive enough in one fell swoop.
- Janis should identify specific situations that present problems for her self-confidence. She should find a trusted colleague with whom she can role-play to prepare for these situations in the future.
- Janis should draw up two lists: a to-do list of things she and her team need to get done and a not-to-do list of things they are not going to do. The not-to-do list can include things that other people outside of Janis's group need to handle, as well as things that do not need to be done at all.
- Janis should practice how to disagree with others or offer an alternate point of view in a polite but effective way.
- Janis should practice applying the good customer skills she has with the outside world to her job internally. She should keep her manager and other key stakeholders regularly informed of both the work she and her team are doing and the work they have decided they cannot do.
- Janis should practice assertiveness in a safe forum, such as role-playing or in a program like Toastmasters.
- Janis has an elevated Diligent profile, so, she should think about whether she is delegating enough and fully leveraging the resources of her team. She should identify specific situations where she will have to delegate projects to others and hold them accountable.

Evaluating Your Need for Change

The following behavioral questions should be considered in conjunction with your low Bold score when evaluating the need for a change in your behavior. A "yes" response to three or fewer items suggests that there is no imminent need for behavioral changes. A "yes" response to four to six items suggests that a low score on the Bold scale should be a watch-out for you. A "yes" response to more than six items suggests that you should take active steps toward making behavioral changes.

Do you:

1. Avoid any appearance of taking personal advantage of the perks offered by the system?   Yes   No   Not Sure

2. Pass up challenging assignments that would be helpful in terms of future career opportunities?   Yes   No   Not Sure

3. Accept tasks that are better suited for individuals at a lower level in the organization?   **Yes   No   Not Sure**

4. Exhibit excessive self-doubt or concern when it comes to accepting what should be routine assignments?   **Yes   No   Not Sure**

5. Consistently set the bar low in terms of goal setting or career aspirations?   **Yes   No   Not Sure**

6. Appear excessively humble to the point others may perceive a lack of self-confidence?   **Yes   No   Not Sure**

7. Gravitate toward the status quo when presented with new opportunities or career options?   **Yes   No   Not Sure**

8. Espouse a poor self-image when it comes to personal skills or abilities?   **Yes   No   Not Sure**

9. Defer to others despite possessing superior knowledge or the skill necessary to address an issue?   **Yes   No   Not Sure**

These items should be considered as behavioral indicators. Similar or associated behaviors to any of those listed that you exhibit likely suggest a "yes" response. They provide additional support that you may be at risk for the negative reputational consequences associated with those scoring low on the Bold scale, such as Janis.

Development Tactics

Development tactics cover a range of approaches and resources that have been found useful in addressing low Bold behaviors. These tactics are typically used in combination to form a custom plan suited to the specific learning needs of a leader. The tactics are divided into four categories: (1) thought-provoking questions, (2) exercises to improve performance, (3) tips and techniques to improve performance, and (4) support resources that can be consulted to gain additional insights in addressing low Bold behaviors.

Thought-Provoking Questions

- What is the cost to your reputation for not asserting yourself?
- What is the worst that can happen if you try asserting yourself more?
- What might be some of the positive consequences of asserting yourself more often?

- If you repeatedly assert yourself, do you think it will gradually become easier to do?
- Do you feel like you are being ignored by key people?
- How will you feel if people more junior or with less experience get promoted over you?
- What is the effect on your direct reports of not speaking up?
- Do you have a responsibility to assert yourself for the good of the organization, your people, or yourself?
- Can you think of times when not pushing back caused things to not go well?
- What is one thing for which you could take a very limited but innovative approach that might also improve things in your area of responsibility?
- What would be a modest next step in your career?

Exercises

- Think about how others may react to your unassertiveness.
- Reenact actual situations that occurred and how they might have been handled differently.
- Rehearse alternate ways of responding to those situations.
- Identify individuals by whom you may feel particularly dominated and develop new tactics about how to deal with these individuals.
- Pick a situation that is coming up and rehearse more assertive ways of dealing with it.
- Pick an area where you have to compete with a peer for resources. Plan how you would make your case.
- Identify several role models in the organization whom you admire. What qualities make them so admirable?

Tips and Techniques

- Set criteria for success at very minimal levels in the beginning. Initially, just trying new behaviors should be the standard for success, regardless of their outcome.
- Remind yourself often that continually avoiding potential failure carries with it the potential for disapproval or ridicule by others.
- Recognize your successes to encourage and reinforce your new behavior, and then build on that to shape even more appropriately assertive behaviors.
- Enlist the aid of others (e.g., manager, HR, other key stakeholders, etc.) as additional sources of encouragement.

Support Resources

Alter, C. H. (2012). *The credibility code: How to project confidence and competence when it matters most.* New Brunswick, Canada: Meritus Books.

Alter describes how readers can use body language, posture, eye contact, intonation, and many other actively controlled cues to project more self-assurance and an aura of credibility and competence.

Beckwith, H., & Clifford, C. (2011). *You, inc.: The art of selling yourself.* New York, NY: Hachette.

Based on the premise that "the most important part of the sale is you," Beckwith and Clifford offer practical, readily applicable advice for marketing oneself (along with a healthy dose of humor).

Bolton, R. (1986). *People skills: How to assert yourself, listen to others, and resolve conflicts.* New York, NY: Simon & Schuster.

In this communication skills handbook, Bolton describes the twelve most common barriers to effective communication and teaches readers how to better listen, assert themselves, resolve conflicts, and find mutually agreeable compromises.

Cuddy, A. (2012). *Your body language shapes who you are* [Video file]. Retrieved from http://www.ted.com/talks/amy_cuddy_your_body_language_shapes_who_you_are

Social psychologist Amy Cuddy explains how "power posing"—using confident body language—can affect mechanisms in the brain capable of positively impacting the likelihood of being successful.

Cuddy, A. (2015). *Presence: Bringing your boldest self to your biggest challenges.* New York, NY: Hachette.

Rather than try to make a fundamental transformation of an individual, Cuddy argues that small tweaks in body language, behaviors, and mind-set can produce more assertive and effective behaviors.

Dotlich, D. L., Cairo, P. C., & Rhinesmith, S. H. (2006). *Head, heart, and guts: How the world's best companies develop complete leaders.* San Francisco, CA: Jossey-Bass.

The authors rely heavily on high profile case studies while discussing the crucial capabilities required of today's leaders and offering readers an actionable plan for stepping outside their "leadership comfort zone."

Harris, R. (2011). *The confidence gap: A guide to overcoming fear and self-doubt.* Boston, MA: Trumpeter Books.

Harris posits that, rather than attempting to "get over" fear and insecurity, readers should try to reconceptualize and stop fighting these emotions. Borrowing liberally from tenets of the well-respected and proven-effective Acceptance and Commitment Therapy (ACT), Harris offers readers a practical plan designed to minimize missed opportunities stemming from insufficient confidence.

Patterson, K., Grenny, J., McMillan, R., & Switzler, A. (2013). *Crucial accountability: Tools for resolving expectations, broken commitments, and bad behavior* (2nd ed.). New York, NY: McGraw Hill.

The authors of the best-selling book *Crucial Conversations* offer readers strategies for dealing with unmet expectations in a manner capable of strengthening, not damaging, relationships.

Summary

Keep Doing

Exhibit good team behaviors like listening, collaborating, and acknowledging others.

Stop Doing

Avoid confrontations, let others take credit for your work, and fail to state opinions.

Start Doing

State your own opinions, and advocate for your own positions on issues.

While leaders who are high on the Bold scale often run the risk of being fired, leaders who are low on the scale run the risk of being passed over or unrecognized for their contributions. Many times they have much to offer an organization, but their full potential goes untapped. However, assertiveness is a skill that they can develop, just like any other skill. Low Bold individuals should take successively more assertive actions, so that eventually this assertiveness may become part of their normal behavioral repertoire. The key success for these leaders is changing their public reputation from one of a lack of self-confidence to one of effective assertiveness. Many times this simple change opens the door for these individuals, allowing others to see their potential for contributing to the success of the organization.

CHAPTER 11

MISCHIEVOUS

HIGH MISCHIEVOUS: BUILDING TRUST

But charisma only wins people's attention. Once you have their attention, you must have something to tell them.

Daniel Quinn

Detecting When It Is a Problem

Mischievous behaviors concern the tendency to appear charming, friendly, and fun-loving but also to seem impulsive, excitement-seeking, and nonconforming. High scorers usually make a favorable first impression, but others find them hard to work with because they tend to test limits, ignore commitments, and take risks that may be ill-advised. Although those with high scores on the Mischievous scale may seem to be decisive, they tend to make fast-and-loose decisions because they are often motivated by pleasure and do not fully evaluate the consequences of their choices. They can gain a reputation for being flighty, for not taking business issues seriously enough, or even for lacking the gravitas needed to be a leader.

Sir Richard Branson, who owns more than 300 companies under the umbrella of The Virgin Group, lives a life and espouses a business vision that illustrate the essence of a high Mischievous character: "In the end, you have to say screw it. Just do it." From the music industry to the airplane industry to commercial space travel and exploration, Branson has made technological leaps. He has also experienced numerous failures, earning him membership in the coveted "famous failures" entrepreneurial club. He says there are two techniques that free him from dreaded routine (which is anathema to the high Mischievous leader): breaking world records and making bets. One striking aspect of Sir Branson's public persona is that he is often thought of as a charismatic leader. High Mischievous leaders are often thought of as charismatic because they approach life with an adventuresome spirit that followers admire.

Tanya from Case 4—Tanya, insurance professional on page 62—provides a good example of a high Mischievous profile (98%).

Tanya's Situational Summary			
Tanya was a successful insurance professional for a medium-sized corporation who was promoted into the role of training manager. The new role looked to be quite challenging because it required a new skill set to be successful, and the insurance industry as a whole was evolving into a highly regulated industry with many new government regulations. Tanya's new role as training manager could potentially be quite stressful given the job demands and industry changes.			
Dimension	**Score**	**Percentile**	**Description**
Excitable	90	▬▬▬▬▬▬▬▬▬	Tanya is a crafty insurance professional who can let her emotions get the best of her (Excitable—90%). She is known for putting big deals together for her corporate clients. Outwardly, she appears very self-confident (Bold—89%). She works her own agenda (Leisurely—80%), and tends to set her own rules (Mischievous—98% and Dutiful—10%) with little regard for consequences (Cautious—20%).
Skeptical	60	▬▬▬▬▬▬	
Cautious	20	▬▬	
Reserved	30	▬▬▬	
Leisurely	80	▬▬▬▬▬▬▬▬	
Bold	89	▬▬▬▬▬▬▬▬▬	
Mischievous	98	▬▬▬▬▬▬▬▬▬▬	
Colorful	70	▬▬▬▬▬▬▬	
Imaginative	50	▬▬▬▬▬	
Diligent	30	▬▬▬	
Dutiful	10	▬	
		0 10 20 30 40 50 60 70 80 90 100	

Tanya's high Mischievous profile contributed to her success in prior jobs that required an entrepreneurial spirit, but in her new position as training manager, this profile can be a derailer, especially because the company has been inundated with a number of new government regulations. These regulations forced company leaders to embark on a culture change initiative to ensure compliance with the new regulations. One of the most important components of the culture change initiative was to ensure that new insurance professionals were well acquainted with the regulations and were scrupulous in their adherence to them in completing their jobs. The culture change initiative presents a significant challenge for Tanya. First, she will come under careful scrutiny because of the importance of the right messages being conveyed to new professionals. Second, it is reasonable to assume that some aspects of her success formula could go beyond stretching the envelope and cross into areas that challenge regulatory compliance. There are also risks associated with how Tanya will react to the regulatory constraints that were not in place when she accepted the position as training manager.

Sample Development Program (Case 4—Tanya)

Tanya's high Mischievous score (98%) shows high elevations on all three subscales: Risky, Impulsive, and Manipulative.

Reputation Change

While Tanya is known as being charming, friendly, and fun-loving, she is also known as being hard to work with because of her tendency to test limits, ignore commitments, and take risks that may be ill-advised. In the new more heavily regulated environment and in her new role as training manager, she needs to take immediate action to combat this reputation of being a maverick. She needs to acquire a reputation of being a role model for her students in scrupulously adhering to regulations and supporting company policy, while still exhibiting a passion for the business and for developing creative, but completely above-board solutions to customers' insurance issues.

Development Actions for Tanya

Development actions for Tanya need to include strategies to curb or redirect her potentially derailing tendencies in order to drive a reputation change.

- Tanya should differentiate and identify a new "success profile" in the new regulatory environment.

  This case is an exploration of the adage "what got you here may not get you there." With respect to Tanya's creative initiative and mischievous resourcefulness, she will have to clearly understand the range of behaviors that will be successful in her upcoming role; moreover, she must understand what will not be tolerated. Tanya should develop a two-column chart that lists "Former Regulatory Environment" and "New Regulatory Environment." She should list responsibilities, behaviors, explicit rules, regulations, decision-making latitude, and so on, to contrast the difference in the two environments of the training manager position. What shifts will she have to make to meet expectations and adjust to the constraints in the newly defined environment? Specifically, with respect to working style, decision-making, creative boundaries, and dealing with impediments or roadblocks, how do the two contexts differ and what will that require for success? What are the boundaries in both versions of the role for the ability to challenge or act expediently? What are the collaborative realities in both scenarios?

- Tanya needs to manage impulsivity and risk taking by transferring those behaviors to a more appropriate activity where creative resourcefulness is an asset.

This is a sublimation or redirection strategy—transfer undesirable or intolerable behavior to another, more acceptable setting. For example, training presentations are greatly enriched and more memorable with a training style that incorporates charismatic behavior, including mischievous ploys.

Tanya should identify and compile a list of ways that she might use her seat-of-the-pants, shake-things-up mentality to liven up what could be staid and formal training content. How could she deliver training with a degree of cleverness and creativity to accomplish learning objectives?

Tanya would be natural at role-playing. She could develop role-play exercises where rule compliance comes into play, with her playing her natural limit-testing and rule-busting self. These sessions could be practiced with a colleague acting as a participant experiencing Tanya's behavior and providing feedback.

- Tanya should develop a flexible style of expression where a level of mischievous behavior can be used in a way that is appropriate to the situation.

This tactic will help Tanya learn to recognize when she has crossed the line on her level of mischievous behavior. Extinction of impulsivity, risk taking, and manipulative savvy is not necessarily desirable, but part of the moderation of these elements is consciously assessing whether these behaviors are invoked for a productive benefit or not. Tanya must make qualitative judgments about the impact of these behaviors and when they cross the line.

Tanya should identify a scenario where she thought she was at her best in making a risky decision, acting opportunistically, being cleverly resourceful and creative, gaining confidence from others quickly, or simply beating the system. Then she should evaluate her behavior along four dimensions of mischievous behavior:

- Did my limit-testing and pushing boundaries (a) help foster creativity and innovation in the end or (b) lead to unintended or unnecessary consequences and risks?
- Did I use my charm and persuasion to (a) achieve a specific, legitimate goal or outcome or (b) show off my personal, engaging style of interacting?
- Did my provocative or cleverly insightful statements or challenges (a) foster a more vigorous, focused debate or help reframe the discussion, or (b) did they really serve no objective other than my own personal amusement of goofing on others?

- When I turn on the charm, is it to (a) genuinely deepen trust and comfort in order to get others comfortable with working with me, or is it to (b) use my ability to talk others into something or convince them about something in the speediest manner possible?

Tanya should tabulate the number of "a" answers versus "b" answers, with "a" representing appropriate uses of mischievous behavior, and "b" representing crossing over the line into reckless, risky, overly manipulative territory. This kind of post-scenario dissection can help Tanya become more deliberate and aware of her mischievous tendencies.

Evaluating Your Need for Change

The following behavioral questions should be considered in conjunction with your high Mischievous score when evaluating the need for a change in your behavior. A "yes" response to three or fewer items suggests that there is no imminent need for behavioral changes. A "yes" response to four to six items suggests that a high score on the Mischievous scale should be a watch-out for you. A "yes" response to more than six items suggests that you should take active steps toward making behavioral changes.

Do you:

1.	Regularly bend the rules of the organization to advance personal agenda items?	Yes	No	Not Sure
2.	Fail to consider the downside when taking actions that have unknown consequences?	Yes	No	Not Sure
3.	Push limits to the point it makes other people uncomfortable with the consequences or outcomes?	Yes	No	Not Sure
4.	Take fast action on the basis of intuition without the necessary facts or contingencies?	Yes	No	Not Sure
5.	Use charm or charisma as a means of avoiding personal responsibility when things go wrong?	Yes	No	Not Sure
6.	Appear to be too impetuous in situations that would likely benefit from a more measured approach?	Yes	No	Not Sure
7.	Rely excessively on political skills or charisma to persuade or influence others?	Yes	No	Not Sure

8. Stretch the truth or embellish the situation in order to look more effective in the eyes of others?   Yes   No   Not Sure

9. Tend to pursue personal self-interests to the point that it results in a trust or credibility gap?   Yes   No   Not Sure

These items should be considered as behavioral indicators. Similar or associated behaviors to any of those listed that you exhibit likely suggest a "yes" response. They provide additional support that you may be at risk for the negative reputational consequences associated with those scoring high on the Mischievous scale, such as Tanya.

Development Tactics

Development tactics cover a range of approaches and resources that have been found useful in addressing high Mischievous behaviors. These tactics are typically used in combination to form a custom plan suited to the specific learning needs of a leader. The tactics are divided into four categories: (1) thought-provoking questions, (2) exercises to improve performance, (3) tips and techniques to improve performance, and (4) support resources that can be consulted to gain additional insights in addressing high Mischievous behaviors.

Thought-Provoking Questions

- What are the triggers for you to test limits or make potshot or provocative statements?
- In what circumstances does taking a risk work well for you?
- Describe a time that you made an impulsive choice that did not turn out well. What would you have done differently?
- How do you ensure you are seeking and getting enough substantive input to your decisions?
- How would you describe the risk tolerance of the organization? How does that align with your risk tolerance? For you to achieve your business and career goals, how might you need to adapt your style?
- How might your credibility change if you enlisted others in arriving at a course of action?

Exercises

- Examine key stakeholders associated with your role, and grade them in terms of the degree to which they trust you.

- Evaluate a key mistake you made in terms of how you handled the aftermath. Consider how that situation could have been handled differently as a trust-building opportunity.
- Take an idea or proposal and analyze the pros and cons from two perspectives: (1) your point of view and (2) others' points of view.
- Consider the challenge and fun of engaging others and moving them from nonsupporters or neutral to supporters. How could this benefit you? Your team? The organization?
- Generate a list of all the positive attributes that might be associated with a high Mischievous person. Look at these attributes through a different, less positive lens, and consider how others may view these attributes.

Tips and Techniques

- There are a number of key messages that help high Mischievous leaders become less impulsive and manipulative:
    - Slow down decision-making to afford time for a realistic appraisal of the likely consequences of alternative courses of action.
    - Recognize career success depends on the support of others. Consider their ideas from their point of view, not yours.
    - Demonstrate loyalty to others by following through on the commitments you made to them.
    - Identify and apologize to those who may have been hurt or disappointed by past actions, rather than trying to explain the situation away.
    - Leverage spontaneity and charm carefully to become a good team player who seeks success for all members of the organization.
- Identify a critical decision-making situation that will occur in the near future. How could this situation be handled including ways that differ from those used in the past?
- Design a process to create a pause before acting on decisions or impulses. Find a trusted partner for feedback.
- Identify a decision-tree process you can use to assess possible options for action and pros and cons. Use this process to evaluate decisions.
- Role-play with a colleague how to accept negative feedback and learn from it, instead of using charm and manipulation to sidestep it.

Support Resources

Covey, S. M. R. (2006). *The speed of trust: The one thing that changes everything.* New York, NY: Simon & Schuster.

Covey asserts that trust is the linchpin of the new global economy and demonstrates that trust—and the speed at which it can be developed with employees, clients, and constituents—is a defining factor within successful, high-performance organizations.

Dotlich, D. L., & Cairo, P. C. (2003). *Why CEOs fail: The 11 behaviors that can derail your climb to the top and how to manage them.* San Francisco, CA: Jossey-Bass.

The authors alternate high profile cases with compelling examples from their coaching practices. The Mischievousness chapter addresses coaching tactics for Mischievous.

Hogan, J., Hogan, R., & Kaiser, R. B. (2010). "Management derailment: Personality assessment and mitigation." In S. Zedeck (Ed.), *APA handbook of industrial and organizational psychology, Vol. 3: Maintaining, expanding, and contracting the organization* (pp. 555–576). Washington, DC: American Psychological Association.

A substantive chapter (also available via Hogan's website) with four main points. First, leadership literature offers few useful generalizations about the distinguishing characteristics of good leaders. Second, the behaviors associated with managerial derailment are well documented. Third, private and public sectors are rife with bad managers. Finally, organizations that observe principles of good management, including how they manage their managers, are more profitable.

Hogan, R., & Warrenfeltz, R. (2011). "Educating the modern manager." *Academy of Management Learning and Education,* 2, 74–84.

This Hogan Press article discusses key terms associated with learning and education often left unspecified, offers a taxonomy of learning outcomes associated with self-knowledge, and concludes noting that executive education proceeds most efficiently and productively when it is preceded by an assessment of capabilities relative to role responsibilities.

Horsager, D. (2012). *The trust edge: How top leaders gain faster results, deeper relationships, and a stronger bottom line.* New York, NY: Free Press.

Based on research likely to resonate with today's leaders, Horsager's highly rated book describes the eight pillars of trust and explains how to build them.

Kouzes, J. M., & Posner, B. Z. (2011). *Credibility: How leaders gain and lose it, why people demand it.* San Francisco, CA: Jossey-Bass.

Building on research described in their best-selling book *The Leadership Challenge,* Kouzes and Posner describe six key disciplines that "strengthen a leader's capacity for developing and sustaining credibility" and provide poignant examples of credible leaders in action.

Maxwell, J. C., & Covey, S. R. (2007). *The 21 irrefutable laws of leadership: Follow them and people will follow you.* Nashville, TN: Thomas Nelson.

While some leadership books encourage leaders to break all the rules, Maxwell and Covey's best-selling leadership book provides readers with specific rules to abide by, in addition to a self-assessment tool and exercises designed to facilitate personal growth.

Summary

Keep Doing

Take prudent risks, and appropriately challenge the status quo.

Stop Doing

Ignore warnings, cautions, and feedback about your unnecessary risk taking.

Start Doing

Avoid impulsive behavior by slowing down and evaluating the consequences of decisions.

Individuals with high scores on the Mischievous scale expect that others will like them and find them charming. Consequently, they expect to be able to extract favors, promises, money, and other resources from people with relative ease. They see others as individuals to be exploited. As a result, they have problems maintaining commitments and are unconcerned about violating expectations. At their best, Mischievous individuals are self-confident and have an air of daring that others find attractive and even intriguing. At their worst, they are impulsive, reckless, faithless, exploitative, and manipulative. Their self-confidence and recklessness lead to many mistakes, but they seem unable to learn from experience. A lack of trust is at the core of the problems they create for themselves. The career consequences for being perceived as untrustworthy include missed opportunities, being passed over for promotion, or even being fired. The essential development focus for these leaders is not to eliminate the impulsivity, risk taking, and savvy influencing skills but to curb these behaviors so they can better use them to achieve productive, trust-building outcomes.

Low Mischievous: Becoming Adventuresome

People who make no mistakes lack boldness and the spirit of adventure. They are the brakes on the wheels of progress.

Dale E. Turner

Detecting When It Is a Problem

The low Mischievous individual can be summed up with two words: unassuming and responsible. Low Mischievous people tend to avoid unnecessary risks and play by the rules, which make them valued corporate citizens. Bosses appreciate their dependability and trust them to think through the consequences of proposed actions. They are cautious by nature and tend to make few mistakes in managing their careers. However, they may not take many chances. When formulating business strategy, they remember past mistakes and try to minimize risk. Warren Buffett, the legendary investor, typifies low Mischievous attributes. Buffett is known for thinking carefully when those around him lose their heads; his low-key, conservative attributes permeate his investing philosophy—he's noted for his adherence to value investing and for his personal frugality despite immense wealth ($65 billion).

What gets low Mischievous leaders in trouble or causes them to be ignored are the attributes on the low end of the charisma dimension: an unwillingness to be adventuresome or try new things, a lack of cleverness or charm, and an inability to influence others. Restrained and muted, these individuals typify the corporate survival rule regarding derailers: "High scores get you fired, low scores get you passed over."

The 1980 presidential debate between Ronald Reagan and Jimmy Carter provides a salient and memorable example of risk taking and quick wit versus risk aversion and personal restraint: Carter stumbled, citing his young daughter Amy's advice that nuclear weapons were the most important issue. Reagan lived up to his reputation for delivering lines, deflating one of the president's criticisms with a chuckling, "There you go again." And Reagan summed up his argument in the end by asking voters in what would become a classic campaign question: "Are you better off now than you were four years ago?"

James's profile from Case 7—James, marketing manager on page 68—provides a good example of a low Mischievous profile (15%).

	James's Situational Summary	
	James was the marketing manager for a small family-owned business that was sold to a well-established technology company. After the sale, James moved on to a small, fast-moving start-up technology company. He had clear challenges with his ability to get things moving in the new company. Combined, his high Cautious score with a low Mischievous score will have a direct impact on the speed with which he makes decisions that may be in conflict with a fast-moving start-up.	

Dimension	Score	Percentile	Description
Excitable	10		James is a laid-back, even-tempered marketing guy (Excitable—10%). It takes him a long time to get to know and trust people (Skeptical—70%), and he is guarded and slow to make decisions (Cautious—85% and Mischievous—15%). James doesn't make a big impression on people. In fact, he is best known for his loyalty and willingness to do whatever the owners asked (Dutiful—90%).
Skeptical	70		
Cautious	85		
Reserved	25		
Leisurely	19		
Bold	24		
Mischievous	15		
Colorful	45		
Imaginative	35		
Diligent	50		
Dutiful	90		

With the sale of his former company and downsizing, James was relocated to a small, high-tech start-up. Unlike his former business, this start-up was a fast-paced business that forced people to make decisions without a lot of guidance or management support. Perhaps the biggest change for James was the fact that he was left to make a lot of important decisions on his own. James's low scores on the Risky, Impulsive, and Manipulative scales contributed to his tendency to carefully analyze ideas and only make decisions when he had all the facts. His slow, methodical approach is likely not to be received well in the new fast-paced environment. Furthermore, James's lack of guidance contributed to his inability to make decisions, as he typically relied on the owners in his previous company to tell him what needed to get done. His early life in the new start-up looked more like a data collection exercise than a newly established marketing function in which steps were being taken to build a high-profile brand. Furthermore, James's low Mischievous score indicated a very unassuming individual who could easily be lost in the entrepreneurial environment of a fast moving start-up.

Sample Development Program (Case 7—James)

James scored low on all the Mischievous subscales—Risky, Impulsive, and Manipulative. His reputation is consistent with what these low scores predict.

Reputation Change

James is perceived by others as rule-bound, predictable, and overly corporate, which can be the kiss of death in a small, fast-moving start-up company. These perceptions have resulted in a growing reputation of being unadventurous and overly compliant. To succeed in the new environment, James needs to quickly turn perceptions around and garner a reputation for being a creative, innovative leader of the marketing function. He needs to be seen as the owner of the marketing strategy who influences the rest of the organization, and as someone who pushes the limits in the marketing realm.

Development Actions for James

To counter his growing reputation of someone who is pretty boring and unexciting, James needs to manifest new, more adventuresome behaviors contrary to his natural tendencies and do so in a sincere manner. His development should include the following activities:

- James needs to identify and evaluate the aspects of the new organizational context that will likely require new behaviors.

  He should plan a number of lunch meetings with various members of his new organization, ostensibly to get to know them, but also to learn as much as possible about the start-up culture, employee climate, the start-up's story, and so on. James should be well prepared for these meetings. He should do the following:

  - Have a well-rehearsed, three-minute infomercial about himself, including who he is, his career highlights, and what excites him about being with the new start-up.
  - Ensure he opens each meeting with a full disclosure of his need to better understand the organization, to see how he can contribute, and to build his network in the company.
  - Have some prepared questions that he can use to gain an understanding of what is expected from the marketing function and from him as the leader of the function.

- Collaborate with key members of the new organization to align with work culture expectations and business objectives.

  After collecting and evaluating data from his initial networking efforts, James should do the following:

  - Develop a profile of strengths he can leverage and weaknesses or shortcomings he may have to address, specifically assessing risk taking, flexibility, building an image, and other interpersonal dimensions of leadership.

- Formalize a job position statement and share it with his boss and key decision makers. When sharing this statement, he should again query these individuals on their expectations for an effective marketing function.
* Identify the important behaviors that must be demonstrated in order to build a reputation for being an effective leader of the marketing function.

With intelligence gathering complete for this stage, James should deploy and demonstrate behaviors and a working style commensurate with that needed for an effective leader of the marketing function. He should do the following:

- Refine and formalize the descriptive profile of what the company deems an ideal marketing person for the enterprise at this stage in its development.
- Identify an in-house confidant or onboarding mentor whom he can use as a sounding board.
- Keep a log of situations that come up weekly in business operations, including how he handled the scenarios, what seems to be working well, and what needs adjustment.
- Seek agenda time, if appropriate or available, for any meetings where successes can be celebrated, and where any adjustments need to be made.

Evaluating Your Need for Change

The following behavioral questions should be considered in conjunction with your low Mischievous score when evaluating the need for a change in your behavior. A "yes" response to three or fewer items suggests that there is no imminent need for behavioral changes. A "yes" response to four to six items suggests that a low score on the Mischievous scale should be a watch-out for you. A "yes" response to more than six items suggests that you should take active steps toward making behavioral changes.

Do you:

1. Rigidly follow the rules of the organization, even when they should be appropriately challenged?   Yes   No   Not Sure

2. Devote an excessive amount of attention and energy to what might fail rather than what might succeed?   Yes   No   Not Sure

3. Stay so far within established organizational limits that it stifles creativity or innovation?   Yes   No   Not Sure

4. Fail to act, even when the evidence is overwhelming that action is called for and needed?   Yes   No   Not Sure

5. Accept blame or become a scapegoat when things go bad due to the actions of others? Yes   No   Not Sure

6. Exhibit an excessive degree of caution in taking action even when the negative consequences are minimal? Yes   No   Not Sure

7. Seem to lack the necessary political skills to persuade or influence others? Yes   No   Not Sure

8. Speak with candor in situations where a more guarded approach would be more appropriate? Yes   No   Not Sure

9. Set aside personal self-interests to the point that others see this as a weakness and take advantage of it? Yes   No   Not Sure

These items should be considered as behavioral indicators. Similar or associated behaviors to any of those listed that you exhibit likely suggest a "yes" response. They provide additional support that you may be at risk for the negative reputational consequences associated with those scoring low on the Mischievous scale, such as James.

Development Tactics

Development tactics cover a range of approaches and resources that have been found useful in addressing low Mischievous behaviors. These tactics are typically used in combination to form a custom plan suited to the specific learning needs of a leader. The tactics are divided into four categories: (1) thought-provoking questions, (2) exercises to improve performance, (3) tips and techniques to improve performance, and (4) support resources that can be consulted to gain additional insights in addressing low Mischievous behaviors.

Thought-Provoking Questions

- In what situations are you most likely to stick with the tried-and-true, and a less risky course of action? What does this indicate about your leadership brand?
- How would you describe the risk tolerance of the organization? How does that align with your fairly low level of risk tolerance? For you to achieve your business and career goals, how might you need to adapt your style?
- How would you describe the "balance point" for leadership behaviors associated with being daring, creative, and charismatic (or, at least, interesting) without engaging in the limit testing, deviousness, and provocative behaviors that can contribute to a reputation of untrustworthiness?

- In what circumstances does avoiding risks or not experimenting with a creative approach work well for you?
- Describe a time when you had to sell others on an idea or secure their buy-in. How did you do that? Provide a camera-ready (i.e., details that a camera would have captured) example of what you did and said.

Exercises

- Define a list of behaviors that contribute to executive presence and identify those you want to incorporate into your leadership style.
- Consider the challenge and fun of engaging others and moving them to be supporters. How could this benefit you? Your team? The organization?
- Map where the organization and specific leaders fall on the risk spectrum and the impact their behavior has had on their careers. Where do you fall in comparison to them?
- Create a Tell-a-Story vignette about a personal experience or business experience, one where you learned something about yourself. The story can even be self-deprecating, but share an experience where you took a risk, went outside conventional boundaries, or did something that might have been embarrassing.
- Identify a situation in your past where you believe others have taken advantage of you. What could you do differently in the future to avoid these situations?

Tips and Techniques

- Try these skill-building steps:
  - Identify circumstances or contexts in which you behave in a cautious and restrained manner and describe the impact of this behavior on your team and overall effectiveness as a leader.
  - Consider the risk of not changing anything and the lost possibilities that result from hesitation. What possibilities could be opened up by changing this behavior?
  - Identify how and what might be done to strengthen your executive presence. List behaviors you could model, starting with the easiest and progressing to those behaviors that are more sophisticated.
  - Role-play a scenario where others have to be sold on an idea that is somewhat risky and where there is hesitance for buy in.

- View risk as a spectrum. What does the behavior at both ends of the spectrum look like? Identify where you fall on the risk spectrum. Identify the potentially positive outcome of moving slightly further along the spectrum.

- Generate a list of positive attributes that might be associated with a low Mischievous individual, and the impact these attributes have on team members. Then, generate another list that describes the high Mischievous leader's approach. Examine the contrasts between the two approaches, and identify the midrange or productive blend of the two approaches.

- Think about how to build a "Leadership Legacy," including how you would want to be described by others in the future with respect to your leadership style and accomplishments. Identify the low Mischievous behaviors that can stand in the way of your achieving the desired legacy and how they could be overcome.

- Develop a stump speech on a specific area of interest or topic of concern. Infuse the speech with anecdotes, humor, and so forth. Identify venues where you can give the speech and a plan to get feedback on the delivery and audience perceptions.

Support Resources

Cain, S. (2013). *Quiet: The power of introverts in a world that can't stop talking.* **New York, NY: Crown.**

Cain discusses the "Extrovert Ideal," how it has contributed to the devaluation of introverted qualities, and the risk we as a society take when we underestimate what introverts have to offer. *Quiet* highlights groundbreaking achievements of introverts from past and present and likely will leave readers seeing themselves and other introverts in a different light.

Cooper, R. (2014). *Decision making: The ultimate guide to decision making!* **[Kindle edition]. Retrieved from Amazon.com**

Decision Making offers practical and proven tactics capable of helping readers efficiently evaluate options, decisively and confidently make decisions, and maintain the self-restraint necessary to see decisions through to fruition.

Glei, J. K. (Ed.). (2013). *Maximize your potential: Grow your expertise, take bold risks & build an incredible career.* **Las Vegas, NV: Amazon Publishing.**

In addition to offering wisdom from twenty-one leading creative minds, this book provides guidance on how to create new opportunities, build creative expertise, cultivate relationships, and take bold, strategic, growth-promoting risks.

Grenny, J., Patterson, K., Maxfield, D., McMillan, R., & Switzler, A. (2013). *Influencer: The new science of leading change,* (2nd. ed.). New York, NY: McGraw-Hill.

Grenny and colleagues offer readers science-based insights about successful influence tactics, inspiring stories about influencing against all odds, and concrete, step-by-step recommendations for enhancing influence skills.

Houpert, C. (2014). *Charisma on command: Inspire, impress, and energize everyone you meet* [Kindle edition]. Retrieved from Amazon.com

Based on a thorough analysis of some of today's most charismatic leaders, *Charisma on Command* teaches readers how to tap into their "charismatic potential" and develop the mannerisms and mentality that others perceive as magnetic and memorable.

Kahnweiler, J. (2013). *The introverted leader: Building on your quiet strength.* San Francisco, CA: Berrett-Koehler.

After discussing common workplace challenges faced by introverts and offering a self-assessment, Kahnweiler provides concrete and readily applicable strategies introverted leaders can apply when on stage, managing up, leading projects, and in many other scenarios.

Pillay, S. (2014, December). "A better way to think about risk." *Harvard Business Review.* Retrieved from https://hbr.org/2014/12/a-better-way-to-think-about-risk

Pillay presents a compelling argument for reframing "risk" in a more favorable (and productive) light.

Summary

> ### Keep Doing
>
> Be a valued corporate citizen who is dependable and thinks through consequences.
>
> ### Stop Doing
>
> Be overly cautious, and minimize risk taking.
>
> ### Start Doing
>
> Take some appropriate risks in terms of being more proactive and innovative.

Leaders with low scores on the Mischievous scale have a reputation for being compliant and risk averse; they conscientiously follow rules and established procedures. They remember past mistakes and incorporate those lessons into their behavior going forward. These leaders are resistant or unwilling to try new, innovative, or experimental approaches to solving problems or attaining objectives. This lack of resourcefulness means they miss opportunities that are outside the box for the team and for themselves. They are unassuming and responsible in their work approach but less likely to motivate others through inspiration due to a muted and restrained personal demeanor. They can be depended upon to handle routine, lower-profile projects with efficiency but with a lack of fanfare.

Development for a low Mischievous leader—manifesting new behaviors that are contrary to his or her natural tendencies and also help him or her display these new behaviors in a sincere manner—is a challenge. Core to the approach is for the low Mischievous leader to view risk, impulsivity, and manipulation as a spectrum of behaviors, with the goal of moving slightly further along the spectrum.

CHAPTER 12

COLORFUL

HIGH COLORFUL: LOWERING YOUR PROFILE

If you deny people a voice ... their own voice, there is no way you will ever know who they were.

Alice Walker

Detecting When It Is a Problem

High Colorful behaviors are readily observed by others, and if not reined in, can earn a leader a reputation as a show-off or a blow-hard in pretty short order. In addition, it can be exhausting to be around high Colorful individuals for an extended period of time due to their high-energy levels and constant chatter. At their best, high Colorful leaders are articulate, friendly, and many times draw followers like moths to a flame. However, when their behaviors are over the top, their larger-than-life personalities can alienate their constituents.

 A good example of a high Colorful leader is Cristina Fernandez de Kirchener, the former high-profile president of Argentina. During her years as a senator and then as president, she constantly drew attention to herself through both her appearance and her actions. Perfectly coiffed, heavily made-up, and dressed in designer clothes (she was rumored to have over 200 "mourning black" dresses in her wardrobe following the death of her husband), she was routinely seen front and center in photographs with other world leaders. She was notoriously vain, and the very public discussion of her cosmetic surgery and collagen injections to ensure she stayed youthful earned her the moniker "The Botox Queen." Quite outspoken and known for dramatics, she sometimes brought her followers to tears through her passionate speeches, while at other times, she shook her fist at her adversaries. She maintained her flamboyant lifestyle despite the fact that her policies brought the Argentinian economy to its knees, and she was the subject of a personal financial scandal. Prone to oversharing, Cristina once tweeted over 61 times in a 9-hour period. Even as she left office (her term ended at midnight), she maintained her penchant for high drama as she quipped, "I can't talk much because after midnight, I'll turn into a pumpkin."

Similar to Cristina Kirchener, most high Colorful individuals thrive on their attention-getting behaviors. That is why convincing a high Colorful leader to dial it down can be so difficult. Typically, high Colorful leaders have received praise and compliments on their outgoing personalities over the years, and they just do not realize when they are over the top with their antics. They find themselves very entertaining and think everyone else does, too.

Mark from Case 6—Mark, district account manager on page 66—provides a good example of a high Colorful profile. The following is Mark's profile summary.

Mark's Situational Summary

Mark is a long-tenured district account manager for a consumer products company. A significant change in his account porfolio brought a number of new government accounts under his control. These customers were no-nonsense type customers who had little interest in his affable nature and tendency to exaggerate to garner attention.

Dimension	Score	Percentile	Description
Excitable	68		Mark is a high-energy person who brings a lot of passion to the business (Excitable—68%). He can be highly colorful (Colorful—91%) to the point of being overbearing at times. His colorful behavior extends into his tendency to exaggerate issues or problems and his role in solving them. He also has a tendency to miss details or fail to follow up on important issues (Diligent—10%).
Skeptical	15		
Cautious	29		
Reserved	42		
Leisurely	19		
Bold	24		
Mischievous	70		
Colorful	91		
Imaginative	29		
Diligent	10		
Dutiful	45		

Mark is a district account manager whose high Colorful behaviors, while earning him a reputation of being a bit of a character, have not been problematic in the past. In fact, they have endeared him to his work colleagues and customers because he is so outgoing. However, given the transactional nature of the work with his new by-the-book government accounts, his high Colorful behaviors, compounded by his low Diligent, low Cautious, and slightly elevated Mischievous and Excitable scores, are likely to become derailers. Further, although Mark has survived a couple of downsizings already, he is not likely to survive the next ones if he alienates his large government accounts.

Sample Development Program (Case 6—Mark)

It is crucial that Mark modify his high Colorful behaviors with his customers. He also needs to be mindful of his interactions with his colleagues as his jokes and bravado might not play as well as they did in the past, and his lack of attention to detail might matter more given the austere financial situation that the company is experiencing.

Reputation Change

Mark's new government customers are the primary stakeholders with whom he needs to do reputation repair. In his new assignment, he has already garnered a reputation with them for being a jokester and a "blow-hard" and for talking a good game but not always delivering on commitments. He needs to be seen as friendly and approachable but also as a serious businessman who is genuinely concerned about his customers' budgetary and regulatory issues. Further, he needs to build a reputation of doing what he says he will do, meeting deadlines, and being attentive to details.

Development Actions for Mark

An examination of Mark's scores on the Colorful subscales reveals that he is high on the Distractible and Self-Display subscales and low on the Public Confidence subscale. Thus, his greatest risks with his new accounts will most likely involve his lack of attention to detail, his failure to deliver on promises, and his coming on too strong with his jokes and anecdotes, as opposed to his having to have the floor all the time. Given the precarious financial situation of Mark's company and the reality that his job could be at stake, development around the Distractible and Self-Display behaviors is imperative to get him off to a good start with his new low Colorful accounts. The steps for Mark's development should address his Self-Display and Distractible behaviors.

Distractible

- Mark should think of examples of when he missed due dates or failed to give sufficient attention to details. He should think about the consequences of his actions, both from a business standpoint (e.g., he provided incorrect information) and from a relationship standpoint (e.g., he disappointed a client). What were both the short-term implications and the long-term implications?

- Mark should describe the circumstances under which the foregoing situations occurred in order to identify any triggers.
- Mark should identify what should have happened. How should he have behaved?
- Mark needs to identify tools to help him deal with details and stay focused:
  - Create a to-do list with electronic reminders.
  - Use a time-management and priority-management system.
  - Find an assistant who is good with details to help keep him organized.
  - Mark should review the details of a project with a direct report, enabling Mark to interact with someone else, rather than having to focus on the tedious details by himself. It will also give Mark the opportunity to see how the direct report thinks and handles things.
- Mark needs to identify upcoming events where he can practice his behavior modifications.
- He needs to seek feedback from others to gauge the effectiveness of his behavior changes.

Self-Display

- Mark needs to think about what he hopes to gain by being the center of attention. Does he want to impress people? Does he want to be admired? Does he feel people will not remember him unless he does *x, y, z*, and so on? He has some personal need that he must satisfy, and understanding that personal need can help him identify other more socially constructive ways it can be met. Also, he should think about other people he knows who operate in a similar fashion. How does he react to being with them and battling for floor time? Is he annoyed by their behavior?
- Mark should identify examples of situations when he has been told that his behavior was over the top and annoyed others. It is important for Mark to have behavioral examples as described by others, because sometimes, high Colorful individuals just do not realize that their behavior is not the norm. Mark's examples should include a description of the situation, what he said (including, if possible, the tone and volume of his voice, and his facial expressions), and how others reacted.
- Mark should look for common themes in the situations to identify any specific triggers for his high Self-Display behavior.

- Mark should analyze how his behavior compares to how others in the organization who are respected and viewed as leader-like would have behaved. How would his customers have behaved? Mark should identify how he could have modified and dialed down his behavior to be less annoying to others. How could he mirror the behavior of the leaders? What behavior would be acceptable in the customer's organization?

- Mark should develop ways to control his Self-Display behavior going forward:
    - Perform a Stakeholder Analysis to identify the styles and business goals of his key stakeholders so that he can determine how best to interact with them.
    - Get ahead of situations, and decide how to behave based on the audience.
    - Use a "cut-it-in-half" or "don't-do-it" mantra, at least initially, to focus on the behavior modifications required. Mark should try to be half as expressive, or not tell any jokes at all, and so on and see what the reactions are.

- Mark should identify upcoming situations where he can practice modifying his behavior and use role-plays if necessary.

- He needs to seek feedback from others to gauge the effectiveness of his behavior changes.

Evaluating Your Need for Change

The following behavioral questions should be considered in conjunction with your high Colorful score when evaluating the need for a change in your behavior. A "yes" response to three or fewer items suggests that there is no imminent need for behavioral changes. A "yes" response to four to six items suggests that a high score on the Colorful scale should be a watch-out for you. A "yes" response to more than six items suggests that you should take active steps toward making behavioral changes.

Do you:

1.	Consistently grab the stage or the limelight when opportunities arise in public settings?	**Yes**	**No**	**Not Sure**
2.	Appear to be compelled to be the first to speak in group situations?	**Yes**	**No**	**Not Sure**
3.	Exhibit poor listening skills because of an excessive desire to express views or opinions?	**Yes**	**No**	**Not Sure**
4.	Lose focus on the task at hand because of an excessive need to engage others in conversation?	**Yes**	**No**	**Not Sure**

5. Become easily bored when the task at hand involves extensive details or the need for a high degree of focus? **Yes   No   Not Sure**

6. Exhibit an excessive need to interact with people even when it results in the neglect of task assignments? **Yes   No   Not Sure**

7. Demonstrate the need to stand out in a crowd or be the center of attention? **Yes   No   Not Sure**

8. Exhibit behaviors or actions that seem intended to draw the attention of anyone within close proximity? **Yes   No   Not Sure**

9. Garner so much public attention that even those who are observing the situation seem to cringe? **Yes   No   Not Sure**

These items should be considered as behavioral indicators. Similar or associated behaviors to any of those listed that you exhibit likely suggest a "yes" response. They provide additional support that you may be at risk for the negative reputational consequences associated with those scoring high on the Colorful scale, such as Mark.

Development Tactics

Development tactics cover a range of approaches and resources that have been found useful in addressing high Colorful behaviors. They are typically used in combination to form a custom plan suited to the specific learning needs of a leader. The tactics are divided into four categories: (1) thought-provoking questions, (2) exercises to improve performance, (3) tips and techniques to improve performance, and (4) support resources that can be consulted to gain additional insights in addressing high Colorful behaviors.

Thought-Provoking Questions

- How socially generous are you? Do you suck the air out of a room, or do you share the floor with others? Do you proactively try to include them?
- How do you focus on listening to others?
- Do you find yourself encouraging others to speak (e.g., bringing them out) or shutting them down?
- How do you learn from others?
- How do you step back to let others step forward? What is the value of this for you?

- How can you shine the light on others?
- How can you make sure you stay focused and meet commitments?

Exercises

- Observe your participation in meetings. How often do you speak first, and what percentage of the time are you speaking?
- Try counting to 10 to give others time to jump in before you respond.
- Make sure you respond to what others have said before you shift gears to what you want to talk about.
- Practice focusing on listening and not speaking. Take notes on the situation, what you observed, and what you learned as a means of controlling your need to immediately interject your views.
- Be curious about the thoughts and perceptions of others. Use open-ended questions that encourage others to express their views, and listen carefully to what they are saying.
- Before you speak up in a meeting, think about the type of contribution that is really needed at that moment and whether what you intend to say will add value.
- Think of the benefits of allowing others to be in the limelight.
- Identify situations where your efforts could be better spent following through on previous commitments or focusing on more strategic issues versus engaging with others.
- Share your development goals with a trusted colleague, and ask for observations of your behaviors in key situations.

Tips and Techniques

- Determine why you demonstrate high Colorful behaviors. What need is being met? Are these behaviors an attempt to impress people? Are they being used to gain approval or admiration? Identifying the underlying need will assist in finding other ways the need can be met that are less disruptive.
- Think about the concept of "social generosity"—that there is give and take in any social situation and that it is the leader's responsibility to make sure the views of others are heard in an atmosphere of respect without unnecessary distractions.
- Describe a situation where your Colorful behaviors dominated a group discussion. Review the purpose of the interaction, the outcomes, and what you contributed. What were others able to contribute? Identify what may

have been achieved by providing opportunities for others to contribute more. What could you have done differently to achieve that?

- Identify a critical situation that is going to occur in the near future. Rehearse how you will approach the situation differently than you would have in the past.
- Identify venues where high Colorful behaviors will add value (or at worst, not detract from others' experiences). Perhaps the venue may be a volunteer project or other nonwork related opportunity.

Support Resources

Bolton, R., & Bolton, D. G. (1984). *Social style/management style: Developing productive work relationships.* New York, NY: AMACOM.

Based on their extensive research uncovering four predominant social styles (amiable, analytical, expressive, and driver), management experts Robert and Dorothy Bolton explain how to assess behavior patterns and use the resulting information to capitalize on strengths, minimize weaknesses, and achieve the desired results during the course of interactions.

Cain, S. (2012, February). The power of introverts [Video file]. Retrieved from https://www.ted.com/talks/susan_cain_the_power_of_introverts

Susan Cain makes a passionate argument that introverts bring "extraordinary talents and abilities to the world, and should be encouraged and celebrated."

Fotinos, J. (2014). *My life contract: 90-day program for prioritizing goals, staying on track, keeping focused, and getting results.* Charlottesville, VA: Hampton Roads.

Based on his popular class, Joel Fotinos provides an easy-to-use, example-based blueprint for helping people achieve their goals.

Nichols, M. P. (2009). *The lost art of listening: How learning to listen can improve relationships* (2nd ed.). New York, NY: Guilford.

Mike Nichols offers true-to-life examples, readily applicable techniques, and practical exercises for enhancing listening skills and communicating more effectively, productively, and empathically.

Tichy, N. (2007). *The leadership engine: Building leaders at every level.* New York, NY: HarperBusiness Essentials.

Based on decades of research and extensive firsthand experience, acclaimed faculty member and consultant Noel Tichy describes a proven system for creating dynamic leaders at every organizational level, emphasizing why the successful organizations of today require nimble, adaptable, and forward-thinking leaders capable of anticipating change and responding decisively.

Treasure, J. (2011). 5 ways to listen better [Video file]. Retrieved from http://www.ted.com/talks/julian_treasure_5_ways_to_listen_better?language=en

In his brief TED talk, sound expert Julian Treasure describes five ways people can "retune" their ears for "conscious listening."

Summary

Keep Doing

Relate to clients and colleagues with verve and enthusiasm.

Stop Doing

Talk past your allotted time, and interrupt others while they are working.

Start Doing

Listen rather than talk, and share the limelight with others.

Leaders' high Colorful behaviors are highly visible to their constituents. Because of the positive aspects of Colorful behaviors, and the positive feedback that leaders often receive about having a great personality, it can be difficult for them to accept that their Colorful behaviors can cross the line. It is important that leaders calibrate the level of "personality" needed in a given situation, and recognize when their high Colorful behaviors are too much of a good thing. Typically, overcorrection is needed for leaders to get in the habit of reining in derailing behaviors. Overcorrection is also important because it helps to convince constituents that leaders are serious about behavior change. In fact, the behavior change itself is likely to draw positive attention for leaders and reinforce their effort to dial back the negative Colorful behaviors.

Low Colorful: Getting Noticed

Be who you are and say what you feel because those that mind don't matter and those that matter don't mind.

Dr. Seuss

Detecting When It Is a Problem

The greatest risk for low Colorful leaders is being overlooked. These leaders are quiet, unassuming, and unassertive. A low Colorful individual's good ideas and contributions can go unnoticed because of his or her nonobtrusive, low-key personal demeanor. A stereotypical example of a low Colorful individual is Caspar Milquetoast, the character introduced in the 1920s in *The Timid Soul* comic strip. Caspar was so weak and ineffectual that the term *milquetoast* has been incorporated into everyday language to mean bland, plain, unadventurous, and easily overlooked. Low Colorful leaders run the risk of being perceived as "quiet" at best, and "invisible" at worst. Typically, they view their more Colorful colleagues as showboats, and recognizing that they need to be more colorful themselves can be a challenge.

Another good example of a low Colorful leader is President Gerald Ford. He was picked for US vice president after the resignation of Spiro Agnew essentially because of his low Colorful, unobtrusive style. Then, when Ford became president after the resignation of Richard Nixon, he served out his term in virtual anonymity. He is the only person in US history to serve as vice president and president without ever being elected by the American people. While it is true he won his party's nomination for president in 1976, he ran what could only be described as a boring campaign. He was beaten by perhaps the second lowest Colorful president in US history, Jimmy Carter. Ford's entire career was built on the notion that he was an everyday guy to whom anyone could relate and trust. His career success is a testament to the fact that leadership success can be achieved despite a low Colorful profile.

Robert from Case 3—Robert, design engineer on page 60—provides a good example of a low Colorful profile. The following is Robert's profile summary.

	Robert's Situational Summary		
	Robert is a design engineer for a manufacturer of commercial aircraft electronic components. He has worked primarily as an individual contributor and was known for getting things done. His hard work resulted in a promotion to project leader on a cross-functional team. His new role will be highly demanding and require effective leadership skills that will be a challenge for his quiet, reserved nature, and tendency to fade into the background in social situations.		

Dimension	Score	Percentile	Description
Excitable	35	▓▓▓▓	Robert is a hard worker who seems very calm and even-tempered under pressure. People view him as task focused with little interest in engaging with people (Reserved—98%). He tends to work long hours and is not bothered by the fact that his attention to detail spills over into work for others (Diligent—80%), which has earned him a reputation as a grinder who gets things done.
Skeptical	50	▓▓▓▓▓▓	
Cautious	75	▓▓▓▓▓▓▓▓	
Reserved	98	▓▓▓▓▓▓▓▓▓▓	
Leisurely	80	▓▓▓▓▓▓▓▓	
Bold	55	▓▓▓▓▓▓	
Mischievous	40	▓▓▓▓	
Colorful	30	▓▓▓	
Imaginative	62	▓▓▓▓▓▓	
Diligent	80	▓▓▓▓▓▓▓▓	
Dutiful	30	▓▓▓	

0 10 20 30 40 50 60 70 80 90 100

Robert's Colorful score is 30 percent, and we typically use a score of 20 percent or below as a red flag that a low HDS score might be problematic. However, when viewed in the context of Robert's new situation as a project leader, along with the rest of his HDS profile, a score of 30 percent on the Colorful scale can definitely derail him. In combination with his extremely high score on the Reserved scale (98%), and his elevated scores on the Diligent (80%) and Cautious (75%) scales, Robert is likely to be seen as task focused, quiet, unassuming, unapproachable, and having little time for small talk. In his new position as the project leader, his low Colorful behaviors could be disastrous as he will need to communicate with his team, build alignment, generate excitement and energy about the project, and be more visible and leader like. Given the tight timeframe of the new project, his team will probably experience quite a bit of stress, and the team could use some levity and cheerleading from Robert. Further, Robert will need to be a successful advocate for his team so they receive credit for their hard work.

Sample Development Program (Case 3—Robert)

Robert's profile indicates a Colorful score of 30 percent. His subscale scores reveal that he is low on all three subscales (Public Confidence, Distractible, and Self-Display), so his development should address his general need to be more visible and demonstrate more personal presence now that he is the project leader.

Reputation Change

Robert needs to rapidly turn around his reputation of being a task-focused worker bee who would rather work on his spreadsheets than interact with people. As the project leader, he needs to gain a reputation with all his constituent groups for being a visible and influential leader. He particularly needs to be known as a good communicator who keeps his stakeholders informed and who generates interest (if not excitement) around the project. Further, among his direct reports, he needs to be known as a confident advocate who speaks up for them and encourages them when the pressure is on.

Development Actions for Robert

To develop his low Colorful tendencies and drive a reputation described above, Robert should:

- Reflect on recent situations with his team that he thinks would have had a better outcome if he had been more confident, energetic, emotive, and assertive.
- Identify how he could have demonstrated more assertiveness or emotion. He needs to identify leaders whose styles he admires and think about what they would have said or done.
- Recall a time when he was more assertive or emotive. What was the situation (e.g., helping his people, or discussing business results)? What did he feel physically (e.g., excited about the topic)? How did his tone modulate? What was his body language? How did his audience react? How can he tap into these positive feelings in more situations?
- Identify ways he can be more visible and approachable:
    - Communicate with team members proactively, including managing by walking around.
    - Lighten up by including humor or anecdotes in interactions with people.
    - Make sure he speaks up at least twice in each meeting he attends.
    - Share the team's accomplishments with senior management.
- Identify upcoming situations where he can practice these behaviors by role-playing with a trusted colleague what he will say, how he will say it, and so on. If he is reluctant to try these at work, he should try them in a low-risk, nonwork situation (e.g., chatting with someone in line at the grocery store, or speaking up at a PTA meeting).
- Select an advocate to give him ongoing feedback. Evaluate the success of his changed behaviors not by how he feels (he will be uncomfortable), but by their impact on others or on the outcome of the situation.

Evaluating Your Need for Change

The following behavioral questions should be considered in conjunction with your low Colorful score when evaluating the need for a change in your behavior. A "yes" response to three or fewer items suggests that there is no imminent need for behavioral changes. A "yes" response to four to six items suggests that a low score on the Colorful scale should be a watch-out for you. A "yes" response to more than six items suggests that you should take active steps toward making behavioral changes.

Do you:

1. Shy away from the stage or limelight when opportunities arise in public settings? **Yes   No   Not Sure**

2. Blend in to the crowd to the point of going virtually unnoticed by others? **Yes   No   Not Sure**

3. Appear awkward or unable to engage in small talk that would put others at ease in public settings? **Yes   No   Not Sure**

4. Appear to remain task focused and unable to change directions even when others are creating significant distractions? **Yes   No   Not Sure**

5. Tend to get immersed in a task to the point that distractions appear to be easily blocked out? **Yes   No   Not Sure**

6. Exhibit little to no tendency to become bored with a task, regardless of the details involved? **Yes   No   Not Sure**

7. Over-prepare for situations that require speaking to a group or in a public setting? **Yes   No   Not Sure**

8. Leave little to no impression upon others you encounter in public settings? **Yes   No   Not Sure**

9. Appear embarrassed or uncomfortable when others call attention to your actions or contributions in public? **Yes   No   Not Sure**

These items should be considered as behavioral indicators. Similar or associated behaviors to any of those listed that you exhibit likely suggest a "yes" response. They provide additional support that you may be at risk for the negative reputational consequences associated with those scoring low on the Colorful scale, such as Robert.

Development Tactics

Development tactics cover a range of approaches and resources that have been found useful in addressing low Colorful behaviors. These tactics are typically used in combination to form a custom plan suited to the specific learning needs of a leader. The tactics are divided into four categories: (1) thought-provoking questions, (2) exercises to improve performance, (3) tips and techniques to improve performance, and (4) support resources that can be consulted to gain additional insights in addressing low Colorful behaviors.

Thought-Provoking Questions

- How do you contribute in team settings?
- How would you like to be seen, and what is necessary to accomplish this?
- What do you do to display executive presence?
- How do you show affirmation so your audience knows where you stand on an issue?
- How can you promote your own and your team's accomplishments?
- What is necessary to achieve your business or career goals?

Exercises

- Prepare for meetings by summarizing key points you want to make in bullet points.
- Arrive at the meeting early to secure a visible seat in the room.
- Find regular opportunities to brag about an individual or team accomplishment.
- Lead or become involved in a project or initiative that will make it necessary for you to demonstrate a strong presence.
- Keep track of your accomplishments and the accomplishments of your team. Plan strategic moments to insert statements about these accomplishments in the presence of superiors.
- Develop a list of interesting stories, anecdotes, or jokes that you can draw upon in social situations.
- Identify a high-profile task or assignment that is within your capabilities. Put a strategy together to advocate to the decision makers that you are the right person for the assignment.

Tips and Techniques

- Reframe the dialed-up Colorful behaviors as necessary for accomplishing business goals and being effective as a leader.
- Determine, "what is executive presence in your company?" Develop a list of behaviors that you can incorporate to build a stronger executive presence.
- Practice using the word "I" in describing an accomplishment.
- Prepare a 30-second elevator speech that can be used to describe your role and contribution to the organization in a clear and compelling way.
- Observe and practice mannerisms of high Colorful people who effectively promote themselves within the organization. Identify situations where you can experiment with these mannerisms and observe the reactions of others.
- Practice the more Colorful behaviors in a low-risk, non-work environment where it will not matter if things do not go smoothly.

Support Resources

Cabane, O. F. (2013). *The charisma myth: How anyone can master the art and science of personal magnetism.* New York, NY: Penguin Group.

Drawing on techniques she originally developed for Harvard and MIT, Cabane breaks charisma down into its components and describes how people can become more influential, persuasive, and inspiring.

Clark, B., & Crossland, R. (2002). *The leader's voice: How your communication can inspire action and get results.* New York, NY: SelectBooks.

Based on over 20 years of communication research and an examination of over 1,100 examples of leadership communication, Clark and Crossland describe their simple but elegant leadership communication model and offer communication principles capable of helping readers communicate authentically, powerfully, and in a manner that inspires others' confidence.

Hedges, K. (2011). *The power of presence: Unlock your potential to influence and engage others.* New York, NY: AMACOM.

Executive and CEO coach Kristi Hedges demystifies the elusive quality often referred to as "presence" and shows readers how they can strengthen their impact irrespective of their personality or hierarchical position.

Hodgkinson, S. (2005). *The leader's edge: Using personal branding to drive performance and profit.* Lincoln, NE: iUniverse.

Based on current research about impression management, executive development, and social networking, Hodgkinson uses familiar language to offer readers profound insights and a readily applicable plan for creating their own personal brands.

Maxwell, J. C. (2010). *Everyone communicates, few connect: What the most effective people do differently.* Nashville, TN: Thomas Nelson.

Based on the premise that anyone can learn how to turn communication into an opportunity for powerful connection, Maxwell guides readers through the process of developing the crucial skills necessary to connect with others.

Weiner, A. N. (2006). *So smart but . . . : How intelligent people lose credibility and how they can get it back.* San Francisco, CA: John Wiley & Sons.

Weiner describes how anyone can find ways to make measurable, credibility-enhancing improvements in how they present themselves.

SUMMARY

> *Keep Doing*
>
> Be a good team player, and use good listening skills.
>
> *Stop Doing*
>
> Be so quiet and unassuming that you forfeit your opportunity to influence others.
>
> *Start Doing*
>
> Speak up with more self-confidence, and promote team accomplishment.

The greatest risk for low Colorful leaders is being overlooked. Not only might they be overlooked personally (e.g., for a promotion or a high-profile assignment), but their good ideas and their team's good work might be overlooked due to lack of strong advocacy. This lack of acknowledgment results in a lose-lose situation for all individuals involved and the organization. Leader "emergence" is perhaps one of the most significant variables in career success. Effective use of Colorful behaviors is one of the hallmarks of leaders who have strong emergent profiles. Development around confidence, energy, and presence in general can help leaders display a more Colorful persona that will raise their emergent profile and increase the probability of greater career success.

CHAPTER 13

IMAGINATIVE

HIGH IMAGINATIVE: CONTROLLING IDEATION

We miss the real by lack of attention, and create the unreal by excess of imagination.

Sri Nisargadatta Maharaj

Detecting When It Is a Problem

Most organizations today are striving to develop leaders who, among other leadership characteristics, have the ability to be strategic and lead innovation. In doing so, they are usually seeking leaders who can think outside the box and can creatively develop strategies or solutions by generating different and new perspectives and ideas. Leaders who score very high on the Imaginative scale, however, can negatively impact their effectiveness and reputation through an excessive number of unconventional ideas and a preoccupation with their own ideas. Further, they can acquire reputations for being impractical and for being disconnected from the business.

    A good example of a leader with high Imaginative behaviors is Ron Johnson, a former Target and Apple executive who is known as a retail genius. Johnson joined JCPenney as CEO in 2011 and was subsequently ousted in fewer than two years. He set out to transform JCPenney by completely changing the customer shopping experience and introducing pricing strategies brand new to this segment of the retail industry. His radical ideas were developed without a solid understanding of the JCPenney customer base, and suggestions by others that these ideas be tested prior to implementation were dismissed. The pricing schemes alone were found to be very confusing and alienated many customers, resulting in a significant drop in sales and the stock price. Johnson was fired and immediately replaced by the former CEO, Myron Ullman.

High Imaginative leaders often consider visionary leadership and creativity essential to success and believe strongly in their own ideas. This mind-set makes it very challenging for them not to push their ideas, particularly in stressful and critical circumstances. Their idea generation can also be perceived as very random and confusing. Hence, they are often seen as eccentric and impractical and are unable to articulate ideas in a way that engages others.

Courtney from Case 8—Courtney, assistant operations manager on page 70—is a good example of a high Imaginative profile. She also has high scores in the Bold (95%) and Mischievous (90%) scales. The following is Courtney's profile summary.

Courtney's Situational Summary				
Courtney successfully completed a plant start-up in Mexico for an electronics manufacturing company. Despite being considered a high potential leader, her superiors had lingering questions about her leadership ability. As a result, she was given the role of assistant operations manager working for one of the best plant managers in the company. Courtney's new manager is known for her high standards, careful attention to detail, hard work, and putting in long hours.				
Dimension	**Score**	**Percentile**		**Description**
Excitable	30	▇▇▇		Courtney is an energetic leader who is known for her confidence in taking on any challenge (Bold—95%). She tends to use her charm and charisma to get her way (Mischievous—90%). She also tends to grab high-profile assignments to keep herself in the limelight (Colorful—80%). Her superiors have put her on the fast track but have some concerns about her ability to be a team player.
Skeptical	50	▇▇▇▇▇		
Cautious	20	▇▇		
Reserved	25	▇▇		
Leisurely	30	▇▇▇		
Bold	95	▇▇▇▇▇▇▇▇▇▇		
Mischievous	90	▇▇▇▇▇▇▇▇▇		
Colorful	80	▇▇▇▇▇▇▇▇		
Imaginative	85	▇▇▇▇▇▇▇▇▇		
Diligent	5	▇		
Dutiful	10	▇		
		0 10 20 30 40 50 60 70 80 90 100		

Courtney's high Imaginative score (85%) has probably been a helpful aspect of her profile thus far in her career. However, she is now working for a plant manager who appears to be a very pragmatic, detail-oriented person who does not take big risks or make big changes without a lot of due diligence. Courtney will have plenty of big ideas, given her high Imaginative score. She will also feel an obligation to put them on the table as she would see that as one way of contributing to the business. Unfortunately, what she considers brainstorming could be seen by her new manager as wild ideas coming from a person who has not thought through how things work in an established plant. Similar to Ron Johnson, Courtney will not be inclined to go through careful due diligence on her ideas before offering them publicly. Her low Diligent score (5%), low Cautious score (20%), and high Mischievous score (90%) will contribute to a tendency to be impulsive and willing to take risks. This could easily run afoul of her new manager's style and damage Courtney's reputation with the new manager.

Sample Development Program (Case 8—Courtney)

Courtney has an elevated score on the Imaginative scale, combined with high scores on the Bold and Mischievous scales. Given that success in her role requires close management of the business and effectively engaging a broader team of people than she has led previously, managing her high Imaginative tendencies is an important area of focus for her development. This development focus is further reinforced by her high Bold and Mischievous scores, which may be contributing to the existing concern that Courtney is not a team player.

Reputation Change

Currently, Courtney has the reputation of being a confident, results-oriented, charismatic "high-flyer" (she is on the high-potential list) who is strategic and innovative. Sometimes, her ideas can be over the top, and she can fail to listen to others' input because she is so enamored with her own ideas. These behaviors have evoked raised eyebrows and questioning looks from her audiences, who have given her feedback that they feel ignored and that she is hard to follow. This has contributed to the concern that she might not be a team player. Now, with her new task-oriented manager who is concerned with the smooth operation of the plant, Courtney needs to quickly combat any reputational rumbles that she is flighty, that she does not listen, that her team cannot follow her ideas, and that she does not do sufficient due diligence prior to taking action. Further, she needs to be seen as someone who acts in the best interest of the team and the plant. Courtney needs to be known as a strong operations manager and team player who can execute as well as she can think up ideas. It is especially important that her new manager and other senior leaders perceive her in this way so she will remain on the high-potential list and dispel any doubts they have about her leadership abilities.

Development Actions for Courtney

With respect to her subscale scores, Courtney scores very high on the Special Sensitivity subscale but scores at lower levels on the Eccentric and Creative Thinking subscales. Based on this, Courtney's development should include the following key steps:

- Courtney should complete a self-reflection exercise in which she will identify situations in the past where she has demonstrated high Imaginative behaviors. It is important for her to look at those situations objectively and make note of each situation and its specific details, such as the purpose of the meeting, people in attendance, and what may have prompted the high Imaginative behavior. She should also describe the behaviors she demonstrated and the impact she believes they had on the effectiveness of the discussion, on others around her, and on her own effectiveness.
- Courtney should review these situations to identify themes or patterns in the circumstances where these behaviors tend to surface. This identification will help Courtney better prepare for those circumstances and reduce the probability that these behaviors will surface.
- Courtney needs to identify some alternate behaviors that she can use that will reduce her tendency to engage in high Imaginative behaviors. The following are some examples:
  - Clarifying in advance the specific objectives or outcomes expected from an interaction or meeting with others.
  - Making a list of the ideas or solutions she wants to bring to the discussion and conducting a preliminary assessment of their relevance to the issue at hand.
  - Identifying questions to ask others in the meeting to gather more input and perspectives and listening effectively to responses.
  - Allowing others to offer their ideas before offering hers and acknowledging the value in those ideas.
  - Having a way to communicate to the group that she is shifting to out-of-the-box thinking.
  - Asking a trusted colleague to give her a signal during the meeting when her high Imaginative behaviors appear.
  - Asking a trusted colleague for feedback on her behavior after the meeting.
- Courtney needs to identify at least one person with whom she is having difficulty communicating about new ideas. Define the specific challenges with that individual and develop some alternate approaches.
- Courtney should keep a journal of situations where her high Imaginative behaviors appeared. She should include a description of the situation, how she responded (effectively or ineffectively), the impact her behavior had on the effectiveness of the interaction, and what she would do differently next time. The goal is to enable Courtney to learn from her own critical incidents.

Evaluating Your Need for Change

The following behavioral questions should be considered in conjunction with your high Imaginative score when evaluating the need for a change in your behavior. A "yes" response to three or fewer items suggests that there is no imminent need for behavioral changes. A "yes" response to four to six items suggests that a high score on the Imaginative scale should be a watch-out for you. A "yes" response to more than six items suggests that you should take active steps toward making behavioral changes.

Do you:

1. Make statements that others find shocking or just plain weird? **Yes No Not Sure**

2. Exhibit behaviors that others would find peculiar or unconventional? **Yes No Not Sure**

3. Appear to be unaware, or at least unconcerned, about how unconventional actions affect others? **Yes No Not Sure**

4. Profess an ability to anticipate what others may say before they actually say it? **Yes No Not Sure**

5. Profess to have special talents or abilities that others do not possess? **Yes No Not Sure**

6. Point out things that tend to go unnoticed by others? **Yes No Not Sure**

7. Often put forth ideas that others find strange or difficult to grasp? **Yes No Not Sure**

8. Tend to leap from one idea to the next, leaving the impression of erratic or irrational thinking? **Yes No Not Sure**

9. Offer ideas that are impractical or undoable to the point that it negatively impacts your personal credibility? **Yes No Not Sure**

These items should be considered as behavioral indicators. Similar or associated behaviors to any of those listed that you exhibit likely suggest a "yes" response. They provide additional support that you may be at risk for the negative reputational consequences associated with those scoring high on the Imaginative scale, such as Courtney.

Development Tactics

Development tactics cover a range of approaches and resources that have been found useful in addressing high Imaginative behaviors. These tactics are typically used in combination to form a custom plan suited to the specific learning needs of a leader. The tactics are divided into four categories: (1) thought-provoking questions, (2) exercises to improve performance, (3) tips and techniques to improve performance, and (4) support resources that can be consulted to gain additional insights in addressing high Imaginative behaviors.

Thought-Provoking Questions

- What is your purpose in sharing ideas? How do you get satisfaction from this?
- How do you communicate that a discussion is intended for brainstorming purposes? How do you communicate that a discussion is intended to focus on identifying and implementing solutions?
- How do you let your team know which ideas represent out-loud thinking and which are to be acted on?
- How do you assess ideas before presenting them in high stakes situations?
- What cues do you look for to assess understanding and to gauge reactions from others?

Exercises

- Find a partner with whom to vet ideas. Practice discussing all the implications and the necessary steps for implementation of the ideas. Practice staying focused.
- Think through an idea you are about to propose and design follow-up questions to check for understanding regarding the idea and the implications associated with implementing it.
- Keep a record of the important ideas you present during meetings. Track which of those ideas are actually implemented and taken to completion. Critically evaluate the ideas in terms of their success and your role in the implementation process.
- Establish operating guidelines for team members to challenge new ideas and push back on ideas that are unclear or inconsistent with the direction of the team.
- Maintain a list of ideas that have been implemented on a whiteboard and track them regularly in terms of progress.

Tips and Techniques

- Think about other related scale results and their impact on the appearance of your high Imaginative behaviors (e.g., Cautious, or Mischievous).
- Consider the impact of excessive idea generation on group decision-making. List specific circumstances when that occurred. Identify alternative approaches.
- Keep a journal of situations where high Imaginative behaviors surfaced and identify key patterns, themes, and triggers. Identify ways to prevent these behaviors in the future.
- With a colleague, role-play a situation where you present a new, groundbreaking idea with the goal of influencing your colleague to adopt that idea.
- Try to slow down your ideation process by evaluating each idea. The remedy could be as simple as putting each idea on a flipchart and rating the idea on its potential impact and practicality. The goal is to self-monitor ideation using more mental evaluation before public disclosure.

Support Resources

Burkus, D. (2013). *The myths of creativity: The truth about how innovative companies and people generate great ideas.* **San Francisco, CA: Jossey-Bass.**

Based on the latest research on successful creative individuals and organizations, Burkus reconceptualizes the concept of creativity and teaches readers how to employ "a practical approach, grounded in reality, to find the best new ideas, projects, processes, and programs."

Drucker, P. F., Christiansen, C. M., & Govindarajan, V. J. (2013). *HBR's 10 must reads on innovation.* **Boston, MA: HBR Press.**

A thoughtfully curated group of articles from the *Harvard Business Review* offer insight about, for example, identifying ideas worth pursuing, innovating "through the front lines" (not just from the top), and how to avoid stifling innovation.

Duarte, N. (2010). *Resonate: Present visual stories that transform audiences.* **Hoboken, NJ: Wiley.**

Resonate teaches readers how to convey messages with "passion, persuasion, and impact," energize and move audiences to "transformative action," and make meaningful connections with people, even from on stage.

Manning, J., & Roberts, K. (2015). *The disciplined leader: Keeping focused on what really matters.* **Oakland, CA: Berrett-Koehler.**

Manning and Roberts offer fifty-two concise lessons designed to help leaders hone in on the "vital few" activities that truly drive results instead of chasing the countless things they "could do."

Palmer, S. A. (2008). *Good in a room: How to sell yourself (and your ideas) and win over any audience.* New York, NY: Doubleday.

Palmer, former director of creative affairs at MGM, uncovers the tactics used by Hollywood's top producers, directors, and writers to win buy-in and financing and describes how readers can apply the same approaches to sell themselves and their ideas in the business world.

Shank, J. K., Niblock, E. G., & Sandalls, W. T., Jr. (1973, January). "Balancing 'creativity' and 'practicality' in formal planning." *Harvard Business Review.* Retrieved from https://hbr.org/1973/01/ balance-creativity-and-practicality-in-formal-planning

This HBR classic uses multiple examples to demonstrate how creativity and practicality need not be at odds during the planning process.

Smith, P. (2012). *Lead with a story: A guide to crafting business narratives that captivate, convince and inspire.* New York, NY: AMACOM.

Smith makes a passionate and convincing case, based heavily on real-world examples in companies like Nike, Merrill-Lynch, 3M, and Proctor & Gamble, for the power of storytelling in corporate settings. *Lead with a Story* teaches readers how to do just that—craft powerful narratives capable of, among other things, energizing people around a vision, marketing ideas, or generating commitment.

SUMMARY

> *Keep Doing*
>
> Provide ideas, insights, and original solutions to everyday business problems.
>
> *Stop Doing*
>
> Offer ideas or solutions without being asked or before the problem has been identified.
>
> *Start Doing*
>
> Check with colleagues about the practicality of ideas before taking them public.

Leaders who have the ability to think creatively and get others to think creatively can be a tremendous asset to their organizations. However, creative thinking must be demonstrated to the right degree and balanced with the realities of an organization. When leaders exhibit excessive ideation or impractical ideation, they can be seen as unfocused, distracting, and even eccentric. If these high Imaginative behaviors can be brought under control by the leader through greater self-awareness and development, they can become an important asset in the leader's achieving career success. If these behaviors go unchecked, the leader's credibility will suffer, and career limitations will follow.

Low Imaginative: Appearing Innovative

Imagination is more important than knowledge.

Albert Einstein

Detecting When It Is a Problem

The ability to think strategically and innovatively has become an important competency for leaders in many organizations. The Imaginative scale provides an assessment of the degree to which an individual thinks and acts in interesting and unusual ways. While those who score high on this scale demonstrate a strong potential to be derailed because of developing a reputation for an excessive amount of idea generation, those who score low also demonstrate a strong potential to be derailed but for different reasons. When leaders score low on the Imaginative scale, they are often seen as lacking creativity, failing to contribute new ideas, and being inflexible. Their major derailment risks stem largely from missing opportunities to innovate, blocking innovation, or not seeing the need for innovation, and from being labeled as "not strategic."

Classic examples of this are Jim Balsillie and Mike Lazaridis, former co-CEOs of RIM/Blackberry. Dan Pontefract, author of *Flat Army: Creating a Connected and Engaged Organization,* wrote about the failure of Balsillie and Lazaridis to create a new and innovative platform for Blackberry when Apple introduced the iPhone. Pontefract described the situation at Blackberry this way: "To many, RIM seemed to morph from an innovative and flexible organization to one that was rigid, blind, egocentric, and hierarchical. The situation at RIM was a lack of perception, and many of its leaders were culpable. The situation has become a vortex with close-minded behavior at the root."

Leaders with low Imaginative scores may be highly successful as long as their roles require them to remain focused on tasks and key metrics, and results can be achieved through a clear, predictable leadership style. If, however, these leaders are required to lead the development of innovative ideas, methodologies, or processes, they may become quite challenged. The challenge at the low end of this scale is particularly strong because it necessitates demonstrating new behaviors that the leader has not likely exhibited before. Taking on or acquiring new behaviors is generally much more difficult than dialing back a behavior. In the case of low Imaginative leaders, the challenge is particularly daunting because ideation (an important behavior lacking in these individuals) is a difficult skill to learn.

Kelly, the CFO of a large clothing retailer from Case 9—Kelly, chief financial officer on page 72—is a good example of the potential impact of low Imaginative. The following is Kelly's profile summary.

Kelly's Situational Summary
Kelly was successfully performing in the role of controller for a large clothing retailer. The CFO passed away suddenly, leaving a big gap on the leadership team. Kelly was promoted into the CFO position despite concerns about her readiness. The new role required expanded job responsibilities, effective working relationships with other members of the leadership team, and a more strategic approach to the business.

Dimension	Score	Percentile	Description
Excitable	20		Kelly is a very calm, even-tempered finance type (Excitable—20%). She is a "trust, but verify" type of person (Skeptical—79%) who can be a bit intimidating in interpersonal situations (Reserved—80%). Kelly also exhibits very high attention to detail and tends to micromanage all aspects of the financial function for which she is responsible (Diligent—95%).
Skeptical	79		
Cautious	70		
Reserved	80		
Leisurely	38		
Bold	60		
Mischievous	30		
Colorful	20		
Imaginative	30		
Diligent	95		
Dutiful	32		

Kelly's Imaginative score is 30 percent. A score of 20 percent or below is typically used as a red flag that a low HDS score might be problematic. However, when viewed in the context of Kelly's new situation as a CFO, accompanied by the rest of her HDS profile, a score of 30 percent on the Imaginative scale can definitely derail her. Scores on three other scales are particularly problematic for Kelly, including Diligent (95%), Skeptical (79%), and Reserved (80%). These high scores combined with her low Imaginative score show a strong potential for Kelly to be seen as very focused on detail, not creative in her thought process, and cynical or mistrusting of others and new ideas or approaches. In her new role as CFO, being successful necessitates that she think flexibly and contribute meaningfully to developing the long-term business strategy, build trusting collaborative relationships with her peers, and lead the development of innovative ideas and solutions. It will be critical for Kelly to understand the significant negative impact that her low Imaginative behaviors, if unchanged, could have on her ability to be a credible leader and successful at the CFO level.

Sample Development Program (Case 9—Kelly)

The role of CFO presents a tremendous opportunity for Kelly to enhance her understanding of the impact of her low Imaginative behaviors on her effectiveness as a leader. While these behaviors did not appear to get in Kelly's way in her role as controller, they could become a derailer in the CFO role.

Reputation Change

In her controller role, Kelly had the reputation for being a stereotypical "numbers person"—quiet, level headed, detail oriented, and excellent at looking out for the financial well-being of the company. While she was not a "people person" or an "idea person," these shortcomings did not significantly impact her reputation, as people appreciated that she watched expenses like a hawk. Now, however, in the CFO role, Kelly needs to have the reputation of someone who can think strategically and articulate that strategy as a senior leader of the business. Further, she needs to be known as someone who contributes ideas and suggests new approaches to the senior leadership team.

Development Actions for Kelly

Because the CFO role will necessitate a stronger ability to think and lead strategically as well as collaborate effectively with other leadership team members, she needs to develop these skills. Her low score on the Imaginative scale (30%) combined with her relatively high scores on the Diligent (95%) scale and the Skeptical (79%) scale would imply the need for significant behavior change for her to be seen as contributing to the strategic aspects of the business. Kelly's scores on the Eccentric and Creative Thinking subscales are particularly low, suggesting that Kelly needs to expand her willingness and ability to consider new and unusual ways of thinking. The following is a proposed approach for Kelly to use for her development.

- To help Kelly understand the need for change in these behaviors, she should identify the impact that contributing more actively in discussions about strategy and innovation could have on her success in the CFO role. How could her contribution in these areas impact her relationships with her peers? How could it impact the performance of her team? What are the consequences of not changing her behaviors in these areas?

- Kelly should examine past experiences where she had the opportunity to contribute to the development of new ideas. What behaviors did she demonstrate that contributed productively? In what ways did she resist new ideas or decline to help move an idea forward? What would she do differently next time?

- Kelly needs to identify a key business issue she has an interest in that requires new ways of thinking. How can she become involved or change the way she is contributing to help advance the innovative thinking of the group?

- Kelly needs to practice the behaviors she wants to demonstrate. With a colleague role-playing one of her team members who is presenting new ideas, Kelly should practice her reactions, the questions she could pose to challenge ideas or encourage further development, and any other behaviors that may be challenging for her. The goal is not only to help Kelly demonstrate the behaviors effectively but also to help her feel authentic in doing so.

- Kelly should identify a specific opportunity to demonstrate some of the new behaviors with her team members. Then, she should review the experience, thinking about what went well, what the key outcomes from the discussion were, what did not go as she hoped, and what she will do differently next time.

Evaluating Your Need for Change

The following behavioral questions should be considered in conjunction with your low Imaginative score when evaluating the need for a change in your behavior. A "yes" response to three or fewer items suggests that there is no imminent need for behavioral changes. A "yes" response to four to six items suggests that a low score on the Imaginative scale should be a watch-out for you. A "yes" response to more than six items suggests that you should take active steps toward making behavioral changes.

Do you:

1. Refrain from offering ideas in situations associated with brainstorming or problem solving?   Yes   No   Not Sure

2. Avoid the appearance of being out of the mainstream or unconventional in any way?   Yes   No   Not Sure

3. Exhibit an excessive concern for how others may react to ideas or thoughts offered on an issue?   Yes   No   Not Sure

4. Appear easily impressed by the ideas of others, when most people would find the ideas pretty conventional?   Yes   No   Not Sure

5. Display a great deal of humility when others point out your personal talents or abilities?   Yes   No   Not Sure

6. Appear firmly grounded in reality, to the point of appearing boring or uninteresting to others?   Yes   No   Not Sure

7. Consistently put forth ideas that others consider practical or blatantly obvious?   Yes   No   Not Sure

8. Lock in on practical solutions to problems in a way that stifles creativity or innovation?   Yes   No   Not Sure

9. Often get described as someone who is a poor or weak strategic thinker?   Yes   No   Not Sure

These items should be considered as behavioral indicators. Similar or associated behaviors to any of those listed that you exhibit likely suggest a "yes" response. They provide additional support that you may be at risk for the negative reputational consequences associated with those scoring low on the Imaginative scale, such as Kelly.

Development Tactics

Development tactics cover a range of approaches and resources that have been found useful in addressing low Imaginative behaviors. These tactics are typically used in combination to form a custom plan suited to the specific learning needs of a leader. The tactics are divided into four categories: (1) thought-provoking questions, (2) exercises to improve performance, (3) tips and techniques to improve performance, and (4) support resources that can be consulted to gain additional insights in addressing low Imaginative behaviors.

Thought-Provoking Questions

- What are the potential negative implications of not engaging in more creative and flexible thinking?
- How can you give yourself permission to explore new ideas that may not have a practical application?
- What might the benefit be of encouraging your team to be more creative? How would you want to encourage your team to be more creative?
- Think about times when you are creative. What are the circumstances? What enabled you to be creative?
- What resources or support do you feel you need to be more creative?
- What causes you to avoid offering new ideas or innovative solutions when you have them? What would make it easier for you to offer them?
- How do you go about preparing in advance to discuss a problem or issue that is likely to come up in discussions with your colleagues?
- When you are convinced that a tried and proven approach to solving a problem is the best, how do you go about building your case to win support?
- How do you define "strategic thinking," and what are your strengths and weaknesses with respect to it?
- What are some alternatives you could pursue to gain a fresh perspective on a problem or issue that you have been unable to successfully address?

Exercises

- Determine when it is best to inject brainstorming into your work and define guidelines you can follow to allow the flow of ideas.

- Identify colleagues who have reputations as innovative and strategic thinkers. Develop a plan to meet with each periodically to learn more about their thought processes and approaches to creative thinking.
- Find new sources of information for one initiative you are working on.
- Identify a problem or issue that has been plaguing your business unit. Set up and facilitate a brainstorming session to identify potential alternatives for addressing the problem or issue. Establish an implementation team to evaluate and implement a plausible solution from among the alternatives.
- Build a what-if journal in which you keep track of problems or issues with which you are challenged. Keep track of what-if ideas that come to you for these problems or issues, and make it a habit to ask others to contribute their what-if thoughts.

Tips and Techniques

- Review other Hogan inventory results and their impact on the appearance of your low Imaginative behaviors, (e.g., Prudence, or Mischievous).
- Engage in a creative brainstorming session, challenging your thinking and forcing yourself to consider alternatives.
- Describe circumstances where you injected brainstorming into the situation. What worked well? What impact did it have on the outcome? What did not work well? What would you do differently in the future?
- Pick a problem or issue that is challenging. Conduct background research and benchmarking to identify potential alternatives or solutions. Develop an implementation plan to address the problem or issue.
- Build the strategic component of your leadership style. Begin by identifying the key stakeholder meetings in which strategic topics are likely to come up. Use a role-play approach to prepare to make specific strategic contributions in these meetings.

Support Resources

Bryan, M., Cameron, J., & Allen, C. A. (1999). *The artist's way at work: Riding the dragon.* **New York, NY: William Morrow.**

Bryan and Cameron, the creators of the country's most successful course on creativity, collaborated with Allen after receiving feedback that their teachings were tremendously helpful in business settings. Underpinned by innovative principles of organizational behavior, the arts, and human development, the authors teach readers how to "release their creative spirit at work and tap reserves of energy, vision, and passion."

Buckingham, M., & Coffman, C. (1999). *First, break all the rules: What the world's greatest managers do differently.* New York, NY: Simon & Schuster.

Based on a large-scale and in-depth examination of exceptional managers working across a wide variety of contexts, the authors identified managers who excelled at harnessing their employees' capabilities and studied them extensively, finding that these exceptional managers all consistently did one thing—break all the conventional "rules." This book explains why, and how readers can learn from their findings.

De Bono, E. (2008). *Creativity workout: 62 exercises to unlock your most creative ideas.* Berkeley, CA: Ulysses.

De Bono, a leading creativity expert, reconceptualizes creativity as a skill anyone can learn, cultivate, and capitalize upon and offers readers sixty-two exercises designed to elicit a creative mind-set and more original thinking.

Gibson, R. (2015). *The four lenses of innovation: A power tool for creative thinking.* Hoboken, NJ: Wiley.

Based on input from some of the world's most prolific innovators (e.g., Steve Jobs, Richard Branson, Jeff Bezos), best-selling author Rowan Gibson offers readers a series of innovation-promoting business perspectives and teaches readers how to "reverse engineer creative genius and make radical business innovation an everyday reality."

Pink, D. (2006). *A whole new mind: Why right-brainers will rule the future.* New York, NY: Berkeley.

Pink makes a strong and convincing case that "right-brained" thinkers will be the successful leaders of tomorrow, describes six research-based abilities required for success and fulfillment in the days ahead, and describes how to develop and enhance the aforementioned abilities in easy-to-digest terms.

SUMMARY

Keep Doing

Offer practical and grounded advice in appropriate problem-solving situations.

Stop Doing

Act as an unnecessary roadblock to innovation that could improve results.

Start Doing

Contribute and facilitate ideas and strategies that will help grow the business.

Low Imaginative behaviors can often result in missed opportunities to contribute new ideas and, in some cases, contribute to the broader organizational direction and strategy. At some organizational levels and in some roles, these behaviors may not negatively impact the leader's performance. However, as a leader advances in his or her career, effectively demonstrating these behaviors becomes essential to being seen as strategic and contributing in a meaningful way to the growth of the business. Leaders with low Imaginative scores must consistently challenge their thinking about innovation and risk taking. They also must work to become good facilitators of strategic thinking among their colleagues and with their teams. It is not essential for them to be the source of great ideas or strategies. However, it is essential for them to be associated with great ideas or strategies. The association alone will help them build a stronger reputation for being a strategic thinker.

CHAPTER 14

DILIGENT

HIGH DILIGENT: EMPOWERING OTHERS

A sure sign of an amateur is too much detail to compensate for too little life.

Woodrow Wilson

Detecting When It Is a Problem

High Diligent leaders are hardworking, careful, detail oriented, superb at follow-through, and able to get results. However, when these behaviors are overused, high Diligent leaders have a tendency to be extreme perfectionists who micromanage their team members and are reluctant to delegate even the simplest of tasks. They often believe that there are only two options when completing tasks: perfection or failure. This all-or-nothing stance leads them to believe that they must do everything equally well. Early in their careers, high Diligent individuals are often rewarded and promoted for the high quality of their work. As their careers progress, these same behaviors can limit their success.

The fundamental problem with high Diligent behaviors is the wasted effort that they cause and the negative effect they have on the morale of team members. High Diligent leaders are typically inflexible, which limits their ability to change when change is needed. Often they think their way is the only way, and they are not open to new approaches. They also do a poor job prioritizing, treating all tasks with equal importance. By making everything a priority, they create situations in which mission-critical objectives are lumped into everything else and, therefore, do not get the attention they deserve.

Steve Jobs is an example of a high Diligent leader. He was obsessed with details his entire professional life. For example, he was concerned about the color of screws used inside products, even though they were not visible to the customer. He was fired from his initial stint with Apple because he was a tyrant and because of his obsessive level of diligence. Most people found him impossible to deal with as a manager. It was only after he surrounded himself with team members who understood his behavior that he became the leader who enabled Apple's success.

Leaders with high Diligent scores see themselves as caring about quality. "We have to get the details right" is something one would hear from high Diligent individuals. Because of their overreliance on their own abilities, they are poor at delegation, which is a critical skill required for being a successful leader. Team members find high Diligent leaders to be demanding, fussy, excessively critical micromanagers. For these leaders, opportunities are lost because their obsession with details prevents them from seeing the big picture. They become mired in the process instead of focusing on the goal.

Perhaps the most damaging behavior associated with high Diligent leaders is their tendency to micromanage their team members. Micromanagement often results in the team members' becoming alienated. When that happens, the team members soon refuse to take any initiative and simply wait to be told what to do and how to do it. Team members with growth potential will not get the development opportunities they need because of the lack of delegation. Top-performing team members will consider leaving the organization because they feel their abilities are being underutilized and unappreciated.

Kelly from Case 9—Kelly, chief financial officer on page 72—provides a good example of an individual with a high Diligent profile. The following is Kelly's profile summary.

Kelly's Situational Summary

Kelly was successfully performing in the role of controller for a large clothing retailer. The CFO passed away suddenly, leaving a big gap on the leadership team. Kelly was promoted into the CFO position despite concerns about her readiness. The new role required expanded job responsibilities, effective working relationships with other members of the leadership team, and a more strategic approach to the business.

Dimension	Score	Percentile	Description
Excitable	20		Kelly is a very calm, even-tempered finance type (Excitable—20%). She is a "trust, but verify" type of person (Skeptical—79%) who can be a bit intimidating in interpersonal situations (Reserved—80%). Kelly also exhibits very high attention to detail and tends to micromanage all aspects of the financial function for which she is responsible (Diligent—95%).
Skeptical	79		
Cautious	70		
Reserved	80		
Leisurely	38		
Bold	60		
Mischievous	30		
Colorful	20		
Imaginative	30		
Diligent	95		
Dutiful	32		

Kelly's high Diligent behavior, which served her well in her role as controller, will become problematic in her new role as CFO. It could derail her in two ways. First, if she continues to micromanage her staff and fails to delegate, both she and her staff will experience burnout, and she will not have the time to function as a CFO. Second, the combination of her high score on the Diligent scale, her elevated score on the Cautious scale (70%), and her lower score on the Imaginative scale (30%) predict that she will be detail focused and miss the big picture. As CFO, Kelly will be expected to bring strategic thinking to the table that will contribute to the achievement of organizational goals. Failure to rise above the details and add strategic value could derail her in the role as CFO.

Sample Development Program (Case 9—Kelly)

Kelly's profile includes a score of 95 percent on the Diligent scale, and all three subscales (Standards, Perfectionistic, and Organized) are elevated. The tendency to micromanage has been noted by her leadership team but did not seem to inhibit her performance as controller. Her score of 79 percent on the Skeptical scale indicates that she has a mistrustful nature with a need to verify everything. With Kelly's promotion to the CFO role, she will have an expanded set of responsibilities. Kelly will need to pull back from her detail orientation and learn to delegate the "what" and leave the "how" to her team members. If Kelly continues to micromanage her team members, she will burn out and be unable to see the big picture and contribute to the strategic aspects of the business. Her high score on the Diligent scale is exacerbated by her elevated score on the Cautious scale (70%), resulting in a tendency to be conservative and risk averse. Her lower score on the Imaginative scale (30%) indicates a tactical perspective that lacks vision and strategic focus.

Reputation Change

Kelly's current reputation as a conscientious "numbers person" who never misses a commitment or overlooks a detail was a driving factor in her promotion to CFO. Now that she is in the CFO role, her micromanagement and failure to delegate are gaining her a reputation with the executive team of "being in the weeds," "not being strategic," and having difficulty setting priorities. Her direct reports have not seen much difference in Kelly, as she has continued to behave with them the same way she did prior to her promotion. However, they are beginning to see signs of burnout because she is doing so much work herself, and she is getting the reputation of someone who is about to "lose it." In the CFO role, Kelly needs to be seen by her colleagues on the executive team as someone who sees the big picture, sets priorities accordingly, and delegates the actual work to her team. She needs to be seen by her direct reports as a supportive leader who sets direction and then empowers and enables them to deliver results.

Development Actions for Kelly

The development initiative for Kelly should help her learn to delegate, stay out of the weeds, and think more strategically. The following are the proposed steps for Kelly to use to make improvements in these areas:

- Kelly should not try to do everything equally well and needs to focus on developing her delegation skills so that she can attend to the broader critical objectives. She should analyze why she does not delegate (e.g., do her team members lack functional skills, the motivation, or the accountability to perform the delegated task?). Kelly needs to create milestones and check-in points for each team member to whom she delegates a task so she can keep track of progress without taking over.

- Kelly should interview her fellow leadership team members and the CEO to determine what they expect and need from her in her CFO role. This discussion will assist her in determining her priorities and how she allocates her time. She should employ a model of "nice to do," "need to do just well enough," and "need to do really well" to classify her priorities and then share those priorities with her team.

- Kelly should actively participate in meetings and come to the meetings prepared with open-ended questions that will help her understand the big picture of the organization.

- Kelly should identify a colleague whose key strength is strategic thinking and spend time with that person to gain a better strategic perspective on the business. Kelly could also ask this individual to be a sounding board for her own strategic ideas before taking them public.

Evaluating Your Need for Change

The following behavioral questions should be considered in conjunction with your high Diligent score when evaluating the need for a change in your behavior. A "yes" response to three or fewer items suggests that there is no imminent need for behavioral changes. A "yes" response to four to six items suggests that a high score on the Diligent scale should be a watch-out for you. A "yes" response to more than six items suggests that you should take active steps toward making behavioral changes.

Do you:

1. Establish performance requirements that are well beyond those necessary for a job to be well done?   Yes   No   Not Sure

2. Appear to be overly picky or critical when it comes to evaluating the work done by others?   Yes   No   Not Sure

3. Seem difficult to work with because nothing is ever good enough?   Yes   No   Not Sure

4. Focus so much on the details of tasks or assignments that the big picture is often missed?   Yes   No   Not Sure

5. Take over or redo tasks assigned to others because of dissatisfaction with the work completed?   Yes   No   Not Sure

6. Miss deadlines or fail to stay on schedule because of excessive attention to detail?   Yes   No   Not Sure

7. Appear to be rigid or inflexible in the way work is completed, to the point of being viewed as change resistant?   Yes   No   Not Sure

8. Often fail to determine the importance of a task or assignment to the point that everything is a top priority?   Yes   No   Not Sure

9. Create unnecessary stress or pressure because of a meticulous approach to work?   Yes   No   Not Sure

These items should be considered as behavioral indicators. Similar or associated behaviors to any of those listed that you exhibit likely suggest a "yes" response. They provide additional support that you may be at risk for the negative reputational consequences associated with those scoring high on the Diligent scale, such as Kelly.

Development Tactics

Development tactics cover a range of approaches and resources that have been found useful in addressing high Diligent behaviors. These tactics are typically used in combination to form a custom plan suited to the specific learning needs of a leader. The tactics are divided into four categories: (1) thought-provoking questions, (2) exercises to improve performance, (3) tips and techniques to improve performance, and (4) support resources that can be consulted to gain additional insights in addressing high Diligent behaviors.

Thought-Provoking Questions

- What are your key priorities at this time? How do you prioritize work on the objectives that are strategic and highly important? How do you reach agreement with key stakeholders?
- What is your model for delegation? How important is this to you? Do all your team members need the same level of oversight?
- Where have you experienced success or failure when delegating to others, and what did you learn from these experiences?
- Think about your focus on details. What are the missed opportunities resulting from this behavior?
- Reflect on the term "micromanager" and the behaviors that are associated with the term. Would you like to work with a person who exhibited these behaviors?
- Do all your tasks and objectives deserve the same amount of attention and focus?
- Do you often get lost in the weeds (details) and not see the bigger picture? Do you sometimes miss the obvious?
- What are your key goals for the future? How will you let go of enough of your current workload to free up time to contribute in new areas?
- Is your pay commensurate with the work you are doing?
- Do you impose or create structure in every situation in order to reduce ambiguity and uncertainty?
- Do you spend so much time micromanaging people that their development needs become secondary or overlooked?
- Do you hold on to work or fail to delegate tasks for fear that they will not be done correctly or the right way? Are you very demanding and hard to please?
- What is the worst thing that could happen if you let go of some control?

Exercises

- Look at the tasks that you and your team perform, and place them into the following three categories:
  - Nice to do.
  - Need to do just well enough.
  - Need to do really well.
- Create a delegation guide and checklist to provide necessary structure while you build your delegation skills.
- Consider a time when the best solution may not have been cost effective, and "good enough" may have been perfectly acceptable.
- Think about a time when the work of your direct reports did not meet your standards. Were your standards unrealistic?
- Ask your manager to create a list of leaders who are good delegators and people developers. Interview them for insights and opportunities to improve your skill in these areas.
- Draw a circle representing the total time in your work day. Indicate where you currently spend your time—supervising the activities of others, doing work yourself, building relationships, and focusing on long-term goals. How do you want to shift where you spend your time?
- Set a limit on the time you spend at work. Choose an activity that gets you out of your office.
- Determine where strengths and weaknesses lie among your team members. Then, identify which tasks currently on your to-do list could be fully delegated to team members, and which ones you could work on with team members to help them develop new skills.

Tips and Techniques

- Build a delegation guide and checklist.
- Analyze the difference between working *on* the business and working *in* the business. Determine the percentage of time you currently spend working *on* the business versus working *in* the business and how your time should be allocated in the future.
- Build awareness that effective leaders strive to develop skilled team members who are motivated and exhibit personal initiative. Recognize how the effective delegation of meaningful assignments could help develop team members who exhibit these characteristics.
- Think about work-life balance and what the impact on your available time would be by improving prioritization and delegation skills.

- Outline the level of trust you have that each team member is able to independently complete tasks at an acceptable level of performance. Identify safe tasks to delegate to team members that, if completed successfully, will strengthen the trust needed for delegating more work in the future.

Support Resources

Blanchard, K., Oncken, W., Jr., & Burrows, H. (1991). *The one minute manager meets the monkey.* New York, NY: William Morrow & Co.

According to the authors, most managers accept and deal with far too many "monkeys"—other people's problems. Experts Blanchard, Oncken, and Burrows offer invaluable advice for managers about how to truly prioritize their priorities, return others' "monkeys," and facilitate their reports' abilities to solve their own problems.

Brown, B. (2010). *The gifts of imperfection: Let go of who you think you're supposed to be and embrace who you are.* Center City, MN: Hazelden.

Brown, renowned speaker, author, and expert on shame, belonging, and authenticity, discusses emotions capable of stifling talent and thwarting courage in this *New York Times* best-selling book about the perils of perfectionism.

Gain, B. (2015). *Stop being controlling: How to overcome control issues, repair your relationships, relieve stress, rebuild your confidence and self-esteem* [Kindle edition]. Retrieved from Amazon.com

Gain describes how to maintain control without being controlling and, among many other topics, teaches readers how to decrease micromanaging, be more trusting, seek help when needed, and improve relationships with others.

Genett, D. M. (2004). *If you want it done right, you don't have to do it yourself!: The power of effective delegation.* Fresno, CA: Linden.

Genett offers readers six simple and practical steps to delegating effectively within the context of a succinct and lighthearted management allegory.

Harvard Business Review (2014). *Delegating work: Match skills with tasks, coach your people, grant them authority.* Boston, MA: HBR Press.

HBR's *Delegating Work* walks readers through the basics of assigning the right work to the right people, effectively handing off responsibility, and overseeing without micromanaging.

Kaplan, B., & Kaiser, R. (2006). *The versatile leader: Make the most of your strengths without overdoing it.* San Francisco, CA: Wiley.

Based on two decades worth of research and extensive executive coaching experience, Kaplan and Kaiser present a cutting-edge approach to diagnosing and remedying lopsidedness in leaders. Chock-full of real-life examples and practical applications, the authors teach readers how to optimally leverage their strengths while steering clear of "too much of a good thing."

Summary

Keep Doing

Provide a role model for hard work, high standards, and quality outcomes.

Stop Doing

Excessively criticize completed work, requiring it to be redone in a certain way.

Start Doing

Effectively delegate tasks to team members, and let them find their own way.

At their best, high Diligent leaders are hardworking, conscientious, detail-oriented implementers. These characteristics, which may have gotten them promoted early in their careers, often lead to perfectionism, micromanagement, failure to delegate, and a lack of the big-picture thinking necessary for today's executives. With development, high Diligent leaders can change these behaviors. They can learn to dial back their overused and inefficient high Diligent behaviors. They can develop greater trust in their team members and become more effective delegators. Most important, they can free up their time to focus on and contribute to the strategic aspects of the business. The transition from an implementer to a leader who possesses bifocal vision with the ability to work in the business as well as on the business is perhaps one of the most difficult to achieve. It epitomizes the age-old business saying: "What got you here won't get you there." It requires giving up behaviors that were once held in high regard and developing new behaviors that do not come naturally. Leaders who make this transition are often among the most valued contributors to the success of their organizations.

Low Diligent: Managing the Details

It's the little details that are vital. Little things make big things happen.

John Wooden

Detecting When It Is a Problem

Leaders with low scores on the Diligent scale are usually relaxed, trusting, undemanding, and action oriented. The speed and impulsiveness associated with their action orientation can result in details being overlooked, a failure to consider or thoroughly evaluate alternatives, and deliverables that miss the mark. These leaders can be very flexible and tolerant of ambiguity, but they may not demonstrate strong planning skills, they may disregard progress monitoring, and they may assume that the results meet the requirements. They are easily distracted, delegate without verification, fail to keep others informed, and are surprised when projects or tasks do not go well.

An example of a low Diligent leader is former Secretary of Health and Human Services Kathleen Sebelius. She was responsible for the rollout of the Affordable Care Act (ACA), perhaps one of the most significant pieces of legislation passed by the US government in the past fifty years. The legislation was designed to reshape the US health care system. It contained more than 2,000 pages of rules, regulations, and procedures. If ever there was a need for a leader with a strong detail orientation, it was the person selected to head up the implementation of this legislation. Ms. Sebelius decided to outsource (delegate) the responsibility for creating the information technology (IT) backbone of the ACA to a Canadian software firm. However, she and her team failed to adequately track progress or test the software before it went live. The cost overruns, delays, and poor service associated with the IT backbone aspect of the ACA continue to this day. Ms. Sebelius was caught completely flatfooted when this failure began to unfold during the initial rollout of the software and user interface. In response to the glitches and failures, she said to Congress in October 2013, "You deserve better. I apologize. I'm accountable to you for fixing these problems and I'm committed to earning your confidence back by fixing the site." It is hard to put into words how much damage the flawed rollout of the ACA did to her reputation as a leader. One certain outcome was that it directly led to her resignation as secretary of Health and Human Services.

Leaders with low Diligent behaviors are perceived as approachable, flexible, and forgiving with respect to performance standards. They often delegate assignments to team members because they do not want to be bothered with the details and trust that the team members will handle them. They see this approach to delegation as empowering the team members, as opposed to abandoning them. The downside, though, is that their trusting natures, lack of planning, and failure to follow up can lead to a multitude of problems. Their team members, depending on their readiness, may be set adrift and proceed as best they can without adequate oversight. The results can run the gamut from a few missed details to a complete train wreck like what occurred with the ACA. Furthermore, without adequate oversight, team members can begin to view a low Diligent leader as a person who just does not care. Such an attitude can become malignant, spreading throughout the team to a point where the team becomes just a collection of individuals with no common standards for performance.

Courtney from Case 8—Courtney, assistant operations manager on page 70—provides a good example of a low Diligent profile. The following is Courtney's profile summary.

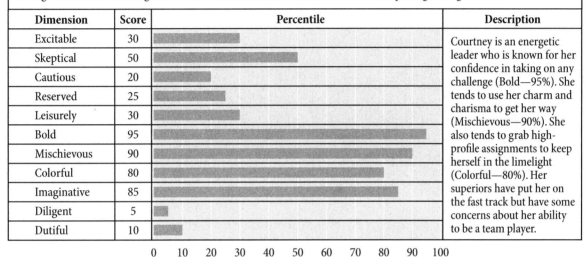

Courtney's Situational Summary
Courtney successfully completed a plant start-up in Mexico for an electronics manufacturing company. Despite being considered a high-potential leader, her superiors had lingering questions about her leadership ability. As a result, she was given the role of assistant operations manager working for one of the best plant managers in the company. Courtney's new manager is known for her high standards, careful attention to detail, hard work, and putting in long hours.

Dimension	Score	Percentile	Description
Excitable	30		Courtney is an energetic leader who is known for her confidence in taking on any challenge (Bold—95%). She tends to use her charm and charisma to get her way (Mischievous—90%). She also tends to grab high-profile assignments to keep herself in the limelight (Colorful—80%). Her superiors have put her on the fast track but have some concerns about her ability to be a team player.
Skeptical	50		
Cautious	20		
Reserved	25		
Leisurely	30		
Bold	95		
Mischievous	90		
Colorful	80		
Imaginative	85		
Diligent	5		
Dutiful	10		

Courtney's low Diligent behavior served her quite well in a fast-paced, entrepreneurial plant start-up in Mexico. She had a good group of independent team members who appreciated her hands-off management style. In her new role, however, poor attention to detail, lack of follow-up, and numerous other behaviors associated with her low Diligent score (5%) may lead to a high probability of running afoul of the management style of the plant manager to whom she now reports. Furthermore, her emergent personality that includes high Bold (95%), high Mischievous (90%), and high Colorful (80%) scores will result in a very visible persona in a manufacturing environment. Such a persona can only serve to magnify her lack of diligence in the eyes of all her constituents, including her manager and peers.

Sample Development Plan (Case 8—Courtney)

Courtney is truly facing "double trouble" given the two changes in her life: a new role (an operations job that requires precision) and a new boss (a woman who is known for her attention to details).

Reputation Change

Courtney currently has the reputation of being an "idea person" and a risk taker who does not like to get into too much detail. She is known for empowering her direct reports, which worked well in Mexico because she had a very experienced team. To succeed with her new manager, who likes details and precision, Courtney needs to dispel her growing reputation of being uninvolved in the business and of giving her direct reports too much latitude without enough supervision. Courtney needs to be known as someone who is on top of the business and understands both the big picture and the details. Further, she needs to be seen as a leader who does sufficient due diligence and who takes prudent risks. She cannot afford to miss a commitment or seem to be unaware of what her team is doing. In order to stay on the high-potential list, she needs to garner a reputation for being operations-savvy in addition to being idea-savvy.

Development Actions for Courtney

Compounding the low Diligent score are Courtney's low score on the Cautious scale (20%) and her high score on the Mischievous scale (90%). These scores indicate that not only will Courtney be inattentive to details, but she will probably be impulsive and make quick and risky decisions that could lead to high-profile disasters. The following are proposed steps for Courtney to take to facilitate her development:

- Courtney needs to understand why her low Diligent behavior can be problematic in her new job (even though it has served her well in the past).
- She should develop a model for delegation that provides the structure needed to ensure her team has adequate oversight and support.
- Courtney should review the projects she is currently responsible for, and determine the ones that are most critical to the business. Then, she needs to determine what level of personal involvement is needed from her in each one.
- Courtney needs to understand that providing oversight is not micromanaging nor is it neglecting. Depending on the situation and the team members to whom she is delegating, the "sweet spot" is somewhere in the middle. She should think about where that "sweet spot" is for each of her projects and each of her team members.
- Courtney should look at her decision process and determine what she needs to do to perform the due diligence required for critical decisions.
- She needs to practice her mental checklist of who needs to be involved in critical decisions or projects and how she plans to communicate with them.
- Courtney should find a mentor who has well-developed skills in delegation and oversight of projects, so she can learn from this mentor's knowledge and experience.

Evaluating Your Need for Change

The following behavioral questions should be considered in conjunction with your low Diligent score when evaluating the need for a change in your behavior. A "yes" response to three or fewer items suggests that there is no imminent need for behavioral changes. A "yes" response to four to six items suggests that a low score on the Diligent scale should be a watch-out for you. A "yes" response to more than six items suggests that you should take active steps toward making behavioral changes.

Do you:

1. Appear to be lackadaisical when it comes to establishing the requirements necessary for a job to be well done?   Yes   No   Not Sure

2. Show little or no concern for the details regarding the way delegated assignments are completed?   Yes   No   Not Sure

3. Seem very relaxed about rules and procedures?   Yes   No   Not Sure

4. Often take a big-picture approach to tasks or assignments, leaving the details to others?   Yes   No   Not Sure

5. Rarely provide feedback or coaching with respect to the way tasks or assignments are completed?   Yes   No   Not Sure

6. Disregard the details of tasks or assignments to the point that work quality suffers?   Yes   No   Not Sure

7. Appear easygoing with respect to timelines and schedules, conveying to others a lack of urgency?   Yes   No   Not Sure

8. Provide poor guidance regarding the importance of tasks or assignments, creating confusion regarding priorities?   Yes   No   Not Sure

9. Overdelegate without follow-up, to the point that others view it as abandonment?   Yes   No   Not Sure

These items should be considered as behavioral indicators. Similar or associated behaviors to any of those listed that you exhibit likely suggest a "yes" response. They provide additional support that you may be at risk for the negative reputational consequences associated with those scoring low on the Diligent scale, such as Courtney.

Development Tactics

Development tactics cover a range of approaches and resources that have been found useful in addressing low Diligent behaviors. These tactics are typically used in combination to form a custom plan suited to the specific learning needs of a leader. The tactics are divided into four categories: (1) thought-provoking questions, (2) exercises to improve performance, (3) tips and techniques to improve performance, and (4) support resources that can be consulted to gain additional insights in addressing low Diligent behaviors.

Thought-Provoking Questions

- How do you delegate and judge when and how to follow up?
- Do you have people on your team who like details?
- What is your assessment of your organizational skills?
- What do your team members need from you to assure that they are working productively?
- How do you create structure and set expectations?
- What would be the result of milestone checkups?
- What is the difference between empowerment and abandonment?
- What is your model for delegation? How important is this to you?
- Do all of your staff need the same level of oversight?
- What are the missed opportunities if you fail to effectively delegate?
- What is the meaning of "trust, but verify"?
- How do you tell the difference between rules and policies that need your close attention versus those you can push to the limit?

Exercises

- Evaluate your team members and determine if you have implementers and detail-oriented people who do not let things fall through the cracks.
- Create a delegation guide and checklist to provide structure while you develop your ability to delegate.
- Work with your manager to create a list of leaders who he or she thinks are good delegators and people developers and interview them for insights and skills that you can apply with your team members.
- Build a list of questions to ask to determine the processes and milestones necessary to ensure the successful completion of a project or work stream.

- Rank your team members on the basis of their ability to handle delegated assignments and your trust in them to perform delegated assignments successfully. Use this rank ordering as a guide to developing your team members through delegation of assignments.
- Practice mentally checking off the individuals who might be affected by actions you plan to take. Determine how you will communicate with them to help ensure that problems do not arise.

Tips and Techniques

- Understand the following key concepts:
    - **Structure**—Individuals have different needs for structure when completing work assignments. Some individuals find it hard to work without structure, while others prefer to determine their own way of doing things. Understanding these individual differences is an important part of building an effective team.
    - **Communication**—Success in completing assignments is only as good as the communication that accompanies the work. It is of little value to complete work that has an impact on others if they resent not being involved. Similarly, failing to check details or not involving key constituents at an appropriate level of detail can result in failure. It always pays dividends to appropriately involve others.
    - **Follow-up**—Perhaps one of the greatest shortcomings a leader can have is failing to follow up on assignments or work delegated. Making the assumption that something was completed as expected is a recipe for embarrassment or even derailment. Follow-up is not a tacit concept. It should be an explicit step in all assignments but especially those that are mission critical.
- Build a delegation guide and checklist that include the capabilities of team members.
- Think about the difference between working *on* the business versus working *in* the business. Determine what percentage of time you spend working *on* the business versus *in* the business. How should these percentages change over time with effective delegation that develops stronger team members?
- Recognize that strong, skilled team members are a critical component to your future career advancement. Review the way tasks are delegated to various team members to determine how they could be more effectively delegated to build team member skills.
- List the Critical Success Factors (CSFs) and top priorities for the business unit. Identify the organizational, team, and personal consequences if these priorities are not met. Conduct a team-building session to help all team

members understand the success factors and priorities, and where they fit in terms of effort.

Support Resources

Blair, G. R. (2009). *Everything counts: 52 remarkable ways to inspire excellence and drive results.* **Hoboken, NJ: John Wiley & Sons.**

Focused on three realms of achievement (professional, personal, and universal), Blair offers readers concrete strategies for inspiring excellence and achieving noteworthy outcomes.

Chandler, S., & Black, D. (2012). *The hands-off manager: How to mentor people and allow them to be successful.* **Pompton Plains, NJ: Career Press.**

Chandler and Black show managers, tenured and green alike, how to mentor and coach instead of hovering and prodding, allowing employees' strengths to be capitalized upon in a "climate of partnership and mutual goal setting."

Kaplan, B., & Kaiser, R. (2006). *The versatile leader: Make the most of your strengths without overdoing it.* **San Francisco, CA: Wiley.**

Based on two decades worth of research and extensive executive coaching experience, Kaplan and Kaiser present a cutting-edge approach to diagnosing and remedying lopsidedness in leaders. Chock-full of real-life examples and practical applications, the authors teach readers how to optimally leverage their strengths while steering clear of "too much of a good thing."

Rock, D. (2009). *Your brain at work: Strategies for overcoming distraction, regaining focus, and working smarter all day long.* **New York, NY: HarperCollins.**

Written with humor and fully relevant to everyday life, Rock's book synthesizes current cognitive neuroscience research and interprets the results in a way that helps readers understand how the brain works and how to make it function more efficiently in personal and professional realms.

Scott, S. (2004). *Fierce conversations: Achieving success at work and in life one conversation at a time.* **New York, NY: Berkley.**

Scott walks readers through "Seven Principles of Fierce Conversations," helping readers learn how to have meaning-filled and enriched dialogue, increase the clarity and digestibility of their messages, and effectively manage strong emotions that inevitably emerge during the course of authentic conversations.

Tracy, B. (2013). *Delegation & supervision.* **New York, NY: American Management Association.**

Tracy offers a quick and easy read, written to help readers master the essential skills needed to delegate effectively and with the intent of helping delegates learn, grow, and become more capable.

Summary

Keep Doing

Maintain a big-picture perspective without losing sight of the details.

Stop Doing

Be too relaxed about adhering to rules, processes, and procedures.

Start Doing

Practice sound delegation and communication techniques.

At first, low Diligent individuals appear to be trusting leaders who want to develop and empower their people. However, low Diligent behaviors can derail leaders in many ways, including inattention to important details, missed due dates, poor-quality deliverables, team members who are adrift because they lack support and oversight, and a failure to build trust with constituents who depend on them. Development can help low Diligent leaders understand the problems that can crop up by focusing on the big picture and relying on others to clean up the details they leave behind. Getting work done through others requires effective delegation skills. Low Diligent leaders need to develop team members using a "trust, but verify" mentality. These leaders also need to realize that their effectiveness depends upon their ability to keep others involved and informed; otherwise, they risk alienating constituents who could play a key role in determining their career success.

CHAPTER 15

DUTIFUL

HIGH DUTIFUL: CHARTING YOUR PATH

Don't depend on anyone in this world because even your shadow leaves when you are in darkness.

Ibn Taymiyyah

Detecting When It Is a Problem

High Dutiful leaders are very much valued by their managers. They offer little resistance, regardless of what is asked of them. They eagerly look for ways to please their superiors. They will even compromise their own values in their efforts to keep the boss happy. Their high Dutiful behaviors can result in a reputation as a follower who has a difficult time charting his or her own course. However, the more salient aspect of high Dutiful behavior is an exaggerated sense of loyalty and eagerness to please those in authority. Most managers desire and appreciate loyalty from their direct reports. The problem with an exaggerated sense of loyalty is that it places high Dutiful leaders in a position whereby they can be taken advantage of by a manager willing to prey upon their dutifulness.

High Dutiful behavior comes in two basic forms. The first form is what might be called the "Scared Puppy." These are individuals who are timid and fearful. They are loyal and eager to please authority figures, but their high level of dutifulness is often driven by a need for self-preservation. They are typically poorly adjusted and very cautious and may have low scores on the Bold, Mischievous, Colorful, and Imaginative scales. They may also be security oriented and not very interested in power or control. The second form of the high Dutiful leader is the "Good Soldier." These leaders may have a good leadership profile, but their high level of dutifulness causes them to exhibit an exaggerated sense of loyalty and eagerness to please authority.

One of the best historical examples of a "Good Soldier" is Lieutenant Colonel Oliver North. Colonel North was part of the National Security Administration during the Iran-Contra scandal in the 1980s. The scandal involved the sale of arms to Iran and the diversion of the proceeds to support the Contra rebel group in Nicaragua. There was a law in place at the time, the Boland Amendment, that specifically prohibited the financial support of the Contras. There are three aspects of this incident that are noteworthy from a high Dutiful standpoint. First, the incident clearly illustrates the lengths to which a high Dutiful leader is willing to go in order to please his or her superiors. Colonel North was well aware of the limits put in place by the Boland Amendment, and yet he broke the law in a clandestine operation that ultimately ended his military career. Second, the public nature of this incident lends considerable insight into the thinking of a high Dutiful leader. During his testimony to Congress, Colonel North is famously (or rather, infamously) quoted as saying, "I thought it was a pretty neat idea." Finally, Colonel North is credited with the second part of the plan—funneling the proceeds of the arms sales to the Contras. This is important because it illustrates that high Dutiful leaders of the "Good Soldier" variety are capable of taking independent action (although often they choose not to do so). In fact, if they are operating under the impression they are fulfilling the agenda of their superiors, they can initiate all sorts of actions in support of that agenda.

The last point with respect to the "Good Soldier" profile is particularly important from a subscale standpoint. The "Indecisive" subscale speaks to the notion of being reluctant to take independent action. In this case, there is every possibility that Colonel North could have a relatively high Dutiful score and yet score low on "Indecisive." If so, it would account for his ingratiating and conforming behaviors flourishing while opening the door for him to take the actions that he took without the knowledge of his superiors. In some ways, the "Good Soldier" profile could be even more insidious than a maxed-out score on Dutiful typically associated with the "Scared Puppy" profile. History is replete with examples of high Dutiful leaders carrying out the wishes of their superiors using their own initiative and decisiveness in very twisted ways.

More typically, high Dutiful leaders fit the "Scared Puppy" profile. James from Case 7—James, marketing manager on page 68—provides a good example. James's highest derailer is his high score on the Dutiful scale (90%). The following is James's profile summary.

	James's Situational Summary			
	James was the marketing manager for a small family-owned business that was sold to a well-established technology company. After the sale, James moved on to a small, fast-moving start-up technology company. He had clear challenges with his ability to get things moving in the new company. His high Dutiful score will have a direct impact on his ability to act independently in an environment that likely lacks structure.			
Dimension	**Score**	**Percentile**		**Description**
Excitable	10			James is a laid-back, even-tempered marketing guy (Excitable—10%). It takes him a long time to get to know and trust people (Skeptical—70%), and he is guarded and slow to make decisions (Cautious—85% and Mischievous—15%). James doesn't make a big impression on people. In fact, he is best known for his loyalty and willingness to do whatever the owners asked (Dutiful—90%).
Skeptical	70			
Cautious	85			
Reserved	25			
Leisurely	19			
Bold	24			
Mischievous	15			
Colorful	45			
Imaginative	35			
Diligent	50			
Dutiful	90			
		0 10 20 30 40 50 60 70 80 90 100		

In James's profile, he is described as "laid-back" and "does not make a big impression on people." These terms, while not directly tied to high Dutiful, leave the impression of a leader who sits in the backseat waiting for others to initiate or direct action. His conduct is quite different from Colonel North, who saw it as his duty to take action in support of his superior. However, similarities remain between the "Good Soldier" and the "Scared Puppy" profiles in that both involve ingratiating and conforming behaviors. The most telling of these for James can be found in the last line in which he is described as "willing to do whatever the owners ask." It is virtually certain that this type of reputation would be appreciated by those in charge. It is equally certain that those in charge would have a tough time viewing James as a person who could take over and lead in their absence.

Sample Development Program (Case 7—James)

James's profile indicates that his highest score is on the Dutiful scale at 90 percent, and all three subscales (Indecisive, Ingratiating, and Conforming) are elevated. The case description indicates that high Dutiful behaviors could be a problem for James in his role as marketing manager—he has joined a technology start-up company in which a premium is placed on employees acting independently and making decisions on their own. James's history suggests that he was quite effective at executing the instructions of the owners of the company he previously worked for, and they appreciated his willingness to follow through on their requests. In his new job, it is unlikely that James will receive a lot of guidance, and, in fact, he will likely be relied upon by others for his expertise in marketing. James's early days at the new company were filled with data-collection activities, with little in the way of tangible actions related to building a marketing function. James had plenty of ideas but was reluctant to take action for fear of making a mistake or doing something that was inconsistent with the wishes of his manager. Also, he had virtually no idea what his manager actually wanted from him in his new role other than to create an effective marketing function.

Reputation Change

The situation described above has resulted in James being seen as a timid follower rather than a dynamic leader of the marketing function. He is rapidly developing the reputation for being indecisive and "waiting in the wings" for his managers to tell him what to do. To succeed, James needs to be seen as a decisive leader who is willing to take independent actions, especially since the marketing function is a new one, and the company is relying upon his subject-matter expertise and influencing skills to successfully build the organization and brand.

Development Actions for James

The following are the proposed steps for James to take that place emphasis on improving his ability to be decisive and take independent action:

- James should work through a series of thought-provoking questions to raise his self-awareness regarding his high Dutifulness and its impact on his role as the leader of the marketing function:
  - How do you see the leader's responsibility to express independent and perhaps opposing points to his superiors or those in authority?
  - How does stating your point of view contribute to your organization? What is the impact of not supporting your point of view?
- James needs to set up a meeting with his manager to establish the Critical Success Factors for his function and discuss the decision-making authority he has in his role.
- James should use the initial marketing plan as a vehicle to practice taking control of his decision-making authority and the resources necessary to be successful. James should outline and execute the marketing plan, making sure he makes the final call on all key steps.
- James needs to establish a series of follow-up meetings with his manager specifically designed for him to keep his manager informed without giving up control of the execution of the marketing plan.

Evaluating Your Need for Change

The following behavioral questions should be considered in conjunction with your high Dutiful score when evaluating the need for a change in your behavior. A "yes" response to three or fewer items suggests that there is no imminent need for behavioral changes. A "yes" response to four to six items suggests that a high score on the Dutiful scale should be a watch-out for you. A "yes" response to more than six items suggests that you should take active steps toward making behavioral changes.

Do you:

1. Require input from superiors before making a decision or taking action?   Yes   No   Not Sure

2. Delay decisions until there is certainty that superiors will support the decisions regardless of the outcome?   Yes   No   Not Sure

3. Appear to go too far when it comes to keeping superiors informed?   Yes   No   Not Sure

4. Say "yes" to virtually any request made by superiors regardless of the consequences for others?   Yes   No   Not Sure

5. Spend an inordinate amount of time stroking the egos of those in power?   Yes   No   Not Sure

6. Tend to tell superiors what they want to hear rather than what they need to hear?   Yes   No   Not Sure

7. Carefully avoid actions that might rock the boat or go against the wishes of superiors?   Yes   No   Not Sure

8. Exhibit loyal support for the actions of superiors, even when those actions are wrong?   Yes   No   Not Sure

9. Often defer personal opinions in favor of those of superiors in order to gain their approval?   Yes   No   Not Sure

These items should be considered as behavioral indicators. Similar or associated behaviors to any of those listed that you exhibit likely suggest a "yes" response. They provide additional support that you may be at risk for the negative reputational consequences associated with those scoring high on the Dutiful scale, such as James.

Development Tactics

Development tactics cover a range of approaches and resources that have been found useful in addressing high Dutiful behaviors. These tactics are typically used in combination to form a custom plan suited to the specific learning needs of a leader. The tactics are divided into four categories: (1) thought-provoking questions, (2) exercises to improve performance, (3) tips and techniques to improve performance, and (4) support resources that can be consulted to gain additional insights in addressing high Dutiful behaviors.

Thought-Provoking Questions

- What behaviors are you demonstrating today that may be contributing to a perception that you are just a follower?
- How do you see the leader's responsibility to express independent and perhaps opposing points of view to superiors or those in authority?
- How does supporting your point of view contribute to your organization? What is the impact of not supporting your point of view?
- To what extent do you challenge your superiors currently? As you take on more senior leadership roles, how does that change?
- What impact would supporting your point of view with senior leaders have on your team and your relationship with them?
- What impact would supporting your point of view have on your peers and your relationship with them?

Exercises

- Identify some leaders you admire and list what they stand for and how they show this. How does standing up for what they believe in contribute to their leadership image?
- List all the reasons why your manager, your team, and your peers would respond favorably to your being more independent in your point of view.
- Think about the organization's culture and tolerance for conflict. How does this compare to yours?
- Rehearse assertively expressing a point of view or challenging a superior on an issue.
- Describe a situation in which you disagreed with a superior, but failed to voice your views. What caused you to hold back? Describe an alternative you could have pursued to ensure that your voice was heard.

Tips and Techniques

- Identify an issue or an initiative where you have control of decision-making authority and the resources necessary to be successful. Outline and execute a plan that places you in the position of making the final call on all key steps.

- Observe and record examples of colleagues or other leaders when they offer challenges or resistance to the ideas of others. Were the approaches they employed effective? Why or why not?

- Identify an issue or decision where you disagree with your manager. Ask a trusted colleague to role-play your manager so you can practice pushing back on your manager and offering a personal perspective.

- Meet with your manager to discuss the scope of decision-making authority, with the goal of establishing a set of boundaries for independent decision-making.

- Work with your team to establish a decision-making charter covering the commitment and use of team resources.

- As part of a stakeholder analysis, include a power rating for each stakeholder, and use it to determine the most effective techniques for working with each stakeholder.

Support Resources

Brandon, R., & Seldman, M. (2004). *Survival of the savvy: High-integrity political tactics for career and company success.* New York, NY: Free Press.

Two of the nation's most successful corporate leadership consultants reveal their proven, systematic program for using the power of "high-integrity" politics to achieve career success, maximize team impact, and protect the company's reputation and bottom line.

DeLuca, J. R. (2002). *Political savvy: Systematic approaches to leadership behind the scenes.* Berwyn, PA: EBG Publications.

DeLuca describes tactics employed by ethical leaders, helps readers identify their own political styles, and offers an efficient and actionable guide to navigating murky political waters.

Goulston, M. (2009). *Just listen: Discover the secret to getting through to absolutely anyone.* New York, NY: AMACOM.

Based on his experience as a business consultant, coach, and psychiatrist, Goulston offers readers science- and practice-backed strategies for winning support and collegiality from unreachable or unyielding people.

Heffernan, M. (2012). Dare to disagree [Video file]. Retrieved from https://www.ted.com/talks/margaret_heffernan_dare_to_disagree

In her brief TED talk, Margaret Heffernan posits that (a) disagreement is often a precursor to progress and (b) echo chambers are not terribly valuable partners.

Matuson, R. C. (2011). *Suddenly in charge: Managing up, managing down, succeeding all around.* Boston, MA: Nicholas Brealey.

This highly rated book teaches readers how to manage up as well as down, take steps to maximize their credibility, and take control of their careers and reputations.

McIntyre, M. G. (2005). *Secrets to winning office politics: How to achieve your goals and increase your influence at work.* New York, NY: St. Martin's Griffin.

Organizational psychologist and corporate consultant, McIntyre, offers an actionable strategy for "increasing your personal power without compromising your integrity or taking advantage of others."

Tulgan, B. (2010). *It's OK to manage your boss: The step-by-step program for making the best of your most important relationship at work.* San Francisco, CA: Wiley.

Based on the premise that employees should take greater responsibility for their most important work relationship, Tulgan challenges antiquated beliefs about how employees should manage up and outlines strategies for helping employees get what they need from their superiors.

Summary

Keep Doing

Communicate with your boss on relevant business developments and problems.

Stop Doing

Check with others before making decisions that are well within your authority.

Start Doing

Support the decisions of your direct reports once you have delegated responsibility to them.

There is a fine line between dependence and loyalty. High Dutiful leaders tend to err on the wrong side of that line, which can have serious career implications. Managers may see high Dutiful leaders as followers, incapable of taking independent action or standing on their own. Peers may see them as sycophants and seek to marginalize them. Direct reports often feel victimized by high Dutiful leaders because of their willingness to accept directives, regardless of their consequences. Direct reports may also resent the tendency of high Dutiful leaders to disregard their need for support and advocacy. While development tactics may vary depending on the way high Dutiful behaviors are manifested, the general approach is for the leader to decrease the perception that he or she is dependent on the manager without undermining the bond that loyalty engenders.

Low Dutiful: Keeping Others Informed

I am reminded how hollow the label of leadership sometimes is and how heroic followership can be.

Warren Bennis

Detecting When It Is a Problem

Low Dutiful leaders often find themselves operating as if they were on an island, taking actions with little to no cover from their superiors. Their behavior goes beyond the need to act independently. They often have a disdain for their superiors, believing that they themselves possess the knowledge and ability to do things better on their own without any support. Low Dutiful leaders almost view it as a sign of weakness to go to their superiors for help. Problems for low Dutiful leaders can come in spectacular fashion. Their independence can put them into high-risk–high-reward situations that have associated potential for high costs. While managers can embrace independent action, it is only human nature to want to be needed to some extent. Low Dutiful leaders rarely give their managers the sense or feeling that they are needed. When things are going well, low Dutiful leaders can thrive. Derailing potentially comes into play when things go bad and the manager provides no cover.

An interesting example of low Dutiful behavior can be found in the actions of President Barack Obama during his second term. Throughout his first term, his inability to work with Congress was well documented. In fact, you could detect a sense of disdain for Congress and resentment toward Congress's constitutional obligation for oversight, particularly as it related to budgetary matters. President Obama installed a group of czars to oversee many aspects of government, resulting in powerful government agencies that could circumvent the will of Congress. They did this by utilizing rules and regulations to manipulate government spending to help President Obama achieve his agenda (high Dutiful behavior on the part of the czars). While these low Dutiful behaviors are not terribly new to presidents trying to get their way, President Obama's in-your-face style in working around Congress is nearly unprecedented in recent history. President Obama's low Dutiful behavior ramped up substantially after being elected to a second term. In a Cabinet meeting on January 14, 2014, he is quoted as saying, "I have a pen and I have a phone." This was a reference (a not-so-veiled threat) to using executive orders to go around Congress to achieve his legislative agenda. There are three important aspects of this example of low Dutiful behavior. First, there is no question as to the president's intent to operate independently of the wishes of Congress. Second, the in-your-face style underscores the notion that he knows best, which he conveys with a degree of disdain. Finally, he has no cover should his initiatives fail or run into trouble. All of these are hallmarks of low Dutiful leaders.

A final point should be made with respect to the impact of low Dutiful behaviors. The importance of failure has been well documented as critical to the growth of a leader. Will Rogers was once quoted as saying, "Good judgment comes from experience, and a lot of that comes from bad judgment." The problem with low Dutiful leaders is that they often do not get second chances. When they fly without cover from a superior, they are exposed, and their mistakes are their own. The ability to recover from a mistake often depends on the willingness of the leader's manager to shoulder a portion of the blame and advocate for second chances. A low Dutiful leader may engender the exact opposite reaction from a manager. This alienation is especially true when the leader's behavior reflects poorly on the manager's judgment. The manager's natural reaction is to put distance between himself or herself and a mistake made by a low Dutiful leader.

Rex from Case 1—Rex, vice president of sales on page 56—provides a good example of a low Dutiful profile. Rex's lowest derailer is his score on the Dutiful scale (5%). The following is Rex's profile summary.

Rex's Situational Summary				
Rex worked in a small company as vice president of sales. In his role, he had considerable autonomy and freedom to make decisions. The company was acquired by a much larger, well-established company with rules, processes, and procedures that often accompany a large bureaucracy. Rex's willingness to take risks and make fast, independent decisions runs counter to the culture that exists in the new company. This issue could be exacerbated by his tendency to follow his own agenda.				
Dimension	**Score**	**Percentile**		**Description**
Excitable	50			Rex is very self-confident to the point of being an arrogant leader (Bold—95%). He is quite willing to take risks (Cautious—10% and Mischievous—90%). He tends to work his own agenda (Leisurely—82%), and prefers to operate independently without a lot of close supervision (Dutiful—5%).
Skeptical	67			
Cautious	10			
Reserved	45			
Leisurely	82			
Bold	95			
Mischievous	90			
Colorful	75			
Imaginative	70			
Diligent	30			
Dutiful	5			
		0 10 20 30 40 50 60 70 80 90 100		

Rex has a classic sales profile, and it is not uncommon to see a low Dutiful score as part of the profile. He is described as having an entrepreneurial approach, which can be an asset in sales situations. The key to the problems that might emerge for Rex with respect to his low Dutiful behavior lies in his high Mischievous score (90%) and low Cautious score (10%). These scores indicate that Rex is a significant risk taker and may bend rules from time to time. Rex's low Dutiful score suggests that he may not do a very good job of keeping his manager informed. If his risk taking leads to a problem, his manager may be caught off guard and may choose to let Rex stand alone to face the consequences. Further exacerbating Rex's situation is that he is now working for a much larger company. Rex's profile suggests he will quickly try to prove himself, and his new manager may want to keep close tabs on him early on until some trust has been built up in the relationship. The perfect storm is set up for a problem to arise—a low Dutiful entrepreneurial sales person out to prove himself, working for a manager who needs to keep close tabs on him as a new employee.

Sample Development Program (Rex—Case 1)

Rex's profile indicates that he has a very low score on the Dutiful scale (5%), driven by depressed scores on all three subscales (Indecisive, Ingratiating, and Conforming), and a strong "Moving Against" profile, which is not uncommon for a successful salesperson. Rex's biggest challenge is that he worked in a relatively small company where his independent style was not only tolerated, it was valued. When his company was acquired by a much larger company, he should have realized that there would be more rules and more processes to follow. Plus, he was going to be working for a new manager who was very unfamiliar with his style or his capabilities. It did not take long for Rex to get sideways with his new manager. He did what might be expected, given his profile, and that was to go out and try to make deals and close business to prove his worth. A key customer to whom Rex was assigned actually called Rex's manager to discuss Rex and what the customer perceived as a very different sales approach in comparison to what he had experienced in the past. It did not take a lot of probing to figure out what was creating problems for Rex. He had simply transferred his aggressive entrepreneurial style from his old company to his new company and assumed it would work just fine.

Reputation Change

Due to Rex's actions described above, he has gained the reputation of being a "loose cannon" and a "lone cowboy" early in his tenure with the new company. His colleagues and manager do not trust him, and they perceive him as doing what he wants when he wants without seeking their advice or counsel. Further, he has the reputation of completely disregarding policies and procedures. To succeed in the new organization, Rex needs to do reputation repair post haste. Initially, he needs to overcorrect his behaviors to ensure that he is garnering the reputation of a team player who builds trust with his colleagues and customers, who keeps his manager informed, who follows procedures, and who puts the company and the brand ahead of his own interests.

Development Actions for Rex

The following development actions may help get Rex back on the right track in his new company.

- Rex should ask one of the senior sales associates to introduce him to a number of the company's long-standing customers and help him become familiar with the sales style to which the company's customers have grown accustomed.

- Rex needs to meet with his manager to establish his Critical Success Factors (CSFs) and Information Sharing plan.

- Rex should review the CSFs and Information Sharing plan to ensure he understands the boundaries of his decision-making authority and the information needs of his manager.

- Rex needs to do an ongoing review of his information sharing to ensure that he keeps it succinct while keeping his manager informed.

- Rex needs to establish a series of follow-up meetings with his manager to explore ways in which he could become more independent and use his entrepreneurial style to benefit the company.

Evaluating Your Need for Change

The following behavioral questions should be considered in conjunction with your low Dutiful score when evaluating the need for a change in your behavior. A "yes" response to three or fewer items suggests that there is no imminent need for behavioral changes. A "yes" response to four to six items suggests that a low score on the Dutiful scale should be a watch-out for you. A "yes" response to more than six items suggests that you should take active steps toward making behavioral changes.

Do you:

1. Regularly make decisions or take actions without keeping superiors or team members informed? **Yes   No   Not Sure**

2. Often go out of the way to avoid input from superiors because it may cause your actions to be constrained? **Yes   No   Not Sure**

3. Prefer to ask for forgiveness rather than permission when it comes to taking action or making a decision? **Yes   No   Not Sure**

4. Display an excessive degree of candor when delivering feedback to superiors? **Yes   No   Not Sure**

5. Challenge the views of superiors and team members, regardless of those who are present? **Yes   No   Not Sure**

6. Often display a lack of sensitivity when delivering bad news to superiors?   **Yes   No   Not Sure**

7. Chart a personal course without seeking the guidance or counsel of superiors?   **Yes   No   Not Sure**

8. Cause superiors and team members to feel ignored because of your willingness to act independently?   **Yes   No   Not Sure**

9. Often contradict or disagree with the views of superiors when outside of their presence?   **Yes   No   Not Sure**

These items should be considered as behavioral indicators. Similar or associated behaviors to any of those listed that you exhibit likely suggest a "yes" response. They provide additional support that you may be at risk for the negative reputational consequences associated with those scoring low on the Dutiful scale, such as Rex.

Development Tactics

Development tactics cover a range of approaches and resources that have been found useful in addressing low Dutiful behaviors. These tactics are typically used in combination to form a custom plan suited to the specific learning needs of a leader. The tactics are divided into four categories: (1) thought-provoking questions, (2) exercises to improve performance, (3) tips and techniques to improve performance, and (4) support resources that can be consulted to gain additional insights in addressing low Dutiful behaviors.

Thought-Provoking Questions

- Are there times when you demonstrate low Dutiful behaviors? What is the impact on your boss, your peers, and your team? Are there times these behaviors work for you? Are there times they work against you?
- How would you describe the cultural norms in your organization relative to acting independently or without close supervision? What are the consequences for not conforming to the cultural norms?
- How do you establish the latitude you have in making decisions? Have you ever exceeded your authority? If so, what were the consequences?
- Have you ever had a dispute with a peer because your actions created a problem for his or her business unit? How did you work through that situation, and what did you learn from it?
- Do you see any advantages to using ingratiating behavior as a means of influencing others?

- Are there any behaviors you are demonstrating today that cause people to think you are not a team player?

Exercises

- Identify an individual in the organization with whom you have had a conflict or dispute. Develop and execute an action plan aimed at rebuilding trust with that individual.
- Meet with your team and discuss the key cultural norms and values for your organization and how they should guide all team members in decision-making.
- Develop a team communication report that can be used by all team members as a quick method of updating you on a regular basis on key activities and that you can use to update your manager on key activities.
- Meet with key stakeholders in your organization and discuss their information needs as they relate to your business unit. Develop an information-sharing strategy that will meet their information needs going forward.
- Identify a controversial issue on which you have a strong opinion and want to influence the actions that will be taken on the issue. Identify the other stakeholders with respect to the issue. Develop and execute an influence strategy that will build support among the stakeholders for the actions you want to take.
- Meet with your manager and outline the Critical Success Factors (CSFs) that the two of you agree upon regarding your performance over the next 6 to 12 months. Include in the discussion the manager's need for an information update on the CSFs and any limits you should be aware of regarding your decision-making authority.

Tips and Techniques

- Identify an issue or an initiative where you need to share decision-making authority and the resources necessary to be successful. Outline and execute a plan with the key stakeholders regarding how decisions should be made and what information sharing needs to occur.
- Observe and record examples of colleagues or other leaders as they offer challenges or resistance to the ideas of others. Think about the effectiveness of the approaches they employed.
- Identify an issue or decision where you disagree with your manager. Ask a trusted colleague to role-play your manager to give you practice pushing back on your manager and offering a personal perspective in a way that is non-confrontational and maintains the manager's self-esteem.

- Meet with your manager and discuss the scope of decision-making authority, with the goal of establishing reasonable boundaries that meet the needs of the manager and give you opportunities to grow in autonomy.

- Work with your team to establish a decision-making charter covering the commitment and use of team resources that emphasizes empowering team members and avoiding leader/team member decision-making conflicts.

- As part of a stakeholder analysis, include a power rating for each stakeholder. Use it to work through the most effective techniques for working with each stakeholder to ensure boundaries and information-sharing needs are clear.

Support Resources

Brandon, R., & Seldman, M. (2004). *Survival of the savvy: High-integrity political tactics for career and company success.* **New York, NY: Free Press.**

Two of the nation's most successful corporate leadership consultants reveal their proven, systematic program for using the power of "high-integrity" politics to achieve career success, maximize team impact, and protect the company's reputation and bottom line.

Burg, B. (2013). *Adversaries into allies: Win people over without manipulation or coercion.* **New York, NY: Penguin Group.**

Best-selling author Burg teaches readers about "Ultimate Influence"—the ability to win people over in a manner that leaves everyone feeling positive about the end result and themselves. Burg describes each component of his five-part framework in succinct but meaty chapters, each rife with actionable tips.

Dotlich, D. L., Cairo, P. C., & Rhinesmith, S. H. (2006). *Head, heart, and guts: How the world's best companies develop complete leaders.* **San Francisco, CA: Jossey-Bass.**

The authors rely heavily on high-profile case studies while discussing the crucial capabilities required of today's leaders and offering readers an actionable plan for stepping outside their "leadership comfort zone."

Gabarro, J. J., & Kotter, J. P. (2005, January). "Managing your boss." *Harvard Business Review.* **Retrieved from https://hbr.org/2005/01/managing-your-boss?cm_sp=Topics-_-Links-_-Read%20These%20First**

Gabarro and Kotter reframe "managing up" in a more favorable, less-deferential light—in their words, "the process of consciously working with your superior to obtain the best results for you, your boss, and the company."

George, B. (2007). *True north: Discover your authentic leadership.* **San Francisco, CA: Jossey-Bass.**

George helps readers understand that being an authentic leader is as simple as following one's own internal compass. Based on extensive research and interviews with 125 of today's acclaimed leaders, *True North* walks readers through a process of developing their own practical and comprehensive leadership development plan.

Grenny, J. (2014, November). "How to disagree with your boss." *Harvard Business Review.* **Retrieved from https://hbr.org/2014/11/how-to-disagree-with-your-boss**

According to Grenny, even in the most stultifying of cultures, there is a subset of people who know how to speak the truth to people in positions of power—he describes the tactics used by these individuals in the above article.

Schrage, M. (2010, April). "Make your boss look good (without becoming a sycophant)." *Harvard Business Review.* **Retrieved from https://hbr.org/2010/04/making-your-boss-look-good**

This brief article likens managing up to "knowing your customer" and provides several readily applicable examples of how to manage up in a subtle yet effective manner.

SUMMARY

Keep Doing

Take the initiative and drive the business according to sanctioned strategies.

Stop Doing

Venture into unchartered waters without manager knowledge or support.

Start Doing

Set expectations about decision-making authority and information sharing.

Dutifulness and loyalty are closely tied to each other. Unfortunately, low Dutiful leaders often fail to recognize the link. They often see their drive for autonomy and independence as strengths and the hallmarks of great leadership. Under the right circumstances, this view may be quite accurate, but it has to be tempered with the needs of those around the leader. Managers may see the behavior of low Dutiful individuals as a sign of disloyalty or abandonment, which reduces the likelihood that the manager will support those individuals if or when that support is needed. Peers may think that low Dutiful individuals are encroaching on their territory, which creates unneeded friction. Direct reports may emulate these behaviors (potentially creating their own problems), or direct reports may experience excessive stress, which can reduce their ability to perform effectively. Attention to expectations about decision-making and information sharing can go a long way to preventing low Dutiful leaders from creating problems for themselves and others.

PART III

CHARTING A PATH FOR CAREER SUCCESS

Chapter 16	Building an Aspiration Plan	263
Chapter 17	Development Tips for All Leaders	283
Chapter 18	Closing Thoughts	291

CHAPTER 16

BUILDING AN ASPIRATION PLAN

INTRODUCTION

Most leaders have experienced building a development plan. The traditional view of a solid development plan includes specific action items, a clear definition of success, and appropriate measurements. It has always been considered the sine qua non for behavior change. If assessment results are the "what" (What do these say about me?) and performance feedback is the "so what" (So what are the implications for my effectiveness as a leader?), then the "now what" is what comes next (Now what do I do?). The development plan is the "now what"—done correctly, it turns a haphazard joyride into a well-mapped journey with a specific destination in sight.

When reputation is the focus of development, we believe leaders would be better served by creating an Aspiration Plan as opposed to a simple Development Plan. An Aspiration Plan is more forward thinking than a Development Plan. It includes all the basic elements of a Development Plan. In addition, the creation of an Aspiration Plan includes numerous components that cause a leader to consider many of the challenges associated with building a winning reputation that will result in positive career outcomes.

Elements of an Effective Aspiration Plan

The basic elements of a successful Aspiration Plan are similar to those for a Development Plan. These elements include:

- *Scope*—which needs to be clearly identified as to what will benefit the leader and organization the most.
- *Customized Plan*—which needs to take into account the leader's Situational Context.
- *Active Commitment, Involvement, and Support*—on the part of the leader's manager.

Each of these elements is described in detail in the sections that follow.

Scope

Too often, development planning is viewed solely as fixing something that is wrong or needs to be improved. However, that is much too narrow a perspective, and individuals and organizations that have this view miss a huge opportunity. While improving areas of weakness is crucial, development activities should also include leveraging key strengths that the leader already possesses. Many times, an organization can benefit much more from a person's leveraging a key strength that will have a broad impact than from a person's trying to improve an area of weakness that is relatively inconsequential.

> *The power of a change in emphasis was illustrated in the case of Joe, a very creative and innovative leader who was being groomed for greater responsibility. He absolutely detested details, and in an organization that was engineering and project-management oriented, this was a huge barrier that resulted in a significant reputational scar for Joe—creative, but a poor project manager.*
>
> *For several years, Joe's development focused on honing his project management skills and attention to details. He read books, took courses, and headed up projects to gain on-the-job experience, all to no avail. Joe was unhappy, and the organization suffered through missed due dates and incorrect data on the projects he led. Finally, Joe and his manager agreed that he was much more valuable to the business as a strategist and innovator. He focused on leveraging his strengths by leading a think tank to develop new products, and he willingly nurtured and mentored new hires to teach them the competitive landscape. This career shift was a win-win for Joe and the organization, as he was happy doing what he did best, and the organization benefitted from the new ideas and the pipeline of new leaders he encouraged. Plus, the reputational scar created by his lack of attention to details was minimized.*

Development activities can also include the leader's venturing into the world of untested and untried competencies. This journey into the unknown is particularly important for high-potential leaders who will need skills at the next level that they might not have had an opportunity to demonstrate, develop in their current job, or build a reputation for effectiveness. It is central to the success of an Aspiration Plan, which, by definition, is focused on future opportunities that likely will require the acquisition of new skills.

> *Lauren, who was relatively quiet and shy, was a marketing manager for a medical devices company. She aspired to be a field sales person, but she just did not know if she was outgoing and persuasive enough to interface with doctors and their staffs, as she had never really spread her wings in these areas. As a development assignment, Lauren's manager arranged for her to spend a month in the field with a seasoned sales rep. At first, Lauren was an observer on the sales calls, but by the end of the month, she was closing sales. She was convinced she had what it took to be successful, and so was her manager who observed her building an effective reputation as a field sales person. When a field sales position opened up, Lauren was selected for the job and regularly exceeded her sales quota.*

In addition to improving areas of weakness, leveraging strengths, and trying untested competencies, there are other compelling reasons for building an effective Aspiration Plan:

- To maximize the effectiveness of both the individual and team.
- To enhance performance on the current job.
- To prepare for a future job.
- To differentiate oneself from others.
- To serve as a role model for direct reports in their development journeys.
- To create and encourage a culture of growth and development.

Most importantly, an effective Aspiration Plan can lay the foundation for enhancing one's reputation and brand, opening the door for future opportunities.

Customized Plan

Just as feedback must be tailored appropriately for each individual, so too must the Aspiration Plan, due to the fact that leaders have diverse needs as far as areas to leverage and develop and the most appropriate ways to approach them.

Although the plan needs to be customized, it certainly is not I-centric ("all about me"). Leaders work in organizations; therefore, development cannot occur in a vacuum. As we saw in Chapter 2, the Situational Context of the leader is critical, especially three components: the organizational culture, the leader's manager, and the leader's role. The Aspiration Plan needs to be created within the person's Situational Context because the same level of competency or the same behavior that is considered a key strength within one context might be considered a liability in another.

The Aspiration Plan also needs to consider the current perceptions of the leader held by others—that is, his or her reputation. This is where the Hogan foundational concept of Strategic Self-awareness, discussed throughout this book, is translated into behavior change and skill building that will enhance a leader's reputation, thereby making the leader more effective and increasing the perception of "readiness" for a position at the next level.

Choosing the Most Impactful Areas to Leverage and Develop

Too often, leaders attempt to address too many development areas, resulting in the dilution of the time, resources, and goal focus. Selecting too many areas to work on is a recipe for delivering disappointing results: developing a new skill, modifying a behavior, and improving one's reputation are hard work, and people have a finite amount of energy to expend. Therefore, the Aspiration Plan should be limited to no more than two or three areas that are crucial for the leader to be more successful. In identifying the areas of focus that will be the most impactful, it is helpful to think of them in terms of *deal breakers* and *game changers*. A deal breaker is a behavior or skill gap that will sideline a leader and severely hamper success. It is often the reason a leader may develop a reputational scar. A game changer is a behavior or skill, usually already somewhat of a strength, that if leveraged or developed further will differentiate the leader from others, providing a competitive edge.

> **Deal Breaker**—*Bill was a midlevel manager in a manufacturing company. He was viewed by all as extremely competent from a technical standpoint, and he routinely delivered solid business results. Both employees and vendors alike thought he was a "genuinely nice guy," and therein was the deal breaker: Bill had developed a reputation for being too nice. He tended to sugarcoat constructive feedback to his direct reports to a degree that the message was obscured. He caved in on negotiations with vendors, which cost the company thousands of dollars. Peers began to think of him as a pushover. Bill had aspirations of being promoted, and he could not understand why he was passed over, given his good results. His boss advised him that no matter how good his results or how much people liked him, he would not be promoted until he demonstrated that he could handle conflict effectively because the ability to do so was not optional at the next level of leadership. Bill took the feedback to heart and built his Aspiration Plan around eliminating his deal breaker.*
>
> **Game Changer**—*Kay was a highly regarded marketing leader who was known for her successful brand-building campaigns. Although she had spent her entire career in the creative side of marketing, she had been a math major in undergraduate school, and she loved numbers. She was the unofficial numbers cruncher in the marketing department. Her colleagues came to her if they wanted data analyzed or profit-and-loss assessments made. Repeatedly, she displayed keen business insights (not just marketing insights), and this became a key strength for her. Her boss recognized this aptitude and advised her that this*

business acumen could be a real game changer for her. If she could demonstrate it to other departments, and they saw that she had an overall business perspective, she could differentiate herself for cross-functional assignments, task forces, and the like. In other words, she could use her math ability to build a reputation for having superior business acumen.

Link Development Areas to the Business

The development areas selected should be tightly linked to the business and should be in alignment with one or all of the following:

- The business goals the leader has to achieve.
- The competencies associated with the current position or the next position to which the leader aspires.
- The needed reputation changes or enhancements.

How Big Is the Gap?

A critical assessment to make is "How big is the gap?" between how the leader behaves now and how the leader should behave, or between the current level of competence and the needed level, or between the way the leader is currently perceived and the desired perception—reputation in the workplace. The size of the gap will help clarify the development goal(s), the actions needed to support them, and the time and resources required. Goal clarity is absolutely critical for effective development.

Active Commitment, Involvement, and Support

Critical to the success of the Aspiration Plan is that the leader's manager is committed to an active, involved, and supportive role. The manager must agree to be an ongoing source of feedback for the developing leader. In addition, the manager must seek opportunities for the leader to practice skills associated with development areas, and if those practice opportunities are not readily available, the manager must create them. Too often the manager's role is not clearly defined, and too much is left to chance. As can be seen in the remainder of this chapter, the leader's manager plays a pivotal role in the success of the Aspiration Plan.

Aspiration Plan Differences

An Aspiration Plan includes a number of additional components to those that would appear in a traditional Development Plan including:

- Position aspiration
- Key stakeholders
- Reputational vision
- SMARTER goals
- Situational Context (barriers and leverage points)

Each of these elements is described in detail in the sections that follow.

Position Aspiration

An Aspiration Plan should be a document that allows a leader to think more broadly about his or her future. Thinking about the future is captured in the notion of a position aspiration. A position aspiration should be a realistic view on the part of a leader as to what he or she sees as a logical progression from a career-growth standpoint. From the leader's perspective, it can be quite motivating because it establishes a focal point for channeling development energy. From the organization's perspective, it can be important from a leader-retention standpoint as it can drive a career discussion between a leader and his or her manager.

Key Stakeholders

Leaders should always consider the key stakeholders when they consider their future development. These are the people who can open doors, shape development needs, provide candid feedback, and even offer advocacy regarding future opportunities. The Aspiration Plan is a great place for leaders to get specific about the key stakeholders who could play an important role in their future success.

Reputational Vision

We have discussed the importance of reputation throughout this book. An Aspiration Plan must include a reputational vision for a leader if it is to be effective. It is one thing for a leader to think through the position to which he or she aspires. However, to be a serious contender for a future opportunity, a leader must strive to shape his or her reputation in a way that those who have a say regarding the future opportunity, perceive the leader to be a viable candidate. A reputational vision is a statement regarding the characteristics the leader wants to be known for that will give him or her a reputational edge in competing for a future opportunity.

SMARTER Goals

A well-recognized framework within the development-planning literature is that of creating SMART goals (Specific, Measurable, Achievable, Relevant, and Time-bound). Using the insights about Strategic Self-awareness gained from assessments like the HDS, leaders can make SMART goals SMARTER. The "ER" stands for "Enhanced Reputation," and that is exactly what an Aspiration Plan should do: address the behaviors and skills that will enhance the reputation and brand of the leader to make him or her more effective. A well-crafted Aspiration Plan should include a definition of success as to what the modified behavior or improved skill looks like, what the business results will be, and what the impact on the leader's reputation will be. As long as the Aspiration Plan contains the elements of SMARTER goals, the format of the plan itself can vary from simple (a few columns) to more complex.

Situational Context (Barriers and Leverage Points)

The Situational Context should always be considered by leaders when they are identifying their development needs. The Situational Context can be quite dynamic and, as changes occur, the strengths and development opportunities of a leader can be impacted—the demand for certain strengths can rise or fall; development needs can be magnified or minimized. An Aspiration Plan should motivate a leader to give serious consideration to Situational Context variables. These variables can act as barriers to development or can be leveraged to facilitate development. The point in giving the Situational Context serious consideration in an Aspiration Plan is that, if effectively managed, it can accelerate a leader's ability to achieve his or her position aspiration.

Operationalizing an Aspiration Plan

An Aspiration Plan is of no use if it just sits on a shelf and is updated once or twice a year at the time of the midyear or end-of-year performance reviews. To facilitate progress, the action items and developmental assignments supporting the goals should be practical real-world activities that are related to the person's day-to-day job so that they have these qualities:

- Able to be repeated often (practice makes perfect).
- Observable by others who can provide ongoing feedback.

Because "leadership is a contact sport" (Goldsmith & Morgan, 2004), the majority of the activities that support the goals should be ones that can be practiced in the context and situations of the leader's everyday job. It is fine to have an action item of a book to read or a course to attend, but these types of activities should not compose the entire plan. Neither should a leader select a development area that he or she just will not have ample opportunity to develop. For example, if a leader makes one presentation every six months, he or she should not select "enhancing presentation skills" as a goal because he or she will not have sufficient venues to practice, or, if "enhancing presentation skills" truly is a critical skill to develop, then the leader's manager will need to find opportunities for the leader to make presentations on a more frequent basis.

Conventional wisdom on how leaders learn has recommended that a good plan consists of the following:

- 70 percent job and task content, including experiences that stretch and test capabilities.
- 20 percent people to study, listen to, and work with, including relationships with people who challenge and stimulate learning.
- 10 percent courses and readings, including structured education and leadership development programs.

The foregoing items can comprise both formal and informal learning experiences to ensure exposure to a wide range of approaches and perspectives. This also keeps the momentum of the plan alive and prevents people from getting bored with monotonous tasks. For example, if the person needs to develop relationship-building skills to be successful, he or she could perform a stakeholder analysis of key colleagues as part of the formal job-and-task category. On an informal basis, the person could attend more functions and work on networking skills. In the people-to-study category, a formal mentor could be assigned, and on an informal basis, the individual could have lunch with an expert in a certain subject. Likewise, in the courses-and-readings category, the individual could attend a formal week-long, instructor-led workshop, and on an informal basis, he or she could participate in a one-hour webinar. With the rise of social media, blogs, Massive Open Online Courses (MOOCs), and other online venues, there are an ever-increasing number of alternatives for both formal and informal learning.

The findings from Development Dimensions International's "Global Leadership Forecast 2014/2015" revealed that the actual ratio of time spent by leaders in various types of learning is as follows:

- 55 percent job and task content
- 25 percent people to study, listen to, and work with
- 20 percent courses and readings

This distribution puts more emphasis on formal learning and learning from others and deemphasizes the on-the-job learning. However, the important point is to integrate learning across the three areas so they are complementary.

Developmental Assignments

Typically, the assignments that provide the greatest growth and development for a leader are the ones that are stretch assignments—the ones that require the leader to step out of his or her comfort zone. Here are some examples of stretch assignments:
- Working in a start-up
- Working in a fix-it situation
- Working on a special project
- Rotating from line to staff or staff to line
- Rotating to a different department or function
- Taking an enterprise-wide view
- Working on a task force
- Developing others
- Being a change agent
- Implementing a new technology
- Managing direct reports who are located remotely
- Leading a merger or acquisition
- Working in a foreign country
- Participating in activities away from work
- Accepting a battlefield promotion—taking a stretch assignment to meet a sudden organization need

Developmental Activities

If a stretch assignment is not a viable option for the individual, then stretch activities within the individual's own job can provide growth:
- Handling unfamiliar responsibilities
- Proving oneself to others
- Starting something from scratch
- Taking a business in a new direction
- Fixing inherited problems
- Making tough decisions about staff
- Dealing effectively with problem performers
- Dealing with high-pressure situations
- Managing multiple, diverse functions
- Working across cultures (either organizational cultures or country cultures)

- Dealing with job overload
- Handling external pressure
- Influencing without authority
- Getting the job done without support
- Dealing with a difficult boss
- Gaining consensus around projects with multiple, competing constituencies
- Participating in projects requiring both a line and staff perspective
- Working with a mentor or advisor who can provide a sounding board
- Working with an internal or external coach who can facilitate development efforts

Monitoring and Modifying an Aspiration Plan

"No news is good news" definitely does not apply when it comes to a development effort. Individuals need ongoing feedback and checkpoints to determine their progress versus their SMARTER goals. In addition, Aspiration Plans do not exist in a vacuum, and they need to be flexible. Often, business conditions change, and the Aspiration Plan needs to change accordingly. Perhaps a behavior that the leader thought would be effective turns out not to work, and the leader needs to dial it up or dial it down. Several tools to monitor progress and determine the need for modifications follow.

Ongoing Feedback

In Chapter 1, we described the Leader Development Cycle and the important role ongoing feedback plays in the development of a leader. Ongoing, timely feedback serves the following key purposes:

- Reinforces the importance of Strategic Self-awareness and Situational Context.
- Gives the leader insight into the differences between Identity (self-perception) and Reputation (perception of others).
- Allows the leader to modify the development actions and behaviors as needed on a real-time basis.

On an informal basis, feedback should certainly come from the boss, but it is also helpful for the leader to seek feedback from trusted others (peers, direct reports, colleagues, etc.). These casual evaluations typically occur on an ad hoc basis and can be quite helpful in identifying which new behaviors are working and which need modification. It is also helpful to seek feedback from people in other functions and areas of the business to ensure that various perspectives are considered.

On a more formal basis, many people find it helpful to identify an advocate. They take the advocate into their confidence and explain to their advocate the behavior change(s) they want to make, and they ask the advocate to consciously observe their behavior and give them feedback, both good and bad. In addition to being trusted by the leader, an advocate needs to be someone who is in a position to observe the leader on a regular or frequent basis—attending the same meetings, for example. Ongoing contact provides the venue for the advocate to give real-time feedback regarding behavior modifications. It is essential that an advocate is someone whose opinion the leader values so the leader will accept the feedback and suggestions and act on them.

Two leading indicators (obtained from timely feedback) can be helpful in determining the efficacy of the Aspiration Plan and in identifying any needed modifications. These are "early returns" and "overcorrection."

Early Returns—*Just as exit polls during an election can give candidates an indication of how they are doing, so too can feedback received early in the implementation of the Aspiration Plan inform leaders of which new behaviors are working well and which ones need to be modified. This early feedback is best obtained on a casual or informal basis by the leader, the manager, or the advocate. Trusted colleagues whose input is valued by the leader can be asked how the leader is doing. The leader can ask, "Did I appear to be listening better in the meeting this morning?" followed by "What could I do to be even more effective?" Or, the manager or advocate can make similar inquiries to determine if people are noticing the leader's behavior changes and if the changes are having the desired impact on the leader's reputation and effectiveness: "Have you noticed a change in the clarity of Bob's written communications?" "What do you think he still needs to do?"*

Overcorrection—*It is not at all unusual for a leader to overcorrect when first trying a new behavior. The old adage "Be careful what you wish for; you just might get it" applies here, as sometimes people are so anxious to improve that they take the new behavior to an extreme. The behavior change should not be so extreme that the person becomes a joke or does more harm than good to his or her reputation. That said, in some cases, especially development areas that concern interpersonal skills such as being too aggressive or too quiet, an overcorrection is necessary in the beginning so that people will notice that the leader has changed. Reputations die hard, and people continue to play old tapes regarding the leader's behavior unless the change is quite noticeable. Ultimately, though, the leader needs to strike a balance regarding the behavior, and early returns feedback can help him or her do that.*

Progress Reviews

As part of formal feedback, the leader's manager and leader should conduct a formal review of progress as measured against the Aspiration Plan at least every six months—or more frequently if the development goals are shorter term in nature or if the plan is part of a time-bound performance improvement program. Results should be documented and modifications to the plan should be noted as needed.

Key Milestones

The key milestones identified on the Aspiration Plan are another gauge of progress. These are typically dates or numbers and are easily quantified as "made" or "missed." The plan can then be modified if needed (e.g., a due date has slipped because of funding and through no fault of the leader), or remedial action can be taken (e.g., a due date was missed because the leader did not fulfill his or her responsibilities).

Coaching Oneself

A very effective tool for monitoring progress and keeping development top of mind is the "Week in Review," which allows the leader to self-coach. It prompts the leader to engage in self-reflection at the end of every week and to evaluate the progress made and what needs to be done differently. The following are the types of questions that could be included in a "Week in Review" of one's development progress:

- What strengths did I leverage?
- What areas for development did I address?
- What actions did I take (e.g., accomplishments, or progress versus plan)?
- What interactions did I have (e.g., direct reports, peers, boss, others, in meetings)?
- What new skills did I use?
- What went well?
- What would I change?
- What feedback did I receive from others?
- What insights did I have? What did I learn?
- How did I impact my reputation?

Modifications to the Aspiration Plan

Many times, the foregoing monitoring tools of ongoing feedback, review of key milestones, and self-coaching reveal that modifications to the plan are necessary. Additionally, modifications might be driven by business reasons, such as a change in the leader's role, a reorganization, or a change in business strategy. Further, a leader might have reached or exceeded a development goal, resulting in the need to retire it and replace it with another development goal. Regardless of the reason, *the Aspiration Plan needs to be a living document* that is not cast in concrete. As long as the leader and his or her manager agree on what the modifications are and why they are needed, and they follow the practices just outlined, then development should continue successfully.

This approach is consistent with the ongoing nature of the Leader Development Cycle that we introduced in Chapter 1. One mnemonic that supports the Leader Development Cycle and that captures the essence of a solid Aspiration Plan is spelled as "FIRST":

- **F**ocus on priorities; identify critical issues and goals.
- **I**mplement something often; stretch the comfort zone.
- **R**eflect on what happens; extract maximum learning from experiences.
- **S**eek feedback and support; learn from others' ideas and perspectives.
- **T**ransfer learning into next steps; adapt and plan for continued learning.

Measuring the Results of an Aspiration Plan

The bottom line for an Aspiration Plan is whether the leader is more effective and his or her reputation is more positive. Results can be measured at two levels—the Individual Level and the Process Level. The Individual Level is relatively straightforward and easy to measure, while the Process Level is more macro and can be quite difficult to measure.

Measuring Effectiveness at the Individual Level

There are multiple ways to measure the success of a leader against his or her Aspiration Plan at the individual level:

Definition of Success—*As noted earlier, sound goals include a definition of success that describes what success looks like. So, a key measure is whether the person is now behaving in the manner articulated as success.*

Multi-rater Assessment—*Before-and-after multi-rater assessments are frequently administered to determine if the leader has moved the needle on his or her development areas. The multi-rater assessment need not be a* time-consuming, multiple-item sophisticated survey. It can be an informal, verbal multi-rater interview consisting of just a few key questions conducted by the leader's boss or coach to see if there is perceived behavior change and increased effectiveness.

Anecdotal "Buzz"— *Multi-rater assessment as just described often does not need to be solicited, as stakeholders will proactively comment on the person's changed behavior, increased effectiveness, or emerging reputation. Similar to Chief Justice Potter Stewart's infamous "I know it when I see it" comment regarding obscenity, people know behavior change and increased effectiveness when they see it. If the word on the street is positive, then that is a positive sign of reputation enhancement.*

Success of the Leader's Team and Organization—*Generally, when a leader becomes more effective as a result of successful development, there is a pull-through effect for team members and the broader organization. This can be seen in both hard numerical business objectives and in the morale within the team and the reputation of the team as viewed by outsiders.*

Measuring Effectiveness at the Process Level

While there is not a body of research on the effectiveness of Aspiration Planning per se, there is quite a bit of evidence on the effectiveness of coaching. Because coaching typically involves development, we can look at the results of coaching studies as a surrogate.

The ROI of Coaching—*The watershed study on the return on investment (ROI) of coaching was published by Manchester Consulting (McGovern et al., 2001). Prior to this study, coaching, still in its infancy, was only measured by anecdotal evidence, if at all. The Manchester study was the first to quantify the results of coaching in monetary terms. In addition, the Manchester study isolated the impact of coaching from other factors that could have improved the leader's performance (e.g., a process or technology improvement, or a new boss). The Manchester study included 100 midlevel and executive-level leaders who were coached between 1996 and 2000. Through a rigorous process designed to isolate the impact of the coaching, executives and key stakeholders were asked to quantify the dollar value of the coaching. Forty-three of the 100 executives could provide quantitative evidence, and the result was an ROI of 570 percent (i.e., the benefit attributable to the coaching was 5.7 times greater than the amount of the investment).*

Total Value—*All 100 leaders participated in the Total Value measurement that Manchester created. The leaders were asked to rate their coaching experience on a scale of −5 to +5.*

- A "+5" indicated the value of coaching was far greater than the investment.
- A "0" indicated the coaching paid for itself.
- A "−5" indicated the value of the coaching was far less than the investment.

Twenty-seven percent of the participants rated the coaching as +5, 27 percent rated it as +4, and 23 percent rated it as +3. In other words, 77 percent of the participants rated it as +3 or above. When key stakeholders were included in the survey, 75 percent rated the coaching as +3 or above.

Goal Achievement—*The coaching participants and key stakeholders who participated in the Manchester Study were also asked about how effectively the participants had achieved their goals. Seventy-three percent of the coaching participants said they had "very effectively" or "extremely effectively" achieved their goals. Fifty-four percent of the key stakeholders assigned these ratings, and 83 percent gave ratings of "effectively" or better. The coaching goals that these ratings address are development goals by another name, so certainly these results support the efficacy of focused development.*

In addition to the Manchester study, several other studies have calculated the ROI of coaching, and they have revealed similar significant paybacks. A study conducted by Merrill Anderson (2001) showed an ROI of 500 percent. A study conducted by Booz Allen Hamilton (Parker-Wilkins, 2006) showed an ROI of 689 percent. Thus, the coaching surrogate for measuring focused development shows it to be a clear winner.

SAMPLE ASPIRATION PLAN

The idea of a leader creating an Aspiration Plan may seem like a bold departure from the traditional concept of a Development Plan. However, we simply view it as a "next generation" tool that can be employed by leaders to achieve greater career success. At the heart of the concept of an Aspiration Plan are two basic ideas that we have consistently referred to throughout this book:

- The development of a leader rests first and foremost with the leader (him- or herself) and, as such, it needs to be forward thinking with future career success as a targeted outcome.
- Reputation is the cornerstone of career success because it results from the perception others have regarding the effectiveness of a leader. Those perceptions drive the decisions that can make or break a leader's career.

With these two ideas in mind, we offer the following simple format (See Table 3) for an Aspiration Plan. Further, we provide an example of a completed Aspiration Plan that includes the type of content that may appear for a leader interested in improving his or her career success.

Name:	Date:
Position Aspiration:	
Key Stakeholders:	
Reputational Vision:	

Performance Model	SMARTER Goals	Development Activities/Timeframe
Leadership Foundations—Predicts the degree to which individuals are able to effectively manage their career, are rewarding to deal with, and are strong organizational citizens.		
Leadership Emergence—Predicts the likelihood that someone will be noticed in the organization, emerge, and be labeled as a leader.		
Leadership Effectiveness—Predicts the ability to lead teams successfully toward productive outcomes.		
Situational Context (Barriers or Leverage Points)		

Table 3—Aspiration Plan Format

The Aspiration Plan has seven components, including:

1. Position Aspiration—This is the position to which the leader aspires. In general, it should be no more than one or two moves beyond the current position of the leader.

2. Key Stakeholders—These are the individuals most relevant to the position aspired to by the leader. They may include the leader's manager, peers, key subordinates, or even higher level leaders.

3. Reputational Vision—This is a vision statement that captures how the leader wants to be perceived by others especially as it relates to the position to which the leader aspires.

4. Performance Model—These are the relevant performance competencies that will be the focal point(s) of the leader's development activities. In this example, we are using three general competency areas, including Leadership Foundations, Leadership Emergence, and Leadership Effectiveness. These can be changed to fit the specific leadership competencies employed by an organization.

5. SMARTER Goals—These are the development goals that will be the focus of the leader's development activities. It is noteworthy that these goals include "ER" for Enhanced Reputation.

6. Development Activities/Timeframe—These are the specific development activities the leader will engage in and the timeframe for completion.

7. Situational Context (Barriers or Leverage Points)—These are context variables that may need to be overcome (Barriers) or called upon by a leader (Leverage Points) in order to achieve plan success.

Again, this is just a sample form that can be modified in a variety of ways to fit the specific needs of an organization.

Table 4 illustrates a completed Aspiration Plan for a case study involving Jane Barnes, senior director of marketing. The following is a description of Jane Barnes's situation and circumstances leading up to the creation of her Aspiration Plan.

Jane Barnes was a senior director of marketing for a Fortune 100 consumer products company. She was the brains behind numerous successful product launches, gaining her a reputation as being one of the best creative minds in the business. However, her organization and implementation skills were sorely lacking. This caused her direct reports to flounder due to lack of task clarity, resulting in her boss's frustration with budget overruns and her peers becoming disgusted with continual last-minute appeals by Jane to borrow resources to keep the project on track. Her stellar reputation for a "creative mind" was being outweighed by a reputation as "Calamity Jane" as far as implementation was concerned.

Jane aspired to become the VP of marketing, a position currently held by her manager. In her performance review her manager clearly indicated that her challenges with respect to project management were a serious barrier to moving beyond her current role. In fact, he pointed out her project-management skills were weak even for a senior director.

Name: Jane Barnes	Date: 2/3/XX
Position Aspiration: VP of Marketing	
Key Stakeholders: Jose Martinez, VP of Marketing; Jan Sikes, CEO; Sal Daniel, VP Operations	
Reputational Vision: A recognized creative leader with solid project-management skills	

Performance Model	SMARTER Goals	Development Activities/Timeframe
Leadership Foundations—Predicts the degree to which individuals are able to effectively manage their career, are rewarding to deal with, and are strong organizational citizens.	Build sound project-management skills that will ensure projects stay on time and on budget, resulting in effective team performance and positive cross-functional relationships.	• Attend the company-sponsored program on the Fundamentals of Project Management (4/1/XX). • Use Project ABC as an application project for skill practice (5/1/XX to 10/1/XX). • Debrief project-managment performance with team and peers (11/1/XX). • Refine skills for application starting (1/YY).
Leadership Emergence—Predicts the likelihood that someone will be noticed in the organization, emerge, and be labeled as a leader.	Identify an internal advocate who can mentor me on my project-management skills and advocate for my emerging reputation as a willing learner with emerging project-management skills.	• Enlist Sal Daniel, VP Operations, as my internal advocate and mentor. • Meet with Sal to build an effective project-management plan for Project ABC. • Establish bi-weekly meetings with Sal regarding Project ABC beginning on 5/1/XX. • Ensure project-management meetings with Sal cover performance on Project ABC and reputational impact. • Use feedback to improve performance.
Leadership Effectiveness—Predicts the ability to lead teams successfully toward productive outcomes.	Continue to build upon my reputation as a creative leader who offers innovative ideas that produce results for the organization.	• Set up a meeting with Jan Sikes, CEO, to establish a formal role in preplanning meetings addressing the company's YY strategic business plan. • Become an active participant in preplanning meetings, focusing on new products and the product launch process (6/1/XX to 1/YY). • Seek feedback from preplanning meeting participants regarding role and performance during meetings.

Situational Context (Barriers or Leverage Points)

- Initiate reputation change regarding poor project-management skills leveraging the Fundamentals of Project Management program.
- Leverage Sal Daniel's offer to be a mentor and advocate in building stronger project-management skills.
- Use opportunities with Sal, Jan, and the preplanning meeting participants to help overcome the reputational scar as a poor project manager.

Table 4—Sample Aspiration Plan for Jane Barnes

Summary

An Aspiration Plan is a forward-looking planning document that can be used by leaders to fully document development activities that, if executed, will result in reputation enhancement and greater career success. It differs from a traditional Development Plan in that it encourages leaders to examine their development more broadly, consider the implications of their reputation, and focus their development efforts on activities that will result in positive career outcomes.

CHAPTER 17

Development Tips for All Leaders

Introduction

In prior chapters, we have made a solid case that in leadership, personality does indeed matter, Strategic Self-awareness and Situational Context are crucial, and armed with these, leaders can change their behaviors, and subsequently their effectiveness and reputations. We also introduced the Leader Development Cycle (see Figure 1), which illustrates how ongoing behavior changes and reputation modifications occur.

As powerful as it is, the Leader Development Cycle does not exist in a vacuum. It must be part of an overall strategy for development that, based on both the individual leader and the situation, is best able to enhance a leader's effectiveness. Further, the Leader Development Cycle must be supported by blocking and tackling development tips and techniques to help a leader build skills and modify behaviors.

This chapter describes five general strategies for development that, when tailored to a leader and the situation, have proven to be effective time and again. Then we turn to development techniques so widely used that we call them universal.

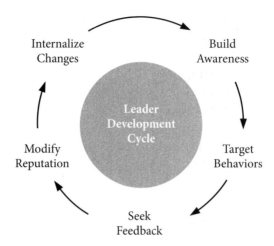

Figure 1   Leader Development Cycle

Five General Strategies for Development

A development strategy is an approach within which skill building, behavior modification, and reputation change occur. Although we often turn to education and training programs as our default development strategy, development is not one size fits all. Many times, a different approach is more appropriate and more effective.

In this section, we outline five development strategies to consider for optimal results depending upon the leader and the situation. These strategies are not mutually exclusive, and they are often used simultaneously to accomplish development. The five strategies are as follows:

- **Develop** through education and training.
- **Leverage** an area of strength.
- **Compensate** with alternative behaviors.
- **Support** the weakness with resources.
- **Redesign** the job or assignment.

Strategy 1: Develop Through Education and Training

A strategy of education and training is well suited for a situation where a leader has an identified skill or competency gap. It is particularly effective when the competencies are business related such as decision-making or strategic planning. This approach takes many forms—formal programs, classes, or workshops; coaching; mentoring; webinars; or on-the-job training, to name a few—all of which can be viable ways to build and reinforce skills and improve performance. Hard skills, such as data-based decision-making, setting priorities, delegating, public speaking, and the like are readily addressed by this approach. Softer, interpersonal skills, such as building relationships and influencing and motivating others can be tougher to develop, but this strategy is still effective with a targeted Aspiration Plan and ongoing feedback.

For example, a leader who struggles with high-quality decision-making can learn and subsequently use a decision-making process that incorporates generating and evaluating alternatives and then selecting a course of action with the highest probability of success. Or a leader who needs to enhance his or her strategic-planning abilities can participate in a strategic planning seminar and then perform an industry Strengths, Weaknesses, Opportunities, and Threats (SWOT) analysis to practice what he or she learned.

Strategy 2: Leverage an Area of Strength

An effective way to compensate for an area of weakness is to leverage an area of strength. Often, an area of strength in one area can be leveraged to offset a weakness in another area.

For example, a leader who wants to improve his or her ability to make an effective public speech can engage and win over an audience by using stories and anecdotes that have their foundation in a good sense of humor.

Another example is a leader who is not creative and innovative (development area), but perhaps is a great team builder and collaborator (strength). The leader can still deliver the desired result of creative and innovative ideas and products through leveraging his or her strength of engaging and encouraging others. In this case, the leader will create an environment that facilitates and nurtures the team's new and different ideas rather than thinking up the new ideas personally.

Strategy 3: Compensate with Alternative Behaviors

This strategy involves using a positive behavior to compensate for a derailing behavior. It can be used to rebuild a reputation of counterproductive behavior. This strategy is most effective when a positive behavior can be identified, incorporated into an ongoing behavioral repertoire, and easily observed by others when it is demonstrated. Repeated demonstration by a leader and observation by others not only helps a leader internalize the new behavior, but it reinforces a leader's reputation change among the observers. Many times, the effectiveness of this strategy increases when a leader uses a physical reminder or awareness builder to ensure frequent and appropriate use of the positive behavior.

For example, a leader who has a reputation for ignoring others' input should make a conscious effort to incorporate nonthreatening "seek" behaviors into team meetings and interactions. As a leader demonstrates the seek behaviors multiple times, his or her reputation will begin to change, and often the new behaviors become a leader's natural behaviors. In this example, as a physical reminder, a leader could change his or her wristwatch from one arm to the other before a meeting as a reminder to engage in the positive behaviors.

Another example is a leader who is known for unstructured free-for-all meetings could start publishing an agenda in advance, keeping the meeting on task and on time, and issuing minutes afterwards. If this process occurs regularly, a leader will gain credibility with the attendees, and his or her reputation will start to change.

Strategy 4: Support the Weakness with Resources

When a leader has a clear weakness that he or she has tried to improve to little or no avail, sometimes the most effective development strategy is to support the individual with resources. Typically, the resource is another team member or employee who possesses the skill a leader lacks. The effectiveness of this strategy increases when the target behavior can be isolated and supported by another person without diminishing a leader's overall effectiveness.

For example, a leader who is disorganized could utilize a well-organized administrative support person to provide a degree of structure and order in the performance of day-to-day responsibilities.

Another example of using this strategy is a leader who struggles with details. This leader could benefit from having a direct report who excels at dotting the *i*s and crossing the *t*s, which will free up the leader to focus on his or her strong suits. The organization will run more effectively, and both the leader and the direct report will be happier.

Strategy 5: Redesign the Job or Assignment

To resolve certain problems, it is sometimes possible to alter a leader's job requirements or scope to remove key roles or responsibilities and assign them elsewhere in the organization. Although this might seem drastic, it is preferable to allowing a leader's performance to lag and possibly losing a valuable contributor. This strategy is most effective when a leader's performance in a role or area of responsibility is ineffective, and it is clear that allowing the leader to struggle will diminish his or her effectiveness further and potentially hurt the overall organization. The effectiveness of this strategy increases when the gap created by removing the responsibilities from the position can be backfilled by expanding the leader's responsibilities in areas in which he or she is strong and that are valued by the organization.

For example, a sales manager might be terrific with customers and product sales but inept at managing direct reports. In this case, a good plan might be to reassign the sales force to another manager who has well-honed managerial skills and then expand the number of accounts that the sales manager handles personally to take advantage of his or her strong suit.

Another example is an entrepreneur who excels at new-product development and start-up scenarios but who is bored by running an ongoing business. Once the start-up morphs into a stable business, the entrepreneur could hire a professional manager to handle the day-to-day company operations. The entrepreneur could then devote his or her time to developing new ideas.

Universal Development Tips

Part II contains 11 chapters detailing a multitude of development tips that are tailored specifically to the high and low ends of each HDS scale. However, there are a number of tried-and-true development tips that have proven effective across all the scales, both high and low scores, and indeed, for behavior change in general. For this reason, we call these universal development tips. These are the go-to tips, including tools and techniques that leaders can use regardless of the development challenge they are confronting:

1. **Build Strategic Self-awareness**, including acknowledgment of the impact the behavior has on others. Leaders need to recognize, accept, and own the behavior that may be negatively impacting their reputation and limiting their career success. Only by acknowledging that he or she does indeed act in a certain way can a leader begin the journey to modify the behavior. Usually, specific behavioral examples and multi-rater assessment are necessary for a leader to understand the full impact of the behavior.

2. **Motivation is half the battle.** A leader who is not motivated to change will not change. A leader who is motivated to change is ready to embrace development. The question for a leader is, "What is motivating me to change?" The only reason to move forward with a plan aimed at improving performance is if there is a clear motivation to change. As part of building Strategic Self-awareness, a leader should consider the factors motivating a behavior change and whether those factors are sufficient to sustain a development effort.

3. **Camera Check Feedback** is a concept first introduced by Brandon and Seldman (2004). Camera Check Feedback is feedback that is so specific that a video camera would see and hear the feedback that is being delivered. This strategy may sound simple, but in practice it can be quite difficult. It is feedback that cannot be denied when it is delivered with this level of accuracy. Leaders who are truly interested in improving performance will embrace the concept of Camera Check Feedback and regularly seek such feedback as part of a development effort.

4. **SMARTER goals** are goals that are specific, measurable, achievable, relevant, and time-bound. We have added the "ER," which stands for "Enhanced Reputation." The ER makes these goals even more relevant when a reputation focus to development is employed. SMARTER goals literally force leaders to consider the reputational aspects of a development effort.

5. **Realize the impact** of the behavior on effectiveness, reputation, and, ultimately, career prospects based on the concept of materialism—that is, how much does the behavior matter? Once a leader understands that the behavior is driving the perceptions of others and limiting his or her

effectiveness and possibly career opportunities, he or she will be more likely to embrace development.

6. **Determine the triggers of the behavior.** Leaders need to identify the people and situations that trigger their derailing behavior. Perhaps it is a particular colleague who gets on a leader's nerves, or perhaps it is all people who are overbearing. The trigger could be meetings in which nothing is decided or a tight due date that must be met. Or it could be a physical phenomenon, such as being tired or hungry. Whatever the trigger, once a leader realizes what it is, he or she can anticipate it and outmaneuver it through various development techniques.

7. **Reframe the behavior change.** Behavior change is difficult, and new behaviors are frequently uncomfortable because they are not in the natural "strike zone" of a leader. Many times a leader will say, "That's just not the way I am," or "I feel like a fake when I do that." Often, taking the behavior change out of the personal realm and reframing it in terms of the demands of the job or the needs of the team will help leaders feel they are not being untrue to themselves or trying to become someone they are not. For example, if a leader needs to speak up and be more assertive but feels it is just not in his or her makeup to do this, the leader can begin to think of the new behavior simply as part of the role of being a leader. While it might not be the leader's natural behavior, it is certainly behavior that a leader needs to exhibit in order to be effective.

8. **Increase Situational Context awareness.** Going hand in hand with Strategic Self-awareness is awareness of the Situational Context—the need for a leader to be aware of his or her surroundings and decide which behaviors will be potential problems. The same behavior is not effective in all circumstances. By evaluating the situation and audience, a leader can decide whether to dial a behavior up or down to be effective. A key tool in understanding the Situational Context is a stakeholder analysis. A stakeholder analysis assists a leader in determining which stakeholders are most critical to his or her success. It also helps a leader determine how he or she can best work with each stakeholder from both a style standpoint (e.g., be more or less talkative, or focus on results or people) and a substance standpoint (e.g., discover common goals, or determine if there is competition for limited resources). The stakeholder analysis can help leaders flex their own style to more closely match the style of each stakeholder in an effort to make the stakeholder more comfortable.

9. **Utilize an advocate.** Ongoing, real-time feedback on the effectiveness of a new behavior is key to a leader's success, and an advocate can play a crucial role in providing this feedback. A leader should select an advocate he or she truly trusts and who sees him or her frequently enough to be aware of and observe new behaviors. The advocate can provide feedback to a leader about how the new behaviors were perceived by others. A leader can then

modify the behaviors as needed. The advocate can also be a leader's eyes and ears in the organization regarding the buzz about him or her, including whether colleagues are seeing a positive difference.

10. **Identify best-case and worst-case scenarios.** Sometimes leaders are leery about trying new behaviors for fear that they will fail. An effective way to confront this apprehension is for a leader to put the consequences of the behavior change in perspective. A leader should ask him- or herself, "What is the best outcome that could occur?" and list the positives. A leader can then ask him- or herself, "What is the worst outcome that could occur?" and list the negatives. Typically, the upside potential is far greater than the downside, and a leader will be more willing to try the new behavior.

11. **Use a tangible reminder to keep the behavior change top of mind.** Given the stress associated with today's fast-moving workplace, it is easy for leaders to put the need for behavior change on the back burner and to revert to the derailing behavior as an expediency. Further, when a leader is under stress, his or her fallback position is to resort to the old, comfortable behavior. Often, something tangible can serve as an ongoing reminder of the need to practice the new behavior. Putting a rubber band around your wrist, moving your watch from one arm to another, and using a special computer screen saver are all examples of tangible reminders.

12. **Identify a role model.** It can be both instructive and motivating for a leader to identify a role model who exemplifies the desired behavior. Finding a colleague who is "best in class" at demonstrating the desired behavior takes the behavior out of the theoretical and grounds it in the practical. A leader can actually see what the behavior looks like in the real world and the reactions others have to the behavior. Sometimes, it is powerful to identify a negative role model (i.e., a colleague who exhibits the same derailing behavior as the leader) so that the leader can feel what it is like to be on the receiving end of the behavior. For example, if a leader has trouble controlling his or her temper, he or she should identify a "hothead" and think about how he or she would like interacting with that person.

13. **Use a Week-in-Review form.** The Week-in-Review form is a tool designed to help leaders coach themselves. At the end of every week, a leader completes the form, which can be customized to a leader's development goals. The form guides a leader through a self-assessment of how he or she did during the week versus the Aspiration Plan. Typically, items covered include strengths leveraged, new behaviors practiced, reactions by others, feedback from others, key learnings, and behavior modifications needed. After a leader has put pen to paper for several weeks and completed the form, he or she can usually start logging events mentally. The important thing is for a leader to make the Week-in-Review part of his or her routine so the development effort stays top of mind.

14. **Evaluate and modify as needed.** A leader should evaluate the effectiveness of the new behavior, and, if necessary, modify it. If a new behavior is delivering the desired results, then a leader should keep it up, thereby internalizing it and reinforcing to others the behavior is going to "stick." However, if the new behavior is off the mark, a leader should modify it. Leaders always need to realize that behavior change is a work in progress, and it might require some adjustment to be maximally effective. Asking oneself what do I need to "stop," "start," and "keep" doing is a simple reminder that leaders should use as a form of self-evaluation.

15. **Do not get discouraged!** This mega-tip needs to be repeated frequently. Behavior change is difficult, and changing people's perceptions is even more difficult. Reputations die hard, and sometimes people continue to "play old tapes" long after a leader has modified the derailing behavior. One way to counter this is for a leader to ask people for feedback and "feed-forward" (e.g., "What can I do in the future to be more effective?") so that those around the leader feel a part of the leader's success in changing his or her behavior. People will embrace a leader who is sincerely trying to make performance improvements. Leaders can capitalize on such positive energy simply by involving others in their development efforts.

Summary

For a leader to modify behavior, increase effectiveness, and ultimately accomplish a reputation change, he or she must actively engage in the Leader Development Cycle on an ongoing basis. The Development Cycle occurs within one or more of five general strategies for development that have proven successful over time. Development is supported by practical development tips and techniques, some of which span multiple strategies and situations and are, therefore, universal. In the sample coaching initiatives described in Part II, the five strategies and universal development tips are often employed with positive results. We strongly believe they should be a part of any effort by a leader to improve his or her performance.

CHAPTER 18

CLOSING THOUGHTS

INTRODUCTION

Our intent in writing this book was to create the go-to guide for personality-based feedback and development that a leader could use to improve his or her reputation and career outcomes. We wanted to share our philosophy, which makes a compelling case for the importance of personality in leadership. We also wanted to offer leaders a practical guide of proven techniques and tips that they could apply to improve their reputation and performance.

Throughout this book, we have taken the position that personality truly is important in matters of leadership. Personality drives behaviors, and behaviors accumulate into a leader's reputation. For a leader's performance to improve, behaviors must change, which will lead to a reputation change. Thus, a change in a leader's reputation, as acknowledged by the leader's constituents, is the acid test for whether real change has occurred.

The question, "Can leaders change for the better?" always comes up in a book devoted to leadership development. Our answer to this is a resounding "yes"—if a leader is motivated and is provided with the appropriate feedback and development opportunities.

Conquering the Dark Side—Let There Be Light!

Using these concepts that leaders can indeed change and that reputation change is real change, we set about describing the most impactful ways to interpret assessment data and feedback and employ proven development tips and techniques to ensure a successful outcome. Our content is based on extensive research accumulated over 30 years and on the best practices of more than 40 coaches we have worked closely with over the past two decades. Our goal is to assist leaders in the pursuit of reputation change and performance improvement. As we looked back over the content covered throughout the book, we thought it would be useful to close with 10 major takeaways we hope were successfully conveyed:

1. Leaders are coaches. Perhaps the most important role for all leaders is that of coach. To be successful, they must pursue their own self-improvement, and they must become proficient in helping those they lead improve their performance. The content of this book is dedicated to all those interested in helping themselves and others become better leaders.

2. Strategic Self-awareness is foundational because without it, the entire development process stalls. Identity is "the you that you know," and reputation is "the you that others know," and it is the latter that is important. It is crucial for leaders to understand how they are perceived by others and why that is the case (e.g., due to their behaviors). Strategic Self-awareness enables them to do this—to understand their key strengths and areas for improvement and how they compare to those of other people. Leaders need to learn to be "awareness consumers" so they are constantly on the lookout for information regarding how they are being perceived by others and can then adjust their behaviors.

3. Situational Context awareness—knowing one's context and being able to adjust behaviors accordingly—is the working partner of Strategic Self-awareness. Leaders must constantly be "reading" the audience or the situation and then dialing up or dialing down behaviors based on what fits the context in which they find themselves. We emphasize three contexts in particular: the role the leader has, the manager to whom the leader reports, and the organizational culture in which the leader works. What is viewed as a key strength in one context might not be one in another. Likewise, what is a derailer in one context might not be one in another. In some instances, a key strength in one context might even be a derailer in another or vice versa. The learning is that leaders need to be constantly vigilant as to their context and adapt their behaviors accordingly.

4. The Hogan Development Survey (HDS) plays a key role in facilitating leaders' Strategic Self-awareness and Situational Context awareness. Because Dark Side behaviors are the ones that derail leaders and negatively impact their reputations, we focused on the 11 scales of the HDS. Two major concepts emerged from the evolution of the HDS:

- Both high and low HDS scale scores can get leaders into trouble and negatively impact their reputations. Although high-end behaviors are more noticeable and memorable, low-end behaviors can be silent killers for leaders as they typically are not very leader-like. The concept that "high scores will get you fired, and low scores will get you passed over" should be kept in mind whenever HDS scores are addressed. The addition of low-score problematic behaviors and development tips and techniques associated with them adds richness to the HDS data that was many times overlooked in the past. Leaders should recognize that many times, it is more difficult to dial up a lower-score behavior than it is to dial down a higher-score behavior. This is because higher-end behaviors are typically so foreign to low-scoring leaders (e.g., a low Excitable leader might have considerable difficulty in being more emotive). Each of the 11 scales has a chapter devoted to it that includes in-depth interpretation and development tips around both the high- and low-end scale behaviors.

- Subscales have been added to the HDS, and they can be invaluable in determining how derailing behaviors will manifest. Each HDS main scale has three subscales that describe different aspects of the main scale, enabling leaders to peel the onion back another layer and specifically target derailing behaviors. This deeper exploration is particularly helpful if an elevated or depressed subscale is part of a main scale that is neither high nor low and typically would not garner much attention. This subscale elevation or depression allows for the identification of problematic behaviors that would not have been noticed by looking solely at a main scale score. In Chapter 3, in the charts for each of the 11 HDS scales, we cover the implications of both high and low scores on the subscales, providing further interpretive nuance.

  For those who are interested in taking the HDS, go to www.hoganassessments.com for more information.

5. People are all wired differently, and it is essential to the success of a performance improvement effort that leaders consider their personality characteristics, receptivity to feedback, preferred learning methods, engagement in the development process, and willingness to take action to make positive improvements.

6. Leaders can often improve their success when undertaking a development effort by enlisting the help of those around them. Superiors, peers, and even direct reports can be quite supportive when they observe a leader who is sincerely interested in improving his or her performance. It may also be very beneficial for a leader to consider engaging a professional coach as a support resource in addressing development challenges.

7. An Aspiration Plan that is well crafted and addresses only two to three areas (either strengths to leverage or watch-outs to improve) is essential to

provide structure for a leader to improve his or her performance. Without an Aspiration Plan that describes what behavior needs to change, what specific actions need to be taken to accomplish this, and what success looks like in terms of greater effectiveness and enhanced reputation, the leader's desired behavior changes are no more than a wish list. Further, a leader's manager must be in alignment with what is outlined in the Aspiration Plan and be committed to providing ongoing feedback to reinforce the leader's behavior change.

8. When addressing Dark Side personality characteristics, we highly recommend that the comprehensive approach outlined in the 11 chapters dedicated to the respective HDS scales be followed. This approach includes detecting when the behavior is a problem, evaluating your need for change based on the leader's presenting behaviors, creating an Aspiration Plan, and utilizing the development tips and resources that are delineated.

9. In addition to the HDS assessment, we strongly encourage leaders to use data from other assessments including multi-rater tools to truly understand the behaviors they may display that could impact their career success. Those interested in other assessment tools can review a number of alternatives at www.hoganassessments.com.

10. The Leader Development Cycle is continuous. Leaders are never finished products but always works in progress, as their context continually changes and with it the need to modify their behaviors to suit the situation. After a development initiative, leaders have come full circle and are back to utilizing their Strategic Self-awareness to understand their reputation and determine what to address next. Nothing takes the place of ongoing feedback in keeping Strategic Self-awareness honed. Too often, especially at higher-level jobs, it becomes very difficult for leaders to obtain objective feedback. It is only with the knowledge of how they are being perceived by others (i.e., their reputation) gained through feedback that they can enhance their performance. Leaders need to proactively seek feedback, and if they feel they are not getting the straight scoop anecdotally from their constituents, they should utilize a more formal means such as a multi-rater assessment or stakeholder interviews.

Summary

In closing, let us recognize that we should never lose sight of *why* we want to enhance leaders' reputations and effectiveness in the first place. It has been shown repeatedly there is a clear line of sight between the quality of an organization's leaders and its business results, including increased financial performance, enhanced employee satisfaction and engagement, less employee turnover, and greater customer satisfaction.

It is our hope that leaders will take to heart and apply what we have put forth in this book, enabling them to deal with their Dark Side head-on and accomplish real behavior changes, reputation enhancements, and greater leadership effectiveness. More effective leaders vastly improve the quality of their constituents' work lives. Let there be light!

BIBLIOGRAPHY

American Psychiatric Association. (1987). *Diagnostic and statistical manual of mental disorders* (3rd ed., rev.). Washington, DC: Author.

Anderson, M. C. (2001). *Executive briefing: Case study on the return on investment of executive coaching.* Retrieved from http://www.true-directions.com/downloads/MetrixGlobalCoachingROIBriefing.pdf

Brandon, R., & Seldman, M. (2004). *Survival of the savvy: High-integrity political tactics for career and company success.* New York, NY: Free Press.

Connellan, T. K., & Zemke, R. (1993). *Sustaining knock your socks off service.* AMACOM: New York, NY.

Crisp, R. J., & Turner, R. N. (2010). *Essential social psychology.* London, UK: Sage.

Goldsmith, M. & Morgan, H. (2004, August). "Leadership is a contact sport: The 'follow-up factor' in management development." *strategy + business, 36.* Retrieved from http://www.strategy-business.com/article/04307?pg=0

Hogan, J., & Hogan, R. (2010). *Motives, values, preferences inventory manual: 2010 administrative and norming updates.* Tulsa, OK: Hogan Press.

Hogan, J., Hogan, R., & Busch, C. M. (1984). How to measure service orientation. *Journal of Applied Psychology, 69*, 167–173.

Hogan, R. (1983). "A socioanalytic theory of personality." In M. M. Page (Ed.), 1982 *Nebraska Symposium on Motivation*, 55–89. Lincoln, NE: University of Nebraska Press.

Hogan, R., & Benson, M. J. (2009). "Personality theory and positive psychology: Strategic self-awareness." In R. Kaiser (Ed.), *The perils of accentuating the positive*, 115–134. Tulsa, OK: Hogan Press.

Hogan, R., & Hogan, J. (1997). *Hogan Development Survey manual* (1st ed.). Tulsa, OK: Hogan Assessment Systems.

Hogan, R., & Hogan, J. (2007). Hogan Personality Inventory manual (3rd ed.). Tulsa, OK: Hogan Assessment Systems.

Hogan, R., & Hogan, J. (2009). *Hogan Development Survey manual* (2nd ed.). Tulsa, OK: Hogan Press.

Jones, W. H. (1988). *User's manual for PROFILE*. Unpublished manuscript.

McGovern, J., Lindemann, M., Vergara, M. A., Murphy, S., Barker, L., & Warrenfeltz, R. (2001). "Maximizing the impact of executive coaching: Behavioral change, organizational outcomes and return on investment." *The Manchester Review, 6*(1), 19.

Parker-Wilkins, V. (2006). "Business impact of executive coaching: Demonstrating monetary value." *Industrial and Commercial Training, 38*(3), 122–127. http://dx.doi.org/10.1108/00197850610659373

Ravasi, D., & Schultz, M. (2006). "Responding to organizational identity threats: Exploring the role of organizational culture." *Academy of Management Journal, 49*(3), 433–458.

Sinar, E., Wellins, R. S., Ray R., Abel, A. L., & Neal, S. (2014). "Ready-now leaders: 25 findings to meet tomorrow's business challenges. Global Leadership Forecast 2014/2015." Retrieved from https://www.ddiworld.com/DDI/media/trend-research/global-leadership-forecast-2014-2015_tr_ddi.pdf?ext=.pdf

Warrenfeltz, R. & Kellett, T. (2016). *Coaching the dark side of personality*. Tulsa, OK: Hogan Press.

INDEX

Note: an *f* indicates a figure; a *t*, a table.

A

Absence of behaviors
   and Change Targets, 19
   and Hogan Development Survey (HDS), 29
Accumulation of incidents and reputational scars, 28–29
Active commitment, involvement, and support for Aspiration Plan, 267
Addition of behaviors and Change Targets, 20
Advocate utilization, 288
Alternative behaviors as development strategy, 284–285
Anecdotal "buzz" for individual level Aspiration Plan measurement of results, 276
Aspiration Plan elements, 264–267
   active commitment, involvement, and support, 267
   customized plan, 265–267
   scope, 264–265
Aspiration Plan measurement of results, 275–276
   individual level, 275–276
   process level, 275
Aspiration Plan monitoring and modifying, 272–275
   coaching oneself, 274
   key milestones, 274
   modifications, 272
   ongoing feedback, 272–273
   progress reviews, 274

Aspiration Plan operationalizing, 269–272
    developmental activities, 271
    developmental assignments, 271
    Developmental Dimensions International's findings, 270
Aspiration Plan samples, 277–281, 278t, 281t
Aspiration plan use for structure, 293–294
Aspiration Plan vs. development plan, 273–274
    key stakeholders, 268
    position aspiration, 268
    reputational vision, 268
    situational context, 268
    SMARTER goals, 268

B

Balsillie, RIM/Blackberry CEO Jim, 217
Best-case and worst-case scenario identification, 289
Bold, 40–41
    behavior range, 40
    high, Rex, Case 1, 158–165
    leadership and reputation implications, 40–41
    low, Janis, Case 5, 64–65, 167–173
    risk summary, 41
Branson, Sir Richard, 175
Building Awareness and Leader Development Cycle (LDC), 10
Bush, President George W., 140

C

Calibration, 20–23
    performance feedback, 20–21
    seeks in place of tells, 23
    and Strategic Self-Awareness, 21
Camera Check Feedback, 287
Career outcomes and reputation, 3
Career success and reputation, 3
Carter, President Jimmy, 184, 202
Case studies, 53–73
    Case 1—Rex, low Cautious, 56–57
    Case 2—Phil, high Skeptical, 58–59
    Case 3—Robert, high Reserved, 60–61
    Case 4—Tanya, high Mischievous, 62–63
    Case 5—Janis, low Bold, 64–65
    Case 6—Mark, high Colorful, 66–67
    Case 7—James, high Dutiful, 68–69
    Case 8—Courtney, low Diligent, 70–71
    Case 9—Kelly, high Diligent, 72–73
    global factors of flawed interpersonal tendencies, 54
Caspar Milquetoast, 202
Cautious, 34–35
    behavior range, 34
    high, James, Case 7, 107–114
    leadership and reputation implications, 34–35
    low, Rex, Case 1, 56–57, 115–122
    risk summary, 35
Change internalization and Leader Development Cycle (LDC), 8–9
Change Targets, 19–20
    absence of behaviors and impact, 19
    addition of behaviors, 20
    elimination of behaviors, 20
    Leadership Formula workshop, 19
    pattern of behavior, 19
Church, Allan, ix–x
Coaching oneself for Aspiration Plan monitoring and modifying, 274
Colorful, 44–45
    behavior range, 44
    high, Mark, Case 6, 66–67, 193–201
    leadership and reputation implications, 44–45
    low, Robert, Case 3, 202–208
    risk summary, 45
Components of performance feedback, 21t
Continuous learning and Leader Development Cycle (LDC), 8
Corleone, Don, 131
Corleone, Michael, 124
Courtney, Case 8
    high Imaginative, 209–216

low Diligent, 70–71
Critical Success Factors (CSFs), 239–240, 246, 254, 256
Culture context, 15–16
    definition, 15
    and employee success, 15–16
    and global factors of flawed interpersonal tendencies, 54
    and reputation, 16
Customized Aspiration Plan, 264–265
    deal breaker, 266
    game changer, 266–267
    gap between behavior and needed changes, 271
    impactful areas to leverage and develop, 270–271
    link between business goals and plan, 267

D

Dark Side assessment, 25–51
    Hogan Development Survey (HDS), 26–29
    Hogan Development Survey (HDS) scales, 30–51
    and reputational scar, 25–28
Deal breaker in customized Aspiration Plan, 266
Dean, Howard, 77
Developmental activities for Aspiration Plan operationalizing, 275–276
Developmental assignments for Aspiration Plan operationalizing, 275
Developmental Dimensions International's findings for Aspiration Plan operationalizing, 270
Diligent, 48–49
    behavior range, 48
    high, Kelly, Case 9, 72–73, 225–233
    leadership and reputation implications, 48–49
    low, Courtney, Case 8, 70–71, 234–241
    risk summary, 49

Direct observation and workplace reputation, 6
Dutiful, 50–51
    behavior range, 50
    high, James, Case 7, James, 68–69, 243–250
    leadership and reputation implications, 50–51
    low, Rex, Case 1, 251–259
    risk summary, 51
Dynamic properties of linear representation of Leader Development Cycle (LDC), 12

E

Early returns for process-level Aspiration Plan measurement of results, 275
Education and training as development strategy, 284–285
Elimination of behaviors and Change Targets, 20
Enlist help of others, 293
Employee success and culture context, 15–16
Evaluate and modify, 290
Excitable, 30–31
    behavior range, 30
    high, Tanya, Case 4, 77–83
    leadership and reputation implications, 30–31
    low, James, Case 7, 84–90
    risk summary, 31
Executive demeanor and reputation, 5
Extrospective issue and reputation, 5

F

Feedback. *See* Ongoing feedback for Aspiration Plan monitoring and modifying; Performance feedback and calibration
Fernandez de Kirchener, former president of Argentina, 193–194
Fontane, Johnny, 131

Ford, President Gerald, 202
Formal feedback, 274

G

Game changer in customized Aspiration Plan, 266–267
Gandhi, Mahatma, 99
Gap between behavior and needed changes in customized Aspiration Plan, 271
General development strategies, 284–286
    alternative behaviors, 285–285
    education and training, 284
    leverage area of strength, 285
    redesign job or assignment, 286
    support weakness with resources, 286
Global factors of flawed interpersonal tendencies, 54
    moving against people, 54
    moving away from people, 54
    moving toward people, 54
Godfather novels and film trilogy, 124, 131
"Good Soldier," 244
Grant, General Ulysses S, 166

H

Hatoyama, Prime Minister Yukio, 107–108
High Bold, Rex, Case 1, 157–165
    development tactics, 162–165
    need for change evaluation, 161–162
    problem detection, 157–158
    sample development program, 160–161
    situational summary, 159
High Cautious, James, Case 7, 107–114
    development tactics, 111–114
    need for change evaluation, 110–111
    problem detection, 107–108
    sample development program, 109–110
    situational summary, 108–109
High Colorful, Mark, Case 6, 66–67, 194–201
    development tactics, 198–201
    need for change evaluation, 197–198
    problem detection, 194–195
    sample development program, 195–197
    situational summary, 194–195
High Diligent, Kelly, Case 9, 72–73, 225–235
    development tactics, 230–232
    need for change evaluation, 231
    problem detection, 227–228
    sample development program, 229–230
    situational summary, 227
High Dutiful, James, Case 7, James, 68–69, 243–250
    development tactics, 247–250
    need for change evaluation, 246–247
    problem detection, 243
    sample development program, 245–246
    situational summary, 245
High Excitable, Tanya, Case 4, 77–83
    development tactics, 81–83
    need for change evaluation, 80–81
    problem detection, 77–78
    sample development program, 78–80
    situational summary, 78
High Imaginative, Courtney, Case 8, 209–216
    development tactics, 211–212
    need for change evaluation, 213
    problem detection, 209–210
    sample development program, 211–212
    situational summary, 210–211
High Leisurely, Rex, Case 1, 139–149
    development tactics, 145–147
    need for change evaluation, 144–145
    problem detection, 139–140
    sample development program, 141–144
    situational summary, 141
High Mischievous, Tanya, Case 4, 62–63, 175–183
    development tactics, 180–183

need for change evaluation, 179–180
problem detection, 175–176
sample development program, 177–179
situational summary, 176
High Reserved, Robert, Case 3, 60–61, 123–130
development tactics, 127–130
need for change evaluation, 126–127
problem detection, 123–124
sample development program, 125–126
situational summary, 124–125
High Skeptical, Phil, Case 2, 58–59, 91–97
development tactics, 95–97
need for change evaluation, 94–95
problem detection, 91
sample development program, 93–94
situational summary, 92
Hogan Developmental Survey (HDS) Profiles, 56–73
Case 1—Rex, Low Cautious, 56–57
Case 2—Phil, High Skeptical, 58–59
Case 3—Robert, High Reserved, 60–61
Case 4—Tanya, High Mischievous, 62–63
Case 5—Janis, Low Bold, 64–65
Case 6—Mark, High Colorful, 66–67
Case 7—James, High Dutiful, 68–69
Case 8—Courtney, Low Diligent, 70–71
Case 9—Kelly, High Diligent, 72–73
Hogan Development Survey (HDS), 26–29
absence of scale behaviors, 29
accumulation of incidents and reputational scars, 28–29
to address dark side, 292
development, 26–27
key role in awareness, 292–294
performance risks and reputational scars, 27–28
personality characteristics and reputational scars, 26
PROFILE use, 26

Hogan Development Survey (HDS) scales, 30–51
Bold, 40–41
Cautious, 34–35
Colorful, 44–45
Diligent, 48–49
Dutiful, 50–51
Excitable, 30–31
Imaginative, 46–47
Leisurely, 38–39
Mischievous, 42–43
Reserved, 36–37
Skeptical, 32–33

I

Image and reputation, 4
Imaginative, 46–47
behavior range, 46
high, Courtney, Case 8, 209–216
leadership and reputation implications, 46–47
low, Kelly, Case 9, 217–224
risk summary, 47
Impactful areas to leverage and develop in customized Aspiration Plan, 265–266
Indirect personal observation and workplace reputation, 6–7
Individual level Aspiration Plan measurement of results, 275–276
anecdotal "buzz," 276
multi-rater assessment, 276–277
success definition, 279
success of leader's team and organization, 281
Informal feedback, 276–277
Informational component of performance feedback, 21
Internalizing Change and Leader Development Cycle (LDC), 12
Interview situation and Self-Monitoring, 18
Intrapsychic approaches to personality vs. Strategic Self-Awareness, 14
Introspective issue and reputation, 5

Involvement of others in development efforts, 290

J

James, Case 7
    high Cautious, 107–114
    high Dutiful, 68–69, 243–250
    low Excitable, 84–90
    low Mischievous, 184–192
Janis, Case 5
    low Bold, 64–65
    low Leisurely, 149–156
    low Reserved, 131–138
Jobs, Steve, 226
Johnson, JC Penney CEO Ron, 209–210

K

Kelly, Case 9
    high Diligent, 72–73, 225–233
    low Imaginative, 217–224
Key milestones for Aspiration Plan monitoring and modifying, 274
Key stakeholders with Aspiration Plan vs. development plan, 268
Kim Jong-Un, 91–92

L

Lazaridis, RIM/Blackberry CEO Mike, 217
Leader Development Cycle (LDC), 7–12, 8f, 53–55
    Building Awareness, 10
    Case Studies Categorized by Contextual Factors and HDS Factors, 55t
    change internalization, 8–9
    continuous learning, 8
    continuous nature of, 294
    continuous process, 10
    dynamic properties of linear representation, 12
    Internalizing Change, 12
    multi-rater assessments, 10
    Reputation Modification, 11
    Seeking Feedback, 11
    steps, summarized, 9
    Targeting Behaviors, 11
Leaders are coaches, 293
Leadership Formula workshop and Change Targets, 19
Leisurely, 38–39
    behavior range, 38
    high, Rex, Case 1, 139–148
    leadership and reputation implications, 38–39
    low, Janis, Case 5, 149–156
    risk summary, 39
Leverage area of strength as development strategy, 285
Lincoln, President Abraham, 166
Link between business goals and plan in customized Aspiration Plan, 267
Low Bold, Janis, Case 5, 64–65, 166–173
    development tactics, 170–173
    need for change evaluation, 169–170
    problem detection, 166
    sample development program, 168–169
    situational summary, 167
Low Cautious, Rex, Case 1, 56–57, 115–122
    development tactics, 119–122
    need for change evaluation, 118
    problem detection, 115
    sample development program, 116–117
    situational summary, 116
Low Colorful, Robert, Case 3, 202–208
    development tactics, 206–208
    need for change evaluation, 205
    problem detection, 202
    sample development program, 203–204
    situational summary, 203
Low Diligent, Courtney, Case 8, 70–71, 234–241
    development tactics, 238–241
    need for change evaluation, 237
    problem detection, 234–235

sample development program, 235–237
situational summary, 235
Low Dutiful, Rex, Case 1, 251–259
  development tactics, 255–258
  need for change evaluation, 254–255
  problem detection, 251–252
  sample development program, 253–254
  situational summary, 252
Low Excitable, James, Case 7, 84–90
  development tactics, 88–90
  need for change evaluation, 87–88
  problem detection, 84
  sample development program, 85–87
  situational summary, 85
Low Imaginative, Kelly, Case 9, 217–224
  development tactics, 221–223
  need for change evaluation, 220–221
  problem detection, 217
  sample development program, 218–220
  situational summary, 218
Low Leisurely, Janis, Case 5, 149–156
  development tactics, 153–155
  need for change evaluation, 152–153
  problem detection, 149
  sample development program, 151–152
  situational summary, 150
Low Mischievous, James, Case 7, 184–192
  development tactics, 188–191
  need for change evaluation, 187–188
  problem detection, 184
  sample development program, 185–187
  situational summary, 185
Low Reserved, Janis, Case 5, 131–138
  development tactics, 134–137
  need for change evaluation, 133–134
  problem detection, 131
  sample development program, 132–133
  situational summary, 132
Low Skeptical, Mark, Case 6, 99–105
  development tactics, 102–104
  need for change evaluation, 101–102
  problem detection, 99
  sample development program, 100–101
  situational summary, 99–100

M

Manager context, 16–17
  definition, 16
  and global factors of flawed interpersonal tendencies, 54
  impact, 17
Mark, Case 6
  high Colorful, 66–67, 193–201
  low Skeptical, 99–105
McClellan, General George, 166
Mischievous, 42–43
  behavior range, 42
  high, Tanya, Case 4, 62–63, 175–183
  leadership and reputation implications, 42–43
  low, James, Case 7, 184–192
  risk summary, 43
Modifications for Aspiration Plan monitoring and modifying, 272
Motivational component of performance feedback, 21
Motivation is half the battle, 287
Moving against people as global factors of flawed interpersonal tendencies, 54
Moving away from people as global factors of flawed interpersonal tendencies, 54
Moving toward people as global factors of flawed interpersonal tendencies, 54
Multi-rater assessment
  for individual level Aspiration Plan measurement of results, 275–276
  and Leader Development Cycle (LDC), 10

N

North, Lieutenant Colonel Oliver, 244

O

Obama, President Barack, 251
Ongoing feedback for Aspiration Plan monitoring and modifying, 272–273
  early returns, 273
  formal, 273
  informal, 272–273
  overcorrection, 273
Other assessments, 294
Overcorrection in Aspiration Plan monitoring and modifying, 273

P

Pattern of behavior and Change Targets, 19
Patton, General George, 158
Peers vs. subordinates and role context, 17
Perception and reality and reputation, 4
Performance feedback and calibration, 21–22
  components, 21t
  informational component, 21
  motivational component, 21
Performance risks and reputational scars, 27–28
Personal bias and workplace reputation, 6, 7
Personality characteristics
  and reputation, 8
  and reputational scars, 26
Phil, Case 2—High Skeptical, 58–59, 91–97
Position aspiration with Aspiration Plan vs. Development plan, 268
Prince Charles, 84
Process-level Aspiration Plan measurement of results
  goal achievement, 277
  return of investment (ROI), 276
  total value, 276–277
Progress reviews for Aspiration Plan monitoring and modifying, 276
PROFILE use and Hogan Development Survey (HDS), 26
Puzo, Mario, 124

R

Reagan, President Ronald, 184
Realize impact of behavior on reputation, 287–288
Redesign job or assignment as development strategy, 286–287
Reference group and strategic self-awareness, 14
Reframe behavior, 288
Refinement, necessity of for workplace reputation, 7
Reputation
  and career success, 3
  and culture context, 16
  definition, 6, 7
  and executive demeanor, 5
  extrospective issue, 5
  and image, 4
  introspective issue, 5
  Leader Development Cycle, 7–12, 8f
  as litmus test for career outcomes, 3
  perception and reality, 4
  personality characteristics and, 8
  realize impact of behavior on, 287–288
  and Strategic Self-Awareness, 15
  in workplace, 4, 6–7
Reputational scars
  and accumulation of incidents, 28–29
  behaviors, 5
  and performance risks, 27–28
  and personality characteristics, 26
  and Self-Monitoring, 18
  as virus, 4–5
Reputational vision with Aspiration Plan vs. development plan, 268
Reputation change pillars, 13–23
  Calibration, 20–23
  Change Targets, 19–20

Self-Monitoring, 18
Situational Context, 15–18
Strategic Self-Awareness, 13–15
Reputation Modification and Leader Development Cycle (LDC), 11
Reserved, 36–37
   behavior range, 36
   high, Robert, Case 3, 60–61, 123–130
   leadership and reputation implications, 36–37
   low, Janis, Case 5, 131–137
   risk summary, 37
Return of investment (ROI) for process-level Aspiration Plan measurement of results, 276
Rex, Case 1
   high Bold, 157–165
   high Leisurely, 139–148
   low Cautious, 56–57, 115–122
   low Dutiful, 251–259
Robert, Case 3
   high Reserved, 60–61, 123–130
   low Colorful, 202–208
Role context, 17–18
   definition, 17
   and global factors of flawed interpersonal tendencies, 54
   with peers vs. subordinates, 17
Role model identification, 289

S

"Scared Puppy," 244
Scope of Aspiration Plan, 264–265
Sebelius, Secretary of Health and Human Services Kathleen, 234
Seeking Feedback and Leader Development Cycle (LDC), 11
"Seeks" in place of "tells" and calibration, 23
Self-Monitoring, 18
   definition, 18
   interview situation, 18
   reputational scar and, 18
Situational Context, 15–18
   with Aspiration Plan vs. development plan, 269

awareness, 292
culture context, 15–16
increasing, 290
manager context, 16–17
role context, 17–18
Skeptical, 32–33
   behavior range, 32
   high, Phil, Case 2, 58–59, 91–97
   leadership and reputation implications, 32–33
   low, Mark, Case 6, 99–107
   risk summary, 33
SMARTER goals, 269, 272, 278, 279, 281, 287
Smith, Captain Edward, 115
Strategic Self-Awareness, 13–15
   building, 287
   and calibration, 22
   definition, 14
   and feedback, 21
   foundational nature of, 292
   vs. intrapsychic approaches to personality, 14
   reference group, 14
   and reputation, 15
   utility, 14–15
Success definition for individual level Aspiration Plan measurement of results, 275
Success of leader's team and organization for individual level as measurement of results, 276
Support weakness with resources as development strategy, 286

T

Takeaways, 292–295
   Aspiration Plan use for structure, 293–294
   enlist help of others, 293
   Hogan Development Survey (HDS), key role in awareness, 292–293
   Hogan Development Survey (HDS) to address Dark Side, 294
   Leader Development Cycle continuous nature, 294

leaders are coaches, 292
other assessments, 294
Situational Context awareness, 292
Strategic Self-Awareness is foundational, 292
willingness to change, 293
Tangible reminders to keep behavior top of mind, 289
Tanya, Case 4
   high Excitable, 77–83
   high Mischievous, 62–63, 175–183
Targeting Behaviors and Leader Development Cycle (LDC), 11
Timid Soul, The, 202
Total value for process-level Aspiration Plan measurement of results, 276–277
Triggers of behavior, 288
Trump, President Donald, 158

U

Universal development tips, 287–290
   advocate utilization, 288–289
   best-case and worst-case scenario identification, 289
   Camera Check Feedback, 287
   evaluate and modify, 290
   impact realization, 287–288
   involvement of others in development efforts, 290
   motivation is half the battle, 287
   reframe behavior, 288
   role model identification, 289
   Situational Context, increasing, 288
   SMARTER goals, 287–289
   Strategic Self-Awareness building, 287
   tangible reminders to keep behavior top of mind, 289
   triggers of behavior determination, 288
   Week-in-Review form usage, 289–290
Utility of strategic self-awareness, 14–15

W

Week-in-review form usage, 289–290
Willingness to change, 293
Workplace reputation, 4, 6–7
   direct observation, 6
   indirect personal observation, 6–7
   personal bias, 6, 7
   refinement, necessity of, 7

ABOUT HOGAN ASSESSMENT SYSTEMS

We are a premium test publishing company that uses a comprehensive suite of personality assessments to help companies select employees, develop leaders, and identify talent. We help organizations maximize their human resources through our vast library of research and scientifically based predictive power. We are the science of personality.

Our history is defined by the business applications of personality. This dates back to the 1930s when assessment centers were used to select individuals for dangerous wartime assignments. Rooted in this tradition, Dr. Robert Hogan developed the Hogan Personality Inventory in the 1970s—it was the first measure of normal personality designed specifically for business applications. He spent more than 15 years accumulating mountains of evidence demonstrating that this personality inventory would predict job performance. And he was right. The first commercial applications of the inventory began in the very early 1980s, and in 1987, Drs. Robert and Joyce Hogan founded Hogan Assessment Systems to make this science available to the business community. Today, we continue to build our position as the innovative leader in providing scientifically based personality assessment, development, and talent management solutions for business and industry.

Quick Facts

- Hogan Assessment Systems was founded in 1987.
- We are a research-based company that is at the forefront of the assessment industry.
- Our research archives cover more than 500 jobs ranging from janitor to CEO.
- Our inventories and services are offered through local distributors throughout the world.
- We have a track record of success working with more than 2,000 companies worldwide.
- Our inventories are currently in use by more than 70 percent of Fortune 100 companies.

Expertise

Employee selection, perhaps more than any other process in an organization, has the power to change a company's destiny. We design and implement selection systems aimed at improving bottom-line business results.

Employee development reports provide important insights to help employees develop to their full career potential. Our assessments help companies determine the right fit for each employee and provide feedback to develop each person into his or her most valuable role within the organization.

Talent management is now recognized by organizations as a key factor in their future growth. Our talent management expertise helps organizations identify talent, which we define in terms of personality, cognitive ability, and leadership potential.

Our employee selection, development, and talent management solutions are backed by a team of highly trained professionals dedicated to delivering the quality solutions necessary to achieve a competitive advantage in today's global market.

Learn more about us at www.hoganassessments.com or call 1-800-756-0632.